Connecticut

FIFTH EDITION

Off
the
Beaten
Path®

David and
Deborah Ritchie

The
Globe
Pequot
Press

Guilford, Connecticut

Maps created by Equator Graphics © The Globe Pequot Press
Illustration credits: Illustrations on pages 11, 58, 78, 169, and 220 drawn from photographs courtesy of the Connecticut Department of Economic Development.
Illustration on page 91 drawn from photograph courtesy of Deborah Ritchie.
Illustration on page 155 drawn from illustration courtesy of Chamard Vineyards.
Illustration on page 158 drawn from photograph courtesy of the Griswold Inn.
Illustration on page 181 drawn from photograph courtesy of Mashantucket Pequot Museum and Research Center.
All other text illustrations by Carole Drong.

ISBN 0-7627-2265-7

Manufactured in the United States of America
Fifth Edition/First Printing

Contents

Acknowledgments vii

Introduction ix

The Heartland 1

The Litchfield Hills 63

Gateway to New England 107

Coast and Country 145

The Quiet Corner 193

Indexes 227

  General Attractions 227

  Kid Stuff 239

  Only in Connecticut 240

  A Taste of Connecticut 241

About the Authors 242

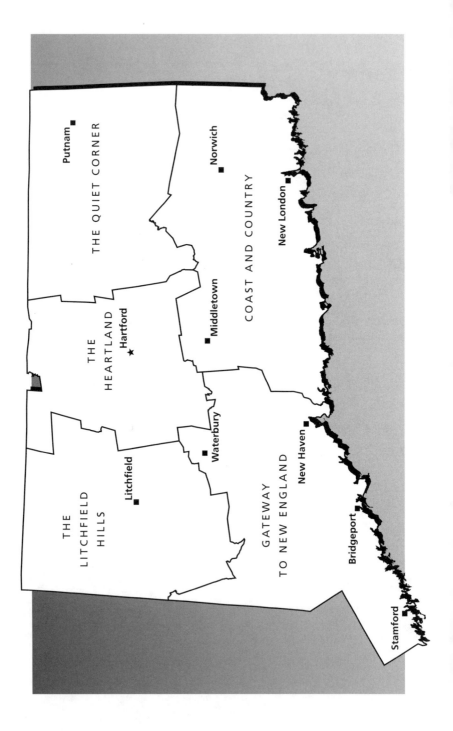

*For my mom, Gwendolyn Jean Montgomery Campbell
(a.k.a. Meem and Meemer Creamer), best mom and best friend.
Thanks for always being willing to read just one more story,
for teaching me to love books and poetry as much you do,
for showing me how to catch fireflys in a pickle jar,
for teaching me how to make the perfect hollandaise sauce
with just a spoon and patience, for scouring church bazaars
and rummage sales for my Nancy Drews,
and for welcoming my husband into our family
and learning to love him as much as I do.*

We love you, Meem.

Acknowledgments

We're truly blessed with friends who generously share their off-the-beaten-path finds with us. Among those are including Anne Goshdigian and Gabriel Kirshnitz, Charles Gilman, Francine Walko-Strazdas, Carol McSheffery, Jo Wood, Carol Bower, and Krystyna Przechorska.

Many thanks to our wonderful neighbors who keep us fed, entertained with their wonderful conversation, and feeling warm and cozy with their care and concern: The Augusts (Bob and Gladys), Bill, Mary and Doc Cuddeback, and Joe Diani. Our much loved friend, neighbor, and Joe's beloved wife, Margaret "Margie" Diani, passed away on December 26, 2001. She is as greatly missed as she was greatly loved.

Special thanks to antiques dealer Barbara Spear (www.yankeelady.com) for the skinny on auctions.

This edition offers special thanks also to intrepid (and tireless) OBPers, Pat and Erasmus "Ray" J. Struglia. Your finds of "must-see" attractions, wonderful letters, cat cards, and, most of all, friendship grace our lives. Your letters always managed to show up just in time to brighten some very dark days.

We appreciate the efforts of the people who staff Connecticut's tourism districts. They are never too busy to share their latest finds or to offer directions.

Our awesome nieces and nephews keep us current with kid and teen stuff so we don't embarrass ourselves too much: R. J. and Daniel O'Kane, Conner and Elise Schliffka, Danielle Crawley, and John Crawley IV.

We would also like to thank Dr. Micha Abelas and the staff of the Rheumotology Clinic at the University of Connecticut Health Center, Dr. Ronald Buonomano and the wonderful people who assist him in his practice, Lorraine Buonomano, Marilyn O'Neil, and Terry Pawling, and the staff of Farmington's Arrow Prescription Center, especially Cathy Gallo, Cathy Dalley, and Roberta Alteri. Their insight, kindness, thoughtfulness, patience, and good cheer keep us up and running off the beaten path.

Jan Cronan, this edition's editor, deserves our thanks for her patience and our sympathy for the gray hairs we gave her. Many thanks to Lesley Rock, this edition's copy editor, for helping to make this a better book.

Introduction

> A good traveler has no fixed plans and is not intent on arriving.
> —*Lao-Tsu* (570–490 B.C.E.)

Nestled like an afterthought between the much larger states of New York and Massachusetts, Connecticut occupies a mere 5,009 square miles along the coast of Long Island Sound. It is, in fact, the third smallest state in the Union. But what a state! Nowhere in America can the traveler find so representative a history, so rich a culture, and so great a physical diversity packed into so small an area.

The Native Americans who lived in the region for millennia before the arrival of the first Europeans called it *Quinnehtukut* ("Beside the Long Tidal River"). About 20,000 Native Americans lived in the area when the Dutch discovered the Connecticut River in 1614; the hundred or so who remain now occupy five reservations. English Puritans from Massachusetts began to flood the Connecticut Valley a couple of decades after its discovery by the Dutch, and in 1638–39, the towns of Hartford, Windsor, and Weathersfield adopted the Fundamental Orders of Connecticut, setting up a government for the new Connecticut Colony. About the same time, the colony of New Haven was

Connecticut River Trivia

- *The Connecticut River is one of fourteen waterways designated an American Heritage River by Vice President Al Gore.*

- *The Connecticut River is 410 miles long—about 5, 551 football fields.*

- *Today's Connecticut River came into being between 10,000 and 13,000 years ago after the Wisconsin Glacier receded from the New England area.*

- *The Connecticut Valley developed about 220 million years ago in the late Triassic period.*

- *Within the ecosystem of the*

Connecticut River watershed, you can find ten endangered or threatened species:

- *Three birds: the piping plover, the peregrine falcon, and the American bald eagle.*

- *One fish: the shortnose sturgeon.*

- *One insect: the Puritan tweed beetle.*

- *One mollusk: the dwarf wedge mussel.*

- *Four plants: the Jesup's milk vetch, small whorled pogonia, Robin's cinquefoil, and the Northern bulrush.*

founded farther west along the coast of Long Island Sound. The two colonies were joined in 1662, and the state gained—roughly—its current outline.

Since then the history of Connecticut has largely marched with that of America. During the past 350 years, the state has played a vital role in American experiences, such as the settlement of the frontier, the winning of the Revolutionary War, the adoption of the Constitution, the Union victory in the Civil War, and that vast upheaval known as the Industrial Revolution.

Connecticut's part in the American pageant has left a lasting mark on the state. Its towns have been ravaged by America's wars. Its language and culture have been molded by the nation's immigration policies. Its geography has been altered by the spread of industrialization. Its economy has been shaped by the growth—and demise—of such industries as whaling, railroading, shipbuilding, and textile manufacturing. It has been, in many ways, a microcosm of America.

Sometimes known as "the Land of Steady Habits," Connecticut has taken as its official designation the title "Constitution State." Washington called it "the Provision State," because it fed his army during the darkest days of the Revolution. It is also called the "Nutmeg State," a sobriquet just as common as the official designation and perhaps more representative of Connecticut's history and culture; the name "Nutmegger" was often applied by the residents of neighboring states to Connecticut peddlers, who were famous for selling bogus nutmegs carved from local wood in place of the imported (and more expensive) real thing.

Whatever you call it, Connecticut is a land of odd contrasts and strange delights that have accumulated over centuries. Modern Connecticut has something to excite the whim and tickle the fancy of almost every traveler. Its diverse geography runs the gamut from the sandy beaches and teeming marshlands of its coastal plains and the fertile meadows of its central lowlands to the forested hills of the eastern and western uplands and the craggy granite cliffs that characterize its northwestern reaches. The many eras of its history are enshrined not only in countless museums, galleries, and restorations but in numerous historical structures that are still part of the everyday lives of its people; this is, in fact, one of the few places in America where you can find real Cape Cod saltboxes, Victorian Gothic mansions, and art deco roadside palaces of the early automotive era all happily residing cheek by jowl.

The densely populated cities along Connecticut's southwestern coast and the navigable portions of its major rivers are home to 90 percent of the state's inhabitants and give the state an urban flavor that is belied by the lightly inhabited uplands. This clustering of settlement along coasts and rivers explains why, even though Connecticut is the fourth most densely populated state in the United States (with an overall density of over 650 persons per square mile), roughly 60 percent of the state is forest land. Most of the trees in these forests are northern hardwoods about sixty to one hundred years old, and they are purely glorious in fall. Another 15 percent of Connecticut is farmland, cultivated by a mere 1 percent of the population. Dairy farming and horse breeding are major Connecticut industries that add their own brand of color to rural areas. So is the cultivation of wrapper tobacco, which is grown under netting and dried in characteristic long wooden sheds that you'll notice dotting the landscape in the northern farming valleys.

In terms of amenities for the traveler, Connecticut has few equals. Though modern accommodations abound, this area, like most of New England, is famous for its quaint inns and bed and breakfasts (or B&Bs), many of which are housed in buildings that have been around longer than the state. The state's robust cuisine, both cosmopolitan and casual, reflects the cultural and gustatory gifts brought by succeeding waves of immigrants. Its great wealth and emphasis on tourism make it a shopping paradise; establishments range from some of America's largest and most attractive malls to ma-and-pa operations offering only-in-Connecticut crafts to factory outlets that fairly shout bargains.

For the traveler who likes to venture off the beaten path, Connecticut is an especially satisfying venue. One constantly discovers the odd, the interesting, and the truly bizarre tucked away in the most unexpected places. Whether it be a mere whimsy like a roadside rock painted to look like a startlingly realistic giant frog, a truly spine-chilling gothic mystery like the deserted village of Bara-Heck Settlement, or something just plain nutty like the weird and wonderful United House Wrecking, you can never be entirely sure what you will find around the next bend.

We like to think of Connecticut as representing all the best of America in vest-pocket size: gilded beaches that would be the envy of California; rolling hills better than any in Virginia; pastoral farmland that makes you think you're in Indiana; downtown chic that rivals New York; and some of the friendliest people on earth. A truly dedicated traveler (and if you're reading this book, you probably fall into that category) could experience the full diversity of the state in one day. You could jump start your day with an espresso at Peter B.'s in West Hartford, drive down to the shore for a few hours of sun and sand capped by a lunch of fried clams at Lenny and Joe's, take an afternoon jaunt up into Litchfield County to browse the antiques shops before driving over to the Quiet Corner for a hayride through its fields and glens, and end your day with one of the best dinners of your life at the Golden Lamb Buttery in Brooklyn.

Geography isn't the only source of variety in Connecticut either. Its northerly location and long coastline conspire to produce a multiplicity of seasonal variations in the weather. Each season brings its own wonders and offers its own characteristic activities. Winter means Olde Weathersfield, all dressed up in the spare elegance of a colonial Christmas, pure white candles glowing in many-paned windows, and the faint sounds of Christmas carols wafting across the green. Spring is the season for strolling along one of eastern Connecticut's back roads, watching farmers plow its rolling farmlands, listening to the first few notes of bird song, and sniffing the green tang of growing things in the air. Summer is a time for the shore; for golden beaches, the hiss of the waves, the crunch of fried clams, and the sweet sugary smell of cotton candy. Fall means Litchfield's amber and cinnabar hills, quintessentially New England, white clapboard churches posed against the fiery reds of nearby sugar maples, the rush of the Housatonic, and the sweet taste of fresh-pressed cider and cider-glazed doughnuts.

Regardless of the season, traveling in Connecticut is easy; interstate highways crisscross the state, with Interstate 95 (formerly the Connecticut Turnpike) running the length of its shore, Interstate 91 bisecting the state from north to south, Interstate 395 winding along its eastern border, and Interstate 84 running from Danbury through Waterbury to Hartford and thence through the northeastern counties to the Mass. Pike. The interstate highway system is complemented by an excellent system of state highways. More often than not, this book takes you off the interstates and the controlled-access state highways and puts you on the smaller roads that evolved with our state's history from Indian trails to two-lane paved roads. Some of these back roads may seem awfully isolated. But never fear; no matter how far into the outback it feels, you're never more than half an hour from a major highway that will quickly return you to more populated areas.

Clearly, no one book can do justice to Connecticut's 350 years of history or to the diverse delights packed into this one small state. Just as an example, we're pretty certain that there's not a township in the state that doesn't have at least one museum located in a restored seventeenth- or eighteenth-century house and decorated with antiques and fittings gleaned from local attics. We could, with some encouragement, write an entire book just on restored buildings.

As in most of life, some judicious editing is necessary. Thus, you won't find herein detailed descriptions of the well-known delights of Mystic or the popular casinos at Foxwoods or Mohegan Sun. Nor do we devote much space to the major attractions in the state's larger cities. These items are well documented in a host of travel books and brochures, many of which are available through Connecticut's tourism division. That office has divided the state into a number of small tourism districts, each of which has a local office that can provide you with maps and information about the area. For further information on popular attractions and tourism in general, write or call the Connecticut Department of Economic Development, 865 Brook Street, Rocky Hill, CT 06067-3405, (800) 282–6863.

This book does not pretend to compete with the state of Connecticut in offering general travel information or describing nationally famous attractions. Instead, we offer a directory of out-of-the-way places that you might not know to look for if you're not native to the area. Where can you get the best pizza or ice cream or chili dog in the state? Where will you find the most interesting pottery or the neatest antiques or the strangest stores? Where can you experience the uniquely Connecticut and the perfectly New England without having to fight the maddening crowd? We may miss some of the major attractions, but if it's funky, funny, little known, or out of the way (and, of course, if it's located in Connecticut), then you'll probably find it here. For convenience, we've divided the state into five sections, matching Connecticut's major geographic, historical, and cultural divisions.

The following state agencies can provide you with other information on travel in Connecticut:

Connecticut State Historical Society
59 South Prospect Street
Hartford, CT 06106
(860) 566–3995

Office of Parks and Recreation
CT Department of Environmental Protection
165 Capitol Avenue
Hartford, CT 06106
(860) 566–2304

Connecticut State Commission on the Arts
227 Lawrence Street
Hartford, CT 06106
(860) 566–4770

Call Before You Go

We've tried to keep the book's contents as current as possible. Businesses and attractions, however, can come and go like snow in July, so it's a good idea to call before hand to make sure that a given establishment is still open (or is open during your trip; many places are open seasonally).

Lost in Connecticut?

A friend, who prefers to be nameless, calls Connecticut the "land that civil engineering forgot." Once our state highways were models on which the national system of interstates were developed, but today it's not hard to get lost. Should you find yourself lost and totally clueless, here are some hints for finding your way:

• Find your way to the town clerk's office and ask for directions. Depending on the size of the town, you may get not only directions but a lesson in the town's history and a suggestion for places to visit, eat, and stay.

• Ask at the post office. Again, depending on the size of the town and the time of year (it's not a good idea to wander in asking for directions the week before Christmas), you can reap a bonanza of travel information, including directions.

• Remember the lesson learned at your mother's knee—ask a police officer. Most of the time, you'll find they are willing and happy to provide you with directions.

• Before leaving home, get door-to-door driving directions at www. mapquest.com.

FYI

The following is a list of some resources an off-the-beaten-path traveler like yourself might find useful. You can find a more encyclopedic listing in the state's *Connecticut State Vacation Guide*.

AGRICULTURE & AGRICULTURAL FAIRS

Much as we'd like to, there's no way we can list all the pick-your-own, cut-your-own, roadside farm-stand or maple-sugaring operations in Connecticut. Fortunately, the Connecticut Department of Agriculture publishes brochures listing everything agricultural from pick-your-own-strawberries patches to cut-your-own Christmas tree farms. Send a self-addressed, stamped, business-size envelope to:

Department of Agriculture, Marketing Division, 165 Capitol Avenue, Hartford, CT 06102. Call (860) 566-3671 or (860) 566-4845 for a list of available brochures. The best way to make sure you get the most recent information is to request the brochure during the time of year it's most appropriate; for example, write for your cut-your-own-Christmas-tree brochure around Thanksgiving.

From late July through October, you could probably attend at least one agricultural fair each week. For a complete list of fairs, send a self-addressed, stamped, business-size envelope to Association of Connecticut Fairs, Box 753, Somers, CT 06071.

Area Codes

We've included phone numbers for most attractions. Connecticut has two area codes: Hartford, Litchfield, Middlesex, New London, Tolland and Windham Counties are in area code 860; Fairfield and New Haven Counties use the 203 area code. Sounds simple? Yep, except that the town of Sherman and the portions of Woodbury with Watertown phone numbers use the 860 area code. The rest of Bethlehem and Woodbury as well as part of Roxbury use the 203 area code. Go figure.

Bed & Breakfast Agencies

Connecticut is chock full of B&Bs, ranging from cozy farmhouses to country estates. B&B reservation services help you to find the inn that's just right for you. The following is a short list of some of Connecticut's best B&B reservation services:

Covered Bridge B&B Reservation Service, P.O. Box 447, Norfolk, CT 06058; (860) 542-5944.

Destinations, 128 South Hoop Pole Road, Guilford, CT 06437; (800) 582-0853.

Four Season International Bed and Breakfast Service, 11 Bridlepath Road, West Simsbury, CT 06092; (860) 658-2181; listings in the Farmington Valley area only.

Nutmeg Bed and Breakfast Agency, P.O. Box 27117, West Hartford, CT 06127-1117; (860) 236-6698 or (800) 727-7592.

Casinos

Foxwoods Resort & Casino on the Mashantucket Pequot Indian Reservation in Ledyard (800-PLAY-BIG) has replaced Mystic as Connecticut's number one vacation destination. The casino—the largest gaming and entertainment complex in North America—offers slot machines, table games, bingo, restaurants, theaters, and hotels and has become a mecca for travelers from all over the world. Connecticut's second casino—the Mohegan Sun Casino in Uncasville (888–226–7711)—offers similar gaming, entertainment, and accommodations and has quickly grown into the third largest casino in the United States.

CRAFTS AND CRAFT CENTERS

Craft shows are a year-round thing in Connecticut, but Mother's Day through Columbus Day is the peak period. For a yearly listing of craft shows in Connecticut, send a self-addressed, stamped envelope to Crafts in Connecticut, Connecticut Guild of Craftsmen, P.O. Box 155, New Britain, CT 06050. For information on how to subscribe to the *Craft Digest*, a publication of the Connecticut Guild of Craftsmen, call (860) 225–8875.

Connecticut also boasts several top-flight centers displaying elegant local crafts. Most centers maintain mailing lists to keep you informed of shows and special events. Try contacting any of the following:

Branford Craft Village at Bittersweet Farm, Branford; (203) 488–4689.

Guilford Handcrafts Center, 411 Church Street, Guilford; (203) 453–5947.

Wesleyan Potters, 350 South Main Street, Middletown; (860) 347–5925; (860) 344–0039.

The Brookfield Craft Center, 286 Whisonnier Road, Brookfield; (203) 775–4526. Web address: www.craftweb.com/org/brookfld/brookfld.shtml.

Farmington Valley Arts Center, 25 Arts Center Lane, Avon; (860) 678–1867.

CYBER TRAVEL

We like the planning and research part of any trip almost as much as the traveling itself. Here are a few of our favorite Connecticut Web sites. A note about Web sites: The Internet is the equivalent of the Wild West with no sheriff in town. Web sites come, go, and move without a lot of notice. If you can't find a Web site we've listed, use your favorite search engine to see if you can track it down.

www.state.ct.us/ecd/research/townprof/index.html

Connecticut town profiles

www.newengland.com/

Yankee Magazine on the Net; a compendium of travel information, Yankee lore, hints, and tips. A good place to find out the weather in the part of Connecticut where you want to travel.

www.cris.com/~Mfedor/cthp/ct.shmtl

Connecticut's highest point Web site and information about Connecticut hiking

www.connix.com/%7Ejfagan/ctfish.htm

Joe Fagan's Web site for the latest and best information about Connecticut fishing

www.mapquest.com/

Door-to-door driving directions

www.state.ct.us/tourism/

Tourism information and the state's tourism guide online

www.inns.com/

B&B information

www.internetweather.com/

The latest Connecticut weather on the Net

search.com/

How to find things fast; combined search engines

www.imbored.com

A great site loaded with travel information about New England.

www.ctwineries.com

All the information you need to follow Connecticut's wine trail.

There are a host of Web sites that give you information about the Connecticut River. Here are some of our favorites:

www.mnh.uconn.edu

www.ctriver.org

www.connix.com/~crm/links.htm

www.ctriverstripers.com

www.fws.gov/r5crc

www.riversalliance.org

www.nu.com/eagles/eagles.htm

www.visitconnecticut.com

www.tnc.org/connecticut

INTRODUCTION

FALL FOLIAGE

In most of Connecticut, fall foliage hits its peak around Columbus Day. Areas in the north, northwest, and northeast see peak color a little earlier. Starting in late September, you can get a daily fall foliage update by calling at (800) CT–BOUND (800–282–6863), ext. 88.

FOOD IN CONNECTICUT

One of our favorite ways to get to know a region is to start with a menu, sampling foods unique to the area. Here in Connecticut, our cuisine is an amalgam of rugged colonial dishes leavened with ethnic foods, the heritage of the immigrants who helped transform our state. It all makes for a diverse and heady cuisine. Try to sample some of these emphatically Connecticut foods when you visit.

Chowder. The origins of its name, *chaudière* (large kettle), may be French, but this hearty soup is all New England. You won't find as many fish chowders in Connecticut as in other parts of New England, but we make stellar clam chowders. **New England clam chowder** is a milk- or cream-based soup full of potatoes, onions, whole clams, and salt pork and seasoned with thyme. It's probably the version you think of when someone mentions clam chowder. **Rhode Island clam chowder** is New England clam chowder lightened with just enough puréed tomatoes to turn the soup a rosy pink. **Southern New England clam chowder** is a bracing, briny broth loaded with clams, potatoes, and onions—no milk or cream. **Manhattan clam chowder** is a tomato-based veggie soup with a few clams. To be shunned. Check out the clam chowder offerings at Abbott's Lobster in the Rough in Noank (page 185) or Lenny and Joe's Fish Tale Restaurant (page 156) in Westbrook and Madison.

Lobster roll. In some New England states, a lobster roll is lobster salad (cold lobster, mayonnaise, seasonings) served on a toasted hot dog bun. But in Connecticut, a lobster roll is a spiritual experience: fresh, hot lobster meat, dripping with melted butter, served on a sesame-seeded hamburger bun or toasted hot dog bun. Both of Lenny and Joe's Fish Tale Restaurants (page 156) excel in the art of the lobster roll. Be sure to try one, and don't forget the extra napkins for wiping butter-drenched chins and fingers.

Grape-Nuts pudding. Baked custard served in a sweet shell of Grape-Nuts cereal, one version features a swirl of Grape-Nuts throughout the pudding. Much better than it sounds. Check out Zip's Diner in Dayville and see page 216 for Zip's recipe for Grape-Nuts pudding.

Indian pudding. A robust dessert dating back to colonial times. It's a mix of cornmeal, molasses, and warm spices cooked for hours at a low temperature until thick and amber-colored. Some heretics add raisins or apples. Served with vanilla ice cream or a rivulet of heavy cream. The Griswold Inn in Essex (page 157) usually has Indian pudding on its fall and winter dessert menu.

Pizza. New Haven is the pizza capital of Connecticut, maybe of the United States. New Haven pizza has a thin and crunchy crust and doesn't wallow in toppings. Don't want anyone to know you're a tourist? Call it a tomato pie, not pizza. Pepe's and Sally's (page 130) are all choice New Haven pizza palaces. In Hartford county, the pizza at Harry's in West Hartford Center is glorious.

FREEDOM TRAIL

The Freedom Trail marks locations in Connecticut that were important in the battle to end slavery. For a complete listing of sites, call (860) 572–5318.

Among the sites on the trail:

Harriet Beecher Stowe Center, Hartford. Home of the author of *Uncle Tom's Cabin*.

John Brown birthplace, Torrington. Where the fiery abolitionist began his life.

First Baptist Church, Milford. A memorial to the African-Americans who fought in the Revolutionary War.

Milo Freeland grave, North Canaan. The gravesite of the first African-American to volunteer for service in the Union Army during the Civil War. His story was depicted in the movie *Glory*.

Paul Robeson house, Enfield. Purchased by the singer and actor at the height of his popularity. His activism on behalf of equal rights helped lead to his banishment from the American stage.

INFORMATION

The Connecticut State Tourism Office, 865 Brook Street, Rocky Hill, CT 06067, publishes a yearly *Connecticut Vacation Guide* and other publications of interest to visitors. These items are available free by calling (800) CT–BOUND. Web address: www.tourism.state.ct.us

Twelve regional tourism districts around the state provide information, guides, and special event listings targeted to their regions.

Southeastern Connecticut Tourism District, 470 Bank Street, New London, CT 06320: (800) TO–ENJOY. Web address: www.mysticmore.com.

Northeast Connecticut Visitors District, P.O. Box 598, Putnam, CT 06260; (860) 928–1228. Web address: www.webtravels.com/quietcorner/index.html.

Greater Hartford Tourism, 1 Civic Center Plaza, Hartford, CT 06114; (800) 793–4480. Web address: www.travelfile.com/get?ghtd.

Connecticut's North Central Tourism Bureau, 111 Hazard Avenue, Enfield, CT 06082; (800) 248–8283 and (860) 763-2578. Web address: www.cnctb.org.

Central Connecticut Tourism District, 1 Grove Street, New Britain, CT 06053; (860) 225–3901. Web address: www.centralct.org.

Connecticut River Valley and Shoreline Visitors Council, 393 Main Street, Middletown, CT 06457; (800) 486–3346. Web address: www.cttourism.org.

Greater New Haven Convention and Visitors Bureau, 1 Long Wharf Drive, Suite 7, New Haven, CT 06511; (800) 332–STAY. Web address: www.newhavencvb.org.

Coastal Fairfield County Tourism District, 297 West Avenue, Norwalk, CT 06850; (800) 866-7925. Web address: www.visitfairfieldco.org.

Housatonic Valley Tourism, P. O. Box 406, 30 Main Street, Danbury, CT 06810; (800) 841–4488. Web address: www.housatonic.org.

Waterbury Region Convention and Visitors Bureau, P. O. Box 1469, 83 Bank Street, Waterbury, CT 06720; (203) 597–9527.

Litchfield Hills Travel Council, P. O. Box 968, Litchfield, CT 06759; (860) 567–4506. Web address: www.litchfieldhills.com.

Farmington Valley Visitors Bureau, Web address: www.farmingtonvalleyvisit.com.

LODGING

You can book accommodations at hotels, motels, inns, and B&Bs throughout Connecticut by calling (800) CT–BOUND. This reservation service is available seven days a week, twenty-four hours a day. For a comprehensive list of lodgings, call the Connecticut Tourism Office, Department of Tourism, at (800) CT–BOUND.

SKIING

Depending on weather conditions, downhill skiing can start as early as November and last until March. Call (800) CT–BOUND for ski conditions. All five of the state's major ski areas have snowmaking capability:

Mohawk Mountain, 48 Great Meadow Road (off Route 4), Cornwall; (800) 895–5222. Downhill and cross-country skiing, snowboarding, ski shop, night skiing, and food service.

Mount Southington, 3995 Mt. Vernon Road (Interstate 84, exit 30), Southington; (860) 628–0954. Downhill skiing and snowboarding, ski shop, night skiing, and food service.

Powder Ridge Ski Area, 99 Powder Hill Road (Interstate 91, exit 17S/18N), Middlefield; (860) 349–3454 and (800) 622–3321. Downhill skiing, snowboarding, ski shop, night skiing, and food service.

Ski Sundown, Route 219, New Hartford; (860) 379–9851. Downhill skiing, snowboarding, ski shop, night skiing, and food service.

Woodbury Ski & Racquet Area, Route 47, Woodbury; (203) 263–2203 and (203) 263–2213. Downhill and cross-country skiing (both with night skiing), snowboarding, ski shop, and food service.

Annual Events

No one volume could do justice to all of the annual festivals, fairs, shows, garden and tag sales, and town hall dinners that make up Connecticut's yearly calendar. Connecticut's regional tourism offices all publish calendars of special events, and you can get on their mailing lists with a phone call. Dates, times, and events change from year to year, so call close to the announced date to confirm information. We've scattered throughout this book information on events we especially enjoy. In addition, we've listed here some of the larger events you might want to make part of a trip to Connecticut.

JANUARY

Early American Hearth Tours, historic homes and museums throughout the Farmington Valley. A celebration to chase away the winter blues with tours, walks, teas, lectures, and dinners at some of the Farmington Valley's most famous museums and historic homes. Usually late January through mid-March. Call (800) WELCOME.

Eagle Watch Cruises. Essex. From mid-January to mid-March. What more spectacular way to see America's national symbol than with a cruise along the Connecticut River. Bring binoculars and dress warmly and be prepared to be dazzled. Call (860) 526–4954 for reservations and more information.

Woodbury Winter Carnival, Woodbury, late January. Almost anything you'd want to do on the snow—snowboarding, tubing, skiing. Good events for kids. Call (203) 263–2203 for more information.

INTRODUCTION

FEBRUARY

Hartford Flower Show, Civic Center, Hartford. Just when you think spring will never come, this fabulous shows reminds you it's just around the corner. Call (860) 529–2123.

Winter Carnival, Winding Trails Cross-Country Ski Center, Winding Trails Road, Farmington. Winter fun for the whole family; lots of children's activities. Usually early February. Call (860) 677–8458.

APRIL

The River Run 5k & 10k Races, Iron Horse Boulevard, Simsbury. Call (860) 651–5917.

MAY

Civil War Battles and Reenactment, Hammonassett Beach State Park. Union and Confederate reenacters re-create Civil War battles, encampments, period music, vintage fashions, children's games. Call (860) 526–4993.

Dogwood Festival, Greenfield Hill Congregational Church, 1045 Old Academy Road, Fairfield. Stroll amid drifts of dogwood and welcome spring. Lots of good stuff to see and do, including garden tours, arts and crafts, a plant and garden sale (very good prices), historic walks, tag and rummage sales, picnic lunches, and an indoor luncheon (reservations required). Usually held mid-May. Call (203) 259–5596.

Lime Rock Grand Prix, Lime Rock Park, 467 Lime Rock Road, Route 112, Lakeville. Spend Memorial Day weekend at the largest race in North America. The racing world is well represented with some of the best drivers from the International Motorsports Association (IMSA) and the Sports Car Club of America (SCCA). Auto-racing-related booths, souvenirs, and food. For the best view, forsake the stands and sit on the slopes overlooking the track. Call (800) RACE–LRP.

Lobsterfest, Mystic Seaport, 75 Greenmanville Avenue, Mystic. Outdoor lobster bake on the banks of the Mystic River. Lobster as you like it, along with all the family entertainment Mystic does so well, such as sea chanteys, demonstrations, entertainment, and food. Usually Memorial Day weekend. Call (860) 572–5315.

JUNE

Taste of Hartford, Constitution Plaza, Hartford. If it's the best to eat, drink, or listen to in the Hartford area, you can sample it at the Taste of Hartford. Usually held in mid-June. Call (860) 728–3089.

JULY

Riverfest, Hartford and East Hartford. A celebration of the Fourth of July and the Connecticut River with show-stopping fireworks over the Connecticut River. Early July. Call (860) 293–0131.

Canon Greater Hartford Open (GHO). Tournament of Players Club, River Highlands in Cromwell. One of the crown jewels on the PGA tour. A great chance to see your favorite links guys up close. The Pro-Am contest before the actual tournament starts offers wonderful chances for photographs and autographs. Usually held in late July. Call (860) 246–4 GHO.

AUGUST

Litchfield Jazz Festival, White Memorial Center, Litchfield. Spend some of Connecticut's hottest summer nights enjoying one of the coolest jazz scenes around. This festival is a real showcase for up-and-coming jazz talent. Music, art, and photography shows, and lots of yummy food (or bring your own picnic). Usually mid-August. Call (800) 593–4446. Web address: www.litchfield.com.clt/lpa.html.

SoNo Arts Celebration, Washington and South Main Streets, Norwalk. For three days the heart of SoNo (South Norwalk)—site of innumerable boutique shops, galleries, and neat restaurants—turns into one huge block party alive with outdoor arts, entertainment, and food. Usually held the first weekend in August. Call (203) 866–7916.

Brooklyn Fair, Route 169 and Fairgrounds Road, Brooklyn. The oldest continuously active agricultural fair in the United States. A real old-fashioned fair with oxen and horse pulls, home-and-garden exhibits, livestock displays, entertainment, and carnival attractions. Usually held in late August. Call (860) 774–7568 or (860) 779–0012 during the fair.

Woodstock Fair, Route 169 and 171, Woodstock. Connecticut's second oldest agricultural fair complete with livestock shows, food-and-garden contests, midway, entertainment, and petting zoo. Usually held the last weekend in August. Call (860) 928–3246.

Goshen Fair, Goshen Agricultural Society Fairgrounds, Route 63, just south of Goshen Center. Our all-time favorite agricultural fair. There are lots of old-fashioned touches, such as blue ribbons for the best corn relish, homemade quilts, and young 4–H kids exhibiting their sheep, cows, and pigs. Lots of midway action to occupy the kids and enough junk food to keep Drew Carey and Mimi happy. Usually the last weekend in August. Call (860) 491–3655.

SEPTEMBER

Norwalk Oyster Festival, Veteran's Memorial Park, Norwalk. Honoring Norwalk's seafaring past and present, this event features oyster shucking and slurping contests, tall ships, adult and kid entertainment, and a nice fireworks display. If you prefer to savor bivalves under less competitive conditions, you'll find plenty of oysters at the food court. Usually held in early September. Call (203) 838–9444 or (888) 701–7785.

Mum Festival, Bristol. It's mum-madness throughout the whole town. Beauty pageants, parades, arts and crafts, antique car show, and of course, mums for sale. Late September to mid-October. Call (860)584–4518

Ferry Park Family Festival, September, Ferry Park, Rocky Hill Food, carnival, steamboat rides on the Connecticut River, arts and crafts, exhibits, musical entertainment. Call (860) 258–2772 for details.

Grandparent's Day at the Beardsley Zoo, September 12, Beardsley Zoo, Bridgeport. Special programs about animal families with crafts for the kids, Call (203) 394-6565 for schedule and details. Free admission for all seniors accompanied by a paying child (age 3 and older).

Schemitzun, September 16–19, Mashantucket Pequot Indian Reservation. Annual feast of green corn and dance with many special events, including drum contests, traditional dance contests, educational exhibits, and more. Call (800) 224–CORN for details.

OCTOBER

Open Cockpit Day, New England Air Museum, just off Route 75, at Bradley International Airport in Windsor Locks. Your chance to visit the museum and, most important, climb into the cockpits of some of its coolest planes. This is a very popular event, so expect to spend some time waiting in line. Usually early October. Call (860) 623–3305. Web address: www.neam.org.

Highland Festival, Edward Waldo Homestead, Waldo Road, Scotland. Our second favorite Scots festival. Bagpipe bands, dancing, athletic competitions, folk music, kid stuff, Scots wares and clothing, and ethnic food but, alas, no haggis. Usually mid-October. Call (860) 456–8627.

Apple Harvest Festival, on and around town green, Southington. Southington is Connecticut's Apple Town, and on this weekend the whole area turns out to celebrate the apple harvest. Apples, apple pies, apple cider, cider-glazed doughnuts, just apples galore as well as a carnival, arts-and-crafts fair, a foot and bed race, and entertainment. Usually held the first two weekends of October. Call (860) 628–8036.

Antiques Show, Connecticut State Armory, Asylum Street, Hartford. One of the country's best shows for American antiques. Dealers transform the armory into elegant rooms full of decorative furnishings and art. There's usually some excellent food catered by one of the area's best caterers or restaurants. Call (860) 247–8996.

Walking Weekend, Northeast Quiet Corner. Historic, cultural, natural history, and scenic guided walks through twenty-five towns in Connecticut's northeast corner. Usually Columbus Day weekend. Call (860) 928–1228.

NOVEMBER

Manchester Road Race, Main Street, Manchester. This $4^7/_{10}$-mile road race—the second oldest in the East—features more than 10,000 runners, some in wonderfully idiosyncratic costumes. It's a Thanksgiving Day tradition full of bands, prizes, and lots of good cheer. Call (860) 649–6456.

Brookfield Craft Center Holiday Exhibition and Sale, Route. 25, Brookfield. An exhibition of quality American crafts, gifts, and holiday decorations displayed throughout three floors of a restored grist mill. Usually mid-November to late December. Call (203) 775–4526.

Festival of Lights, Constitution Plaza, Hartford. Hundreds of thousands of twinkling fairy lights are fashioned into fanciful shapes to celebrate the holiday season. The day after Thanksgiving, the lights go on and the Big Guy (Monsieur Kringle, that is) arrives by helicopter. OK, the helicopter *is* lame, but the lights are cool. From 4:00 P.M. to midnight daily, late November to early January. Call (860) 728–3089.

Holiday Festival of Crafts, Guilford Handicraft Center, 411 Church Street, Guilford. Innovative and unusual crafts from more than 500 of the country's leading artists. Usually November and December. Call (203) 453–5947.

"Dickens of a Christmas" House Tour, Farmington village homes and Stanley-Whitman House, 37 High Street, Farmington. Tour historic "Old Farmington" homes all dressed up for Christmas. Plus catch the

Christmas boutique and a varying menu of special events. Usually early November. Call (860) 677–9222 or (860) 673–6791.

DECEMBER

Christmas at Mystic Seaport, Mystic Seaport, 75 Greenmanville Road, Mystic. You'll swear you've been transported back to the 1800s as Mystic really goes all out to make the holidays of yesteryear come alive. Don't miss the evening "Lantern Light Tours" (by reservation only). Throughout December. Call (860) 572–5315.

First Night, many locations throughout downtown Hartford. A family-friendly (no alcohol) New Year's Eve celebration, live entertainment and foods throughout the afternoon and evening. Early fireworks for the rug rats and midnight fireworks for adults. New Year's Eve. Call (860) 728–3089.

Connecticut Firsts

- 1639: Connecticut adopts the country's first written constitution, the Fundamental Orders of Connecticut.

- 1647: Hartford hangs the first witch in the colonies at what is now the corner of Albany Avenue and Garden Street.

- 1656: New Haven creates the first public library from a gift of books from Theophilus Eaton.

- 1660: Hopkins Grammar School established, the first private secondary school.

- 1727: Samual Higlley mints the country's first copper coins in Simsbury.

- 1740: The Pattison brothers (Edward and William) of Berlin make tinware, which they sell door to door. This enterprise inaugurates the tradition of the "Yankee peddler," that slippery Connecticut character responsible for relieving countless residents of neighboring colonies of their excess cash.

- 1764: Publication of the *Connecticut Courant* (now the *Hartford Courant*), the nation's oldest continuously publishing newspaper.

- 1771: The colony forms the Governor's Footguards, oldest military unit in America.

- 1775: David Bushnell launches the first submarine, the *American Turtle.*

- 1776: Nathan Hale, a Nutmegger and the country's first martyr, is executed in Manhattan.

- 1777: First trimmed and illuminated Christmas tree in Windsor Locks.

- 1780: Benedict Arnold of Norwalk becomes the new nation's most famous traitor.

- 1783: Noah Webster's blue-backed speller printed in Hartford by Hudson & Goodwin.

  Jupiter Hammond of Hartford becomes the first African-American poet to be published.

- 1784: America's first law school—Tapping Reeve—established in Litchfield.

- 1796: Hartford's Amelia Simmons, who styled herself "an American Orphan," publishes America's first cookbook, *American Cookery.*

- 1801: A Mrs. Prout of South Windsor makes America's first cigars, the "Long Nines."

- 1803: Salisbury establishes the first children's library.

- 1806: Noah Webster publishes America's first dictionary.

- 1809: Mary Kies receives a patent for weaving silk with straw or thread. She is the first American woman to receive a patent.

- 1814: Eli Terry patents the first shelf clock in Thomaston.

- 1817: First school for the hearing impaired—the American School for the Deaf—founded in Hartford.

- 1844: Charles Goodyear of New Haven receives the patent for vulcanization of rubber.

- 1854: City of Hartford votes to create Bushnell Park, America's first municipal park.

- 1873: The first football game is played at Yale.

- 1878: The world's first telephone exchange and directory opens for business in New Haven.

INTRODUCTION

- 1881: P. T. Barnum introduces the three-ring circus.

- 1889: Stamford's George C. Blickensderfer invents the first portable typewriter.

  William Gray of Hartford invents the world's first coin-operated pay telephone.

- 1897: The automobile industry is born when Albert Pope and Hiram Maxim show off their electric car.

- 1904: First submarine base established at Groton.

- 1906: Hartford's Alfred C. Fuller makes the housewife's life a little easier when he starts selling door to door the first twisted-in wire housebrush.

- 1909: Hiram P. Maxim invents the gun silencer.

- 1917: John Browning invents the automatic pistol, Browning machine gun, and the Browning automatic rifle, all for Hartford's Colt Firearms.

- 1919: Homogenized milk first sold in Torrington.

- 1920: Stamford's Pitney Bowles introduces the first U.S. Postage meter.

- 1931: First electric shaver made in Stamford.

- 1934: Consumer advocate (and one of our personal heroes) Ralph Nader was born in Winsted.

- 1937: Margaret Rudkin puts on her apron and bakes the first loaf of Pepperidge Farm bread in Fairfield.

- 1939: Igor Sikorsky builds the first helicopter in Stratford.

- 1949: James Wright of New Haven invents Silly Putty, delighting kids and frustrating moms everywhere who find the stuff impossible to remove from the family dog's fur.

- 1954: First nuclear submarine—the *Nautilus*—launched in Groton.

Famous Nutmeggers

Then...

David Bushnell, inventor of the submarine

Samuel Colt, revolver

Peter Goldmark, long-playing record and color television

Charles Goodyear, vulcanization of rubber

Elias Howe, sewing machine

Edwin P. Land, Polaroid camera

Igor Sikorsky, helicopter

Horace Wells, nitrous oxide anesthesia

Eli Whitney, cotton gin

Now...

Larry Kramer, AIDS activist and author

Dominick Dunne, author

Frank McCourt, author

Jacques Pepin, chef and author

Bill Blass, designer

Glenn Close, actress

Placido Domingo, musician

Michael J. Fox and Tracey Pollan, actors

Dustin Hoffman, actor

Henry Kissinger, diplomat

Arthur Miller, writer

Paul Newman and Joanne Woodward, actors

Keith Richards, musician

Maurice Sendak, author and illustrator

William Stryon, author

Diane von Furstenberg, designer

The Heartland

The upper Connecticut River Valley is a broad, fertile meadow-land ideal for farming and grazing, and the state's Puritan settlers were naturally drawn to it. It was the first part of Connecticut to be colonized, and those original settlements thrived and expanded until they finally merged to form what is today Greater Hartford, a vibrant metropolitan area of more than 832,000 people at the center of the state's most populous county. Bounding Hartford County's urban and suburban core on the north and west are the rural Farmington and Tobacco Valleys. To the east is pastoral Tolland County. Within these rural boundaries is Connecticut's heartland, the seat of its government, and one of its most important commercial centers. As you might suspect, the majority of the attractions in this area are historical and cultural or are the commercial activities and entertainment found in any large metropolitan area.

The Capital

Formerly the site of the old Dutch Fort Good Hope (1633), Hartford was the first city in Connecticut. It was famous in the nineteenth century as a center of the abolitionist movement and the tobacco industry and as the home of the Colt Firearms Factory, manufacturers of the Colt Revolver, "the gun that won the West." In more recent times Hartford has tamed down its reputation considerably, and it is now known as the "Insurance City."

In keeping with the city's new image, we suggest beginning any tour of Hartford with a visit to an insurance company. The Hartford Insurance Group on Asylum Avenue has opened *The Hartford Exhibit,* a collection of multimedia presentations and displays that chronicle the company's history back to the start of the insurance business in America. In most cities that wouldn't be of much note, but this is where the insurance industry was born. The first policies covering shipping were written here way back in 1810 (by, who else, the Hartford). By 1898 the first auto insurance policy, at the staggering cost of

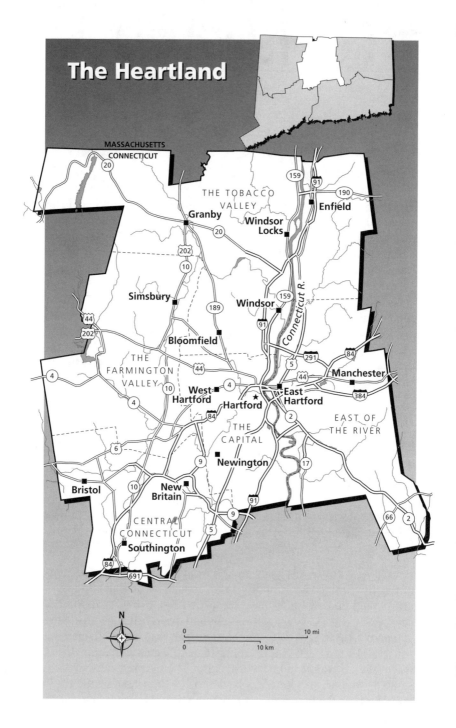

The Heartland

MASSACHUSETTS
CONNECTICUT

THE TOBACCO VALLEY

Granby

Windsor Locks

Enfield

Simsbury

Windsor

Bloomfield

THE FARMINGTON VALLEY

Manchester

West Hartford

East Hartford

Hartford

EAST OF THE RIVER

THE CAPITAL

Newington

Bristol

New Britain

CENTRAL CONNECTICUT

Southington

Connecticut R.

N

0   10 mi
0   10 km

two cents, had been issued by the Travelers Insurance Company in Hartford, and the rest, as they say, is history. Today, even with consolidation and downsizing, Hartford is still the place to be if you want to live long and prosper in insurance.

The Tourist Board may think that the Wadsworth Atheneum and the Old State House best symbolize what Hartford is all about, but natives know that The Hartford Exhibit captures the real soul of the city. Contrary to popular belief, though, UConn's football team is *not* nicknamed "the fighting insurance salesmen." Open to the public weekdays, 9:00 A.M. to 4:00 P.M. Call (860) 547–5000.

The Travelers Insurance Companies also offer visitors an insurance museum in Batterson Hall, 700 Main Street. At the museum you'll find a history of the Travelers from the 1860s through the present. Open Monday through Friday, 7:45 A.M. to 4:00 P.M. Closed holidays. Free.

Having set a proper mood, why not head into the center of the city to the traditional starting point for a tour of Hartford? The *Old State House* at 800 Main Street was built in 1796 and is the oldest state house in America. After a recent $12-million renovation, the building houses a number of exhibits, some inspiring and others just wonderfully silly. It all adds up to great fun in the least stuffy historical site/museum you're likely to come across. For travelers off the beaten path, the big draw is a re-creation of *Joseph Stewart's Hartford Museum* with its surfeit of odd and unusual offerings. Mr. Stewart's original museum, a collection of "natural and artificial curiosities," opened in the Old State House in 1797. In today's museum, you'll see a stuffed "Royal Tiger from Bengal, the largest ever seen," "A Calf with Two Perfect Heads," "A goat with three horns," and, well, you get the drift. For the more serious minded, there are various historical displays and a famous portrait of George Washington by Gilbert Stuart. There's also a gift shop and a fairly extensive tourist information center. The latter is a good place to start a tour of downtown Hartford; you'll find directions to enough museums, homesteads, galleries, and such to keep you busy for at least a week. You could, for example, start with the nearby *Wadsworth Atheneum,* 600 Main Street, the nation's oldest continuously operating art museum; now home to more than 45,000 works, it celebrated its 150th anniversary in 1992.

Art lovers should make a point of seeing two famous pieces of art in the downtown area. Alexander Calder's *Stegosaurus* is a huge steel construction that towers over Burr Mall, a small pocket park between the Wadsworth Atheneum and Hartford City Hall. And watch for Carl Andre's

Hartford Trivia

Before he donned his rumpled trench coat and found fame as TV's Inspector Columbo, actor Peter Falk toiled as an efficiency expert for the state's budget bureau, where it would have been very inefficient to ask "just one more question...."

Founded in 1764, the Hartford Courant (once the Connecticut Courant) is our country's oldest continuously publishing newspaper. The Courant's been around long enough to report the Boston Tea Party as breaking news. In 1796, a Virginia farmer named George Washington advertised in its real estate section.

The Reverend Thomas Hooker is honored as the founding father of Connecticut. These days Hartford celebrates his memory with its laid-back and fabulously flamboyant "Hooker Day" parade, usually held the first weekend in October.

Stone Field sculpture on Gold Street across from the Atheneum and beside the Ancient Burying Ground. This $87,000 sculpture has always been a subject of conversation in Hartford. It consists of thirty-six large rocks. Some critics consider it a statement of minimalist art; some friends of ours call it "Hartford's Meadow Muffins." You decide what it really is.

After you check out Stone Fields, walk over to the **Ancient Burying Ground** on Main Street behind Center Church. This cemetery was created in 1640 and holds the bones of some of Hartford's most prominent citizens, including Thomas Hooker. If you're a fan of early American art, the tombstones are a treasure trove of Colonial death imagery and epitaphs. It's a pleasant place for a lunchtime stroll in downtown. The cemetery is open during daylight hours.

While strolling through the downtown area, look up at the architecture. Hartford has many buildings with some lovely Gothic ornamentation that are certainly worthy of a second look. We've been fans of gargoyles, grotesques, greenmen, and chimeras for a couple of decades, and we always do a gargoyle hunt in every city we visit. In Hartford we particularly like the gargoyles protecting **Christ Church Cathedral,** 45 Church Street (860–527–7231) and the winged gargoyle ornamenting the Richardson Building, 942 Main Street.

Downtown Hartford is home to a pair of small museums that are worth at least a short stop. The **Connecticut Sports Museum and Hall of Fame** in the Civic Center Mall celebrates Connecticut's contribution to sports history. It's free and open Monday through Friday, 10:00 A.M. to 2:00 P.M.; (860) 724–4918.

The **Hartford Police Museum,** 101 Pearl Street, was the first police museum in the Northeast. It chronicles the 136-year history of Hartford's Police Department. Kids like it because they can feel what it's like to sit behind the wheel of a police car and listen to real police dispatches. Free. Open to the public Monday through Friday, 9:00 A.M. to 3:00 P.M. Call (860) 722–6152 for more information or to arrange a group tour.

THE HEARTLAND

FAVORITE PLACES THE HEARTLAND

1. *Dinosaur State Park*
2. *Old New-Gate Prison and Copper Mine*
3. *New Britain Museum of American Art*
4. *Governor's Horse Guards*
5. *Bloomfield Seafood*

That huge, garish, gold-domed monstrosity that greets your eyes when you come into Hartford across Interstate 84 is the **State Capitol Building,** 210 Capitol Avenue. It's been called, with some justice, "the most beautiful ugly building in the world." It's also been said that this gleaming edifice is a mixture of architectural styles. A riot of architectural styles is closer to the truth, though the 1879-vintage building does seem to be vaguely Gothic in intent.

In addition to the state executive offices and the chambers of the state legislature, this recently renovated pile of stone contains a variety of historical exhibits, including some bullet-riddled battle flags and the Marquis de Lafayette's camp bed. There's also a gift shop. And located on the first floor is the Capitol Cafeteria, famous for its chili dogs.

Visitors can take a one-hour guided tour of the State Capitol Building on weekdays between 9:15 A.M. and 1:15 P.M. and on Saturdays from April through October between 10:15 A.M. and 2:15 P.M. Go to the League of Women Voters information desk on the first floor by the west entrance (Capitol Avenue). The cafeteria is open weekdays, 7:30 A.M. to 2:00 P.M. Call (860) 240–0222.

Next to the State Capitol Building on Jewell Street is **Bushnell Park,** 166 Capitol Avenue, the first plot of land in America taken by eminent domain for use as a park. As you would expect, the park's forty-one acres include manicured lawns, towering shade trees, and the obligatory monuments (including one to Dr. Horace Wells, the man who, in 1844, discovered the anesthetic properties of nitrous oxide); but it is also home to some unusual extras, including the 1914-vintage **Bushnell Carousel,** whose forty-eight antique Stein and Goldstein horses revolve beneath 800 twinkling lights. The band organ is a refurbished 1925 Wurlitzer, and, yes, you really can try to catch a brass ring. The park is open year-round, but the carousel operates only mid-May through September. Carousel hours are kind of odd, so call (860) 728–3089 to get the straight stuff. There's a small charge to ride.

Horticulturists may find the half-hour guided Tree Tours of Bushnell Park of interest. The tours explore the rare and native trees in the park and are guided by volunteers. Wear good sturdy walking shoes for the tours. Free self-guided maps of the park and the tree tours are available from the Hartford Convention & Visitors Bureau, located in the Civic Center, or the Connecticut Department of Environmental Protection.

Bushnell Park Trivia

For more information, call the Greater Hartford Tourism District at (860) 244–8181.

Completed in 1932, the **Trinity College Chapel** on Summit Street boasts stained-glass windows, a cloister, arches, and carved pews in keeping with the best medieval tradition. The chapel's most interesting elements are seventy-eight hand-carved oak pews that face each other across the nave. It took more than thirty years to complete all the carvings. Most of the pews were the work of Gregory Wiggins of Pomfret, who taught Latin, Greek, and German before he decided to become a full-time wood carver. The Charter Oak Pew shows Captain Joseph Wadsworth hiding the Connecticut Colony's royal charter in an ancient oak tree to prevent its recall by Royal Governor Edmund Andros (not a beloved figure in Connecticut history).

A nifty lunch spot in the vicinity of Trinity College is **Timothy's** at 243 Zion Street. This place serves some of the cheapest, best, and most plentiful home cooking in Hartford. There's also a certain charm to the decor, with its classic swivel-stooled, Formica-topped diner counter, booths upholstered in the finest vinyl, black tin ceiling, and a handwritten menu that changes almost every day.

The weirdest thing about Timothy's is that it operates out of two side-by-side frame buildings that have no interior communications. The kitchen, the counter, and a booth area occupy one building; there's a dining room in the other. If you sit in the dining room, be prepared for your server (and your food) to hotfoot it from the kitchen onto the sidewalk before entering the dining room from the main street entrance.

Timothy's is usually knee-deep in students and faculty from nearby Trinity, but it's a congenial crowd, and newcomers are graciously welcomed. As for the food, just try any of the soups or sandwiches. It doesn't matter what; they're all good. Timothy's is known for its desserts, among which is a dense, moist, coffee-kissed Black Magic cake that comes highly recommended. Portions are humongous, so pace yourself if you want dessert. Open Monday throughThursday, 7:00 A.M. to 8:00 P.M.; Friday, 7:00 A.M. to 9:00 P.M.; Saturday, 9:00 A.M. to 9:00 P.M. No credit cards. Call (860) 728–9822.

After indulging yourself at Timothy's, you may need to walk off a few calories. One of the most pleasant walks in Hartford is through the **Cedar Hill Cemetery** on Maple Street down on the Hartford/Wethersfield town line. Laid out in 1864 by Jacob Weidenmann, who also did the honors for Bushnell Park, Cedar Hill is a classic Victorian city of the dead, full of ostentatious granite monuments, odd carvings, and strange sentiments. The terrain is hilly enough to be interesting, and the grounds are beautifully planted. This is, after all, the final resting place of such captains of industry and commerce as Sam Colt and J. P. Morgan. Open during daylight hours.

Weidenmann also laid out the beautifully land-scaped grounds and gardens at the **Butler-McCook Homestead** at 396 Main Street. This lovely house-museum is a terrific place to walk off your worries or sit a spell to restore your spirit and rest your mind. Hours were unavailable at press time as this facility was completing renovations. Call (860) 522–1806 for more information.

The Phoenix Mutual Life building in downtown Hartford is popularly known as the "boat building" because it reminds many of the locals of a graceful, green-glass boat.

In the mid-1700s, the men who lived along the Connecticut River and accumulated vast wealth from the West Indies trade were known as "River Gods." You can see a re-creation of a formal parlor belonging to one of the River Gods at the Atheneum. For the 1700s, those River God boys lived very well indeed.

The Publications Office of the **Natural Resource Center** (Department of Environmental Protection), 79 Elm Street, may be the most off-the-beaten path attraction in this book. We love this place, and most visitors we've sent to it are equally entranced. It's a bonanza for hikers, fishers, and armchair geologists. Connecticut's Department of Environmental Protection has produced over 1,300 publications about the state and its environment, including some dynamite maps for hikers, naturalists, and birders and some publications from not-for-profit and private presses. The office also sells some not-so-serious offerings like Smokey the bear t-shirts. It's open Monday through Thursday from 9:30 A.M. to 3:30 P.M. Call (860) 424–3555 for a free catalog and information. Fax: (860) 424–4058. Web address: dep.state.ct.us.

Hartford's **Institute of Living,** 400 Washington Street, the state's first hospital (1822), was one of the first mental health facilities to practice more humane treatment of those afflicted with mental illness. While it seems shockingly inhumane today, the first lobotomy, then considered a leading edge procedure, in the country was performed here in 1939. The Institute has had it fair share of rich and famous recoverers like Bing Crosby (who used to hop the fence to drink in neighborhood bars), but its permanent exhibit, "Myths, Minds and Medicine," is a sober look at just how cruelly mentally incapacitated people were once treated. It's strong stuff and includes information on some less-than-humane treatments like cold wet wraps and induced insulin shock, leavened by a bit of nonsense such as movies of "guests" from the 1930s larking about at fashion shows. This is probably not a good place to visit with younger kids.

If you visit the Institute, take time to tour the grounds. They were laid out by Frederick Law Olmstead in 1861. Take special note of the trees, some of which are among the largest in New England. A brochure for a self-guided tour of the grounds is available at the guard station at 400 Washington Street. Please respect the privacy and confidentiality of the patients. Call (860) 545–1888 for more information.

If you're looking for Hartford's signature food, then head to Franklin Avenue. This is Hartford's street of Italian restaurants, grinder shops, groceries, and bakeries, and practically any place you wander into will have something to delight your palate. Although it hasn't replaced the late, lamented LiVecchi's in our hearts, Hartford's **Mozzicato De Pasquale's Bakery and Pastry Shop** at 329 Franklin Avenue is a warm, dark cafe with a distinctive old-world feel. Just the right place to spend a rainy Saturday afternoon dawdling over a cappuccino and a

Hartford's Trashy Museum

*C*onnecticut is a little too buttoned-up to host truly trashy attractions like a Sleazy Lingerie Museum (housed in the Grantmoor on the Berlin Turnpike in Newington). The closest we could come to a trashy attraction was this way-cool temple of trash.

There are times in January when we're skating down our steep driveway carrying a full recycling bin when we wonder "Why do we bother?" Well, after a visit to Hartford's own garbage-atorium, you'll understand the benefits of recycling. The garbageatorium's real name is the visitor's center at the **Mid-Connecticut Resources Recovery Authority.** Your tour starts with what is called the "Temple of Trash," an area devoted to the cool stuff that people

throw out. After goggling at all the neat junk (and wishing you could take some home), you move on to where the real work happens. From a viewing area, you get a bird's-eye view of the ultimate in dumpster diving: watching colossal bins of trash being sorted and then rushed off via conveyor belts to recycling heaven. The wonderful Rube Goldberg silliness appeals to most kids, especially the ones who harbor a secret desire to dig through trash cans. The Mid-Connecticut Resources Recovery Authority is located at 211 Murphy Road (exit 27 from I–91). The visitor's center is open from Wednesday through Friday from noon to 4:00 P.M., September to June, and Tuesday through Saturday from 10:00 A.M. to 4:00 P.M., July and August. (860) 247–4280. No admission.

pastry or a cup of chocolate hazelnut gelato while entertaining fantasies of Venice. The bakery arm churns out rich pastries and beautiful traditional Italian cakes, tortes, and cookies. Open every day from 7:00 A.M. to 9:00 P.M. Call (860) 296–0426 for more information.

Many years ago, a good friend treated us to dinner at the **Polish National Home,** 60 Charter Oak Avenue, Hartford, and gently but firmly warned us, "If you write about this place, I will hunt you down and kill you." We didn't, but recently Jane and Michael Stern outed the Polish National Home in *Gourmet,* so we're assuming we can now tell you about it. When you visit, don't be intimidated by the brick ark in which the restaurant is located, and don't be deterred by the usually locked front door. You'll find the entrance at the back by the parking lot. Once inside, follow your nose. While you will find some familiar American dishes on the menu (fried chicken, turkey, and so forth), the real stars are the Polish dishes like the crunchy, toothsome *placki* (potato pancakes) and *pierogi* (half-moon shaped little dumplings filled with meat, potato and cheese, sauerkraut and mushrooms, or blueberries). For a taste of Poland, try the "Polish plate," which is a mini-buffet including everything from pierogi to *golabki* (stuffed cabbage) to *bigos* (sauerkraut braised with kielbasa and pork). Do we have to mention portions are huge? Don't miss the Saturday polka parties. Full bar. Open Monday through Saturday from 10:00 A.M. to early evening ("about 7:00 or 8:00," later if there's an event scheduled), Sunday from 11:00 A.M. to 3:00 P.M. Call (860) 247–1784 for hours and more information.

The most striking thing about the **Historical Museum of Medicine and Dentistry** (230 Scarborough Street) is just how far we've come in a couple of centuries. It was not that long ago that doctors were universally known as surgeons, carried their few instruments wrapped in pieces of leather or cloth, and mainly performed amputations. Well into the nineteenth century, doctors were still treating patients by bleeding them, and Pasteur began to work on the germ theory of disease only in 1850.

The museum records the medical profession's progress toward more modern and effective practices in displays of equipment, medications, instruments, and implements of destruction used by doctors and dentists from the eighteenth through the twentieth centuries. There are examining tables and chairs, anesthesia machines, and early X-ray machines. Some rooms contain glass cabinets of instruments; others are set up as doctors' offices of their era. There are also some gloomy portraits of Hartford's early medical men, a medical library open to researchers, and, of course, a display on the discovery of anesthesia. Open weekdays, 10:00 A.M. to 4:00 P.M. Admission is $2.00 for adults, $1.00 for children. Call (860) 236–5613.

If you've eaten a chocolate mousse cake in an upscale restaurant or have stared longingly at one in a gourmet market, the chances are it's a David Glass Chocolate Mousse Cake, made by Hartford's premier dessert-meister himself. Few people know that you can buy seconds and irregulars of his desserts at **Desserts by David Glass,** 140–150 Huyshope Avenue (The Colt Building). Here, most of the fabulous David Glass desserts, such as the Passion Fruit Mousse Cake or the Espresso Walnut Cake, are for sale, and seconds and irregulars of the signature chocolate mousse cake are turned into Chocolate Mousse Balls. Savings are excellent, sometimes as much as 50 percent off retail. The cakes available depend on what's being baked, so call ahead. Open 8:00 A.M. to 5:00 P.M., Monday through Friday. Call (860) 525–0345.

Elizabeth Park Rose Gardens on Prospect Avenue was the first municipally owned rose garden in America. More than 14,000 roses grace the park. There are also perennial gardens, greenhouses, nature walks, and a rock garden. The park offers something special during every season, but it's late June and early July when the roses are at their peak. In those few brief weeks, Elizabeth Park is an experience that overwhelms the senses. The many varieties of roses come in all sizes and hues to excite the eye, and the mingled scents, from the sweetly scented traditional American hybrids to the elegantly fragrant Damask roses, are indescribable. The Pond House on the premises contains a snack bar, lounge, and auditorium. Open daily, dawn to dusk. Call (860) 722–6490.

Back in 1874 the great American humorist and novelist Mark Twain (a.k.a. Samuel Langhorne Clemens) began summering in Hartford in a rambling, three-story, nineteen-room, red-brick Victorian mansion that he had built to his eccentric specifications; in 1881 he had the place redecorated in an even more eccentric style by Louis Comfort Tiffany. For the next quarter century, this was the Twain family summer home, which he often described as "part house, part steamboat." It was the place where Twain wrote some of his best works, including *Tom Sawyer, Huckleberry Finn, The Prince and the Pauper,* and *A Connecticut Yankee in King Arthur's Court.*

The restored **Mark Twain House,** 351 Farmington Avenue, is a museum and storehouse of Twain memorabilia. The unmistakable red-brick building, with its startling three-colored slate roof, its many gables, its monumental chimneys (it has eighteen fireplaces), and its flamboyant exterior walls painted in red and black Chinese stripes and trimmed in dark red, looms over the Farmington Avenue commuter traffic, almost like a lingering sardonic comment from the famous humorist. Inside, each of the mansion's unique rooms has been restored to as close to its

1881 condition as possible. About half of the original furnishings remain, including Twain's Venetian bed, whose ornate headboard so intrigued the author that he slept with his head at the foot of the bed so that he could see the intricate carvings. Open Monday and Wednesday through Saturday, 9:30 A.M. to 5:00 P.M., Sunday, noon to 5:00 P.M. Guided tours begin at the visitor center; the last one leaves at 4:00 P.M. Gift shop. Admission. Call (860) 493–6411.

When he designed his Hartford home, Mark Twain put the servants' quarters at the front so they could hear all the gossip on the street, and report the latest dish to him. The cost of building his home was—for those days—a mind-boggling $131,000.

Mark Twain really didn't say: "If you don't like the weather in New England, wait twenty-four hours." What he really said: "In the spring I have counted one hundred and thirty-six different kinds of weather in New England inside of four and twenty hours."

If you like Mark Twain, you probably have the kind of mind that revels in literary extravagance and appreciates the innate humor of frogs. If so, toddle on down to 589 Prospect Avenue in West Hartford. There you'll find our favorite rainy-day bookstore, **The Jumping Frog.** This is one of those antiquarian booksellers that are so popular in New England. Most of the really rare stuff is kept behind the counter, but there's also an excellent stock of plain old used books, both fiction and nonfiction, in ceiling-high shelves where you can get at them. There are 65,000 volumes in all, making this the largest used-book seller in the state. The shop also has an excellent collection of old ads and illustrations. What makes the Jumping Frog really neat, though, isn't the books. It's the frogs. Everywhere you look, on counters and shelves and walls

Mark Twain House

A Walk in the Center

*W*e aren't mall crawlers, but we love strolling and window shopping along city or village streets. In fact, had it not been for a wintry walk in West Hartford Center, this book probably would have different authors. The Center was our first off-the-beaten-path exploration. In 1983 in the midst of one of the coldest Decembers on record, we moved to Connecticut from Wisconsin, and we were not happy campers. The moving van carrying our furniture was AWOL. We, and two very cranky cats, were bunking in a hotel with all the charm of Moscow's infamous Lubyanka Prison. And it was just a week before Christmas. After several nights of hotel dining, we rambled up to West Hartford Center ("the Center") in search of a decent restaurant. In case you haven't heard the term, in Yankee-speak, center means a town's core business district; in the Midwest, we called it "downtown" or "down street."

At first look, we were smitten with the Center. It looked like Christmas in Connecticut. Big, puffy flakes of snow were falling, and the trees lining the street were swathed in fairy lights, just like a Currier and Ives engraving. Happy shoppers, laden with packages, bustled along the street, bopping in and out of prettily decorated stores. So we strolled, had a nice dinner, and on the way back to the hotel decided this Connecticut thing might just work out after all.

Since then a Center stroll along South Main, Farmington Avenue, and LaSalle Road has been one of our favorite fall and winter activities. Although the

Center's become something of a Westport clone in the last few years, it still offers welcome relief from cookie-cutter mega malls. In early December, Center merchants launch the holiday season with a festive walk, and usually in mid-June, the Center celebrates West Hartford Days with some attractive sales. Here are just a few of our favorite Center haunts: Coffeehouses have mushroomed along Farmington Avenue in the Center. So if you're hit with a yen for strong coffee, try **Peter B.'s Espresso Company**—Hartford's own coffeemeister; or **Michaele's Coffee and Tea,** the GenXer's favorite hangout. On LaSalle Road, you can stoke up on caffeine at the ubiquitous **Starbucks.**

The **Three Dog Bakery,** 967 Farmington Avenue; (860) 232–6299. Yep, a bakery just for dogs, or as one of our grandmothers would have said "People have too much money." A wonderful bit of silliness, perfect for the West Hartford Center ambiance and a zoo at the holidays when perfectly civilized people fight over the last doggy gift basket, this is a place to take your favorite pooch for a treat. We like the cutely named Snickerpoodles for our closest canines companions. So far, we've had no luck persuading the owner to add cat treats.

Spiritus Wines, 984-B Farmington Avenue; (860) 236–3515. Knowledgeable wine people, tastings on Saturdays.

The Elbow Room, 986 Farmington Avenue, is the latest hot dining spot to show off and to be shown off in. Fortunately there's some substance with all *the high style. The menu changes seasonally, but we've enjoyed pork tenderloin with Marsala and lemon tea tart with raspberry sorbet. Open for lunch and dinner, seven days a week. Dinner reservations advised. Visit The Elbow Room on the Web at: www.viewzone.com/elbowroom.*

***Eiko Japanalia,** 990 Farmington Avenue; (860) 523–7722. West Hartford's home-grown couturier. Joyous, beautifully cut, eminently wearable clothes in lush fabrics and colors for women built like Kate Moss or those somewhat more zaftig.*

***Pfau's Hardware,** 982 Farmington Avenue; (860) 523–4201. An old-fashioned, wooden-floored hardware store with all types of cool stuff in every nook and cranny. Kids love this place.*

***War & Pieces,** 7 South Main Street; (860) 232–0608. A superior source of hard-to-find military history, strategy and fantasy role-playing games, models, miniatures, books, and endlessly fascinating trains for the kidlets.*

and woodwork, there's frog art, frog cartoons, and frog artifacts, all mixed up with vintage *New Yorker* cartoons and, of course, books. Open Tuesday through Saturday from noon to 8:00 P.M. and Sunday and Monday from noon to 6:00 P.M. Call (860) 523–1622.

The University of Hartford's **Museum of American Political Life** (located at the university's Henry Jack Gray Center in West Hartford) houses a miscellaneous collection of political memorabilia, including 60,000 campaign artifacts, covering political life from the days of George Washington to the present. All this material is organized into half a dozen thematic exhibits covering such subjects as "The Presidency and the Press" and "Log Cabin to White House." The largest of these, "The History of Presidential Elections," covers the entire 70-foot-long east wall of the museum and serves as a reference point for all of the others. The most amusing exhibit is a life-size 3–D tableau of a nineteenth-century torchlight political parade that greets you as you enter. Near the head of the parade, on the main floor, there's a minitheater where you can view a ten-minute context-setting film on the history of political campaigns. Open Tuesday through Friday, 11:00 A.M. to 4:00 P.M., Saturday and Sunday, noon to 4:00 P.M. No gift shop, but the university bookstore next door has gift shop-type items connected with the museum. Call (860) 768–4090.

West Hartford also has a couple of those restored houses that are ubiquitous in Connecticut. The **Sarah Whitman Hooker House** (1237 New Britain Avenue) is a lovely 1720 saltbox named for a resident heroine of the American Revolution. Outside there's an herb garden and an antique (heritage) rose garden. Open Monday and Wednesday, 1:30 to 3:30 P.M. Special tours by appointment. Call (860) 523–5887.

The **Noah Webster Museum** (227 South Main Street) is lodged in the restored home of Noah Webster, the man who, at the age of seventy, wrote the first dictionary. The house is furnished much as it would have been when Webster lived there in the eighteenth century. The delightful thing about this house is that there's always a staff of "interpreters" on hand to answer questions. They dress in colonial garb, and they actually perform tasks such as baking in the kitchen fireplace; you may even get to taste the result. Open September through June daily (except Friday), 1:00 to 4:00 P.M. Open July and August, Monday, Thursday, and Friday, 11:00 A.M. to 4:00 P.M., Saturday and Sunday, 1:00 to 4:00 P.M. The gift shop on the property sells locally created craft items. Admission. Call (860) 521–5362.

West Hartford is also home to a fine little eatery out of another era. Located at number 319 on Park Road, the **Quaker Diner** is the special labor of love of Harry Bassilakis, whose grandfather built it in 1931.

Quaker Diner Meat Loaf

1 medium onion, chopped fine
1 carrot, chopped fine
2 stalks celery, chopped fine
$^1/_2$ green pepper, chopped fine
2 tablespoons butter
2 pounds ground beef (for a lower-fat meat loaf, use half lean ground beef and half ground turkey)
$^1/_3$ cup ketchup
$^1/_4$ to $^1/_3$ cup freshly grated Parmesan cheese
2 eggs
$^1/_2$ to $^3/_4$ cup flavored dry bread crumbs
salt, pepper, garlic powder to taste

Serves 6 to 8.

Melt butter in medium skillet over medium heat.

Add chopped celery, carrot, onion, and green pepper. Season to taste with garlic powder.

Saute for five to seven minutes, stirring frequently, until soft and onion is translucent. Remove from heat; let cool.

Season ground beef with salt, pepper, and garlic powder to taste.

Add ketchup, Parmesan cheese, eggs, bread crumbs, and sautéed vegetables to ground beef.

Mix lightly until all ingredients are combined.

Pat gently into meat-loaf shape and place in lightly greased baking dish or pat into lightly greased loaf pan.

Bake at 350 degrees until done. Start checking it after an hour; depending on your oven, total cooking time can vary between one hour and one hour and fifteen minutes. Let cool a little before slicing.

Serve with brown gravy and real mashed potatoes.

Harry gave up a career with a local insurance company in 1987 to restore the place to its original state, and many of the fittings—the high-backed wooden booths, counter stools, and the black and white deco tile in the hall leading to the bathrooms—are carefully tended original equipment. Other furnishings are from Harry's personal collection of antiques.

Aside from being a fine restoration, the Quaker's main claim to (local) fame is that it offers some of the best diner food in New England. Harry's mom, Agnes, does much of the cooking, including most of the specials and desserts. Just about everything is made from scratch, and some of the recipes, such as Agnes's justly famous meat loaf, are quite elaborate. The breakfasts are also first-rate. We especially like the Hole-in-One: French toast with the center cut out and replaced with a fried egg (the circular section of toast that was removed to make way for the egg goes back on as a hat).

The Quaker is open Monday through Friday, 6:00 A.M. to 2:30 P.M.; Saturday, 6:00 A.M. to 1:30 P.M.; Sunday, 6:00 A.M. to 1:30 P.M. Saturdays and Sundays, breakfast only. Call (860) 232–5523.

The Park Road area is another neighborhood that's pleasant for walking and window shopping. You'll find a couple of good antique shops, a used book store, and a bakery, **Your Just Desserts,** which specializes in extravagant cake. Not far from the Quaker, you'll find another equally delicious sampling of Connecticut's melting-pot cuisine. **Pho Tuong Lai** (206 Park Road) is a simple, storefront, family-run place, but we think you'll find some of the best Vietnamese cooking at bargain basement prices in the state. We're big fans of their *cha gio tom,* triangular-shaped, deep-fried shrimp rolls stuffed with shredded carrots, ground pork, and shrimp. Less adventurous palates will feel well fed and well satisfied with any of the ginger dishes, for example, the chicken and ginger with steamed broccoli cooked in a tasty reduction of soy with lots of snappy ginger flavor. Meat and potatoes lovers can chow down on the *bo luc lac* or "shaken beef," which is stir-fried cubes of filet mignon and onion in a savory sauce, served on a bed of cold, crunchy watercress. The "house dish" is *Pho,* the beef and noodle soup that's the national soup of Vietnam. Pho bears absolutely no resemblance to the Campbell's beef noodle soup of childhood. The soup part may look familiar to you (tender, buttery beef and noodles are served in a clear broth), but what makes this dish special are the accompaniments of lime wedges, bean sprouts, fresh basil, and chilis served along side, so you can doctor your soup to fit your taste. On weekends, check out the off-menu specials: hot and spicy soup (Friday evenings and Saturdays); a rice-paper dumpling dish; and chicken and rice noodle soup

(Sunday). No liquor license, BYOB. Open daily from 9:00 A.M. to 8:00 P.M. Call (860) 523–9134 for more information.

Connecticut pizza partisans all have one thing in common: every one of them just knows that *their* favorite pizza palace makes the best pie in the state. We won't make that claim here, but we will say that our personal favorite is **Harry's Pizza** (1003 Farmington Avenue). Harry's has one great advantage over most pizza shops you'll meet: Pizza is all that it does. Oh, you can get a very nice side salad with Harry's special peppery dressing. But you won't find the usual selection of dubious sandwiches and ho-hum pasta to distract the guys in the kitchen. Their eyes are firmly on the pie, and they turn out an excellent one. Harry's standard pie is a traditional tomato and mozzarella number, with a crisp thin crust and an eclectic selection of toppings. Besides the standard sausage, mushrooms, and pepperoni, you can choose from embellishments such as sun-dried tomatoes and the veggie of the day. Harry also makes splendiferous clam pizzas and shrimp pizzas and a surprisingly good Hawaiian pizza with Canadian bacon and pineapple. The shop doesn't exactly serve dessert, but it does deliver complimentary dollops of pink grapefruit ice as a palette cleanser, an absolutely perfect touch. Open Monday through Wednesday, 4:30 to 10:00 P.M.; Thursday, 11:30 A.M. to 2:00 P.M. and 4:30 to 10:00 P.M.; Friday, 11:30 A.M. to 2 P.M. and 4:30 to 11:00 P.M.; Saturday 2:30 to 11:00 P.M.; and Sunday 2:30 to 9:30 P.M. Call (860) 231–7166.

On the fringe of West Hartford Center at 950 Trout Brook is the **Science Center of Connecticut,** one of Connecticut's premier science museums (and we don't say that because The Powers That Be at the museum seem to appreciate dinos as much as we do). Kids can explore the wonders of science and technology close-up and hands-on. Most kids of our acquaintance like the giant walk-in kaleidoscope, the computer center, and the marine life touch tanks. The center mounts some very interesting exhibits throughout the year with lots of hands-on kid activities. Open Tuesday through Saturday, 10:00 A.M to 5:00 P.M.; Sunday, noon to 5:00 P.M. Longer hours and open Mondays in the summer and during school holidays. Closed major holidays. Admission for adults and children three or older. Additional admission for special exhibits, the planetarium, and laser light shows. Call (860) 231–2824.

South of Hartford is the township of Wethersfield. Once known as "Onion Town" because the crop grew so well within its confines,

THE HEARTLAND

Rocky Hill Trivia

You can see about 500 sets of dinosaur tracks (that's about 2,000 individual dino footprints) at Dinosaur State Park in Rocky Hill.

Wethersfield boasts the motto of "the most ancient towne in Connecticut." It was an important port on the Connecticut River until the river changed its course and left Old Wethersfield behind. Today **Olde Weathersfield,** the remnants of the original town, consists of half a dozen eighteenth- and early nineteenth-century homes, a museum, a church, and a seventeenth-century graveyard. Most of these places are on Main Street, and all are within easy walking distance of each other. This small area was the setting for the wonderful young adult book *The Witch of Blackbird Pond,* by Elizabeth Speare, as well as for two amusing novels of Gothic horror—*The Other* and *Harvest Home*—written by Wethersfield native Thomas Tryon.

The three restored eighteenth-century homes making up the **Webb-Deane-Stevens Museum** (211 Main Street) are the heart of this attraction. Washington stayed in the 1752-vintage **Joseph Webb House** in 1781, and it was there that he and Rochambeau met to plan the Yorktown campaign. The **Silas Deane House** (1766) belonged to a member of the First Continental Congress (and America's first envoy to France). These houses and the **Isaac Stevens House** (1788) contain a collection of furnishings and decorative elements spanning the years 1690–1840. There are five acres of open ground and a couple of herb gardens behind the houses. Open daily except Tuesdays, 10:00 A.M. to 4:00 P.M. (last tour at 3:00 P.M.) from May to October; during the winter, open weekends only from 1:00 to 4:00 P.M. Admission. Call (860) 529–0612.

There are three other restored homes in the neighborhood: the **Captain James Francis House,** about 3 blocks away at 120 Hartford Avenue; the **Buttolph-Williams House** on the corner of Marsh and Broad; and the **Hurlbut-Dunham House** at 212 Main Street. The **Old Academy Museum,** with changing historical exhibits, is across the street from the Webb-Deane-Stevens Museum at 150 Main Street. Also across the street from the museum at 250 Main Street is the **Meetinghouse,** a famous 350-year-old brick church whose congregation of more than 2,000 still worships there each Sunday; you can view the interior with its original hand-carved pulpit on weekdays from 9:00 A.M. to 5:00 P.M. Behind the Meetinghouse are the Old Burying Grounds; thousands of headstones, dating from 1648 onward, record the thoughts, philosophies, and attitudes of generations of local citizens.

It's not normally treated as a historic site, but at 263 Main Street, you'll find **Comstock, Ferre & Company,** the oldest continuously operating seed company in the United States. Since 1820, it's been a source for seeds and plants. It also stocks specialty craft items and gifts. The chestnut post-and-beam structures date from the late 1700s. Open Wednesday, Friday, and Saturday from 10:00 A.M. to 6:00 P.M.; all other days from 10:00 A.M. to 5:00 P.M. Call (860) 571–6590.

In 1966, while clearing some ground for the construction of a new state building in Rocky Hill, bulldozer operator Ed McCarthy uncovered some strange rocks. They seemed to have strange markings and scorings on them. Later examination proved these were the tracks of dinosaurs that prowled the area 185 million years ago. In those days this part of Connecticut was a mud flat on the shore of a huge lake, rich in fish and small crocodilians; good eating for a growing dino.

After covering the initial excavation of 1,500 tracks to preserve them, the state excavated another 500 tracks, enclosed them in a geodesic dome, added an AV facility that offers a neat presentation on dinos, and called the result **Dinosaur State Park.** The inside of the dome is dominated by a full-sized reconstruction of a carnivorous dino called *dilophosaurus,* but the big attraction is tracks. Most of the impressions are three-toed, and they run up to 16 inches long. The park lets visitors make plaster casts of the tracks and posts instructions for doing so; take along a quarter cup of cooking oil, about ten pounds of plaster of paris (for casting giant dino tracks, take along twenty pounds of plastor

A Huguenot Haunting

*A*ny Connecticut guide book will tell you that the **Huguenot House**, in East Hartford's Martin Park (307 Burnside Avenue), is an excellent example of a restored colonial house. They'll talk about the gambrel roof and the vaulted dormer windows. What they won't tell you is that the Huguenot House has a ghost, albeit a friendly one. When the house was moved from its original location to the park, workers started reporting seeing the ghost of a lady in a blue dress. As construction started to restore and anchor the house to its new site, work was frequently disrupted by the loud sounds of crashing, knocking, and hammering, even when the house was empty. The occurrences became so constant, workers dubbed the haunt Benny, and the foreman made out a daily work list for the ghost. Some believe the ghost or ghosts are the original builders of the house. The house was built in 1761 by a family of French Huguenots, a Protestant sect, known for their carpentry. Call Greater Hartford Tourism for more information on the house: (800) 793–4480. Web address: www. travelfile.com/get?ghtd.

of paris), sticks or paint stirrers for stirring the plaster of paris, a bucket, and paper towels for each cast. Open Tuesday through Sunday, 9:00 A.M. to 4:30 P.M. Admission. Call (860) 529–8423.

When you're in Rocky Hill, you're very close to Cromwell and the site of one of our favorite animal parks, **Amy's Udder Joy Exotic Animal Farm Park** at 27 North Road. As animal lovers, we're very careful about recommending petting zoos and animal parks, and we've checked this one out fairly carefully. The park is licensed by the United States Department of Agriculture under the Animal Welfare Act, the Connecticut Department of Environmental Protection, and the state and federal Fish and Game Service, so the animals are well taken care of. You'll find lots of such exotic critters as llamas, peacocks, emus, and Tennessee fainting goats (our favorites). There's a good guided tour, pony rides on Saturday and Sunday, and a picnic area for lunch or snacks. Admission. Open May through Labor Day, Wednesday through Saturday, 11:00 A.M. to 5:00 P.M., and Labor Day through the end of October from 11:00 A.M. to 4:00 P.M. (weather permitting). Call (860) 635–3924.

In 1687 Governor Edmund Andros, appointed by the British Crown to oversee Connecticut, demanded colonists return the royal charter that made Connecticut a separate colony. Hartford colonists hid the charter in a towering oak tree called the Charter Oak. When the Charter Oak finally toppled in 1856, it was 1,000 years old.

East of the River

New England's population has swelled from numerous waves of immigrants over the years, and as each ethnic group has been assimilated, it has left behind a host of bakeries, restaurants, and similar establishments. In the 1970s, the Vietnamese came to Connecticut, bringing with them a cuisine that incorporates elements of Chinese, French, and Malaysian cooking (among others) yet manages to remain unique and delightfully fresh.

Dedicated to preserving the artifacts of the fireman's life, **The Fire Museum** at 230 Pine Street in Manchester has everything having to do with fire fighting, from old leather fire buckets and ornate marching hats to wooden water mains and a rare eighteenth-century fire warden's staff. There's even a collection of old prints and lithographs of fires, from the prephotographic era when the artist and lithographer were as important as the reporter to the process of communicating the news. It's all displayed inside a big old firehouse that was built in 1901 to protect the Cheney Brothers silk mills, at the time the main industry of this, the "Silk City."

There's a good deal of large equipment on display, with the emphasis on the hand-operated and horse-drawn. Some of the hand pumpers needed as many as thirty men to operate them. There's also a horse-drawn hose wagon, a steam-operated pumper, and an ornate hand-pulled, four-wheeled hose reel designed mainly for use in parades, a reminder of an age when the local firehouse was a center of social and political activity.

The museum is open mid-April through mid-November, 10:00 A.M. to 5:00 P.M. on Friday and Saturday, and noon to 5:00 P.M. on Sunday. Take exit 60 off Interstate 84 and head east up Center Street to the sixth traffic light. Bear right going up the hill; the museum is about ½ mile from the light. No admission; donations requested. Call (860) 649–9436.

A few blocks away, at 106 Hartford Road, is another museum. This one, the **Cheney Homestead,** is the birthplace of the brothers who launched the silk industry in Manchester (and whose factory the firehouse was designed to protect). The house is filled with eighteenth-and nineteenth-century furnishings, and there's an eighteenth-century schoolhouse on the grounds. Open Thursday and Sunday, 1:00 to 5:00 P.M. Adult admission. Call (860) 643–5588.

Far removed in time and space from the Cheney Homestead is the **New England Jukebox and Amusement Company,** which operates out of a storefront next to its warehouse at 77 Tolland Turnpike in Manchester. For thirty years this company has been servicing and repairing juke

What's in a Name?

*H*artford has been dubbed the "Insurance City," but other Connecticut cities have been nicknamed for the industries that once dominated them. Can you match up the city with its nickname? You'll find answers below.

1.	Bristol	A.	Research City
2.	Meriden	B.	Thread City
3.	Naugatuck	C.	Brass City
4.	Stamford	D.	Silver City
5.	Waterbury	E.	Clock City
6.	Willimantic	F.	Rubber City

Some Connecticut cities are famous for the flowers grown there. Norwich, for example, is the "Rose City," Bristol is the "Mum City," and Winsted is the "Laurel City." All three cities have festivals that celebrate their city flowers. Call the regional tourism office or the Connecticut State Tourism office for more information. You'll find these phone numbers on pages xxi–xxii.

1. E; 2.D; 3.F; 4. A; 5.C; 6.B.

boxes, pinball machines, and other coin-operated amusements. In the mid-1980s the owners decided to augment their service operation with a retail business in nostalgia, with a special emphasis on the coin-operated items that were already the core of their business. Today New England Jukebox and Amusement Company purchases coin-op amusements and other mechanical devices from all over America, refurbishes them, and sells them to the general public. While the firm is little known locally,

In Connecticut signs commemorating historical events are literally in your face. A while back, just to show they didn't take things too seriously, some wags in South Glastonbury erected a billboard that read 357 YEARS AGO ON THIS SPOT, NOTHING HAPPENED.

coin-op enthusiasts come to Manchester from across the United States to look, listen, and purchase.

For such an unpretentious store, the breadth of merchandise on display here is amazing. There are antique phones, radios, postcards, and ephemera all jumbled up with neon signs and clocks, comics, pinball machines, and old 45-r.p.m. records. There are also all kinds of coin-operated goodies. On one visit, we saw a lovely old popcorn machine; a 1930s-vintage "Flying A Gasoline" pump; an antique bubble gum machine; a 1927 Mills 5-cent slot machine; and half a dozen jukeboxes, not to mention a player piano with neat carved griffin legs. The stars were two original deco-styled Wurlitzer 1015 O.M.T. jukeboxes, complete with working bubble tubes and rotating color cylinders.

New England Jukebox and Amusement Company is particularly difficult to find unless you know what you're looking for. Take Interstate 84 to exit 63 and get on the Tolland Turnpike heading west. Turn left into the shopping area just past the Acadia Restaurant. Beside the National Speed Center and set back from the road is New England Jukebox and Amusement Company. Open weekdays, 10:00 A.M. to 6:00 P.M., Saturday 10:00 A.M. to 2:00 P.M., or by appointment. If the place seems deserted, ring the bell; they may be in the warehouse. Call (860) 646–1533.

Also in Manchester, you'll find **Shady Glen,** 840 East Middle Turnpike. Shady Glen is one of those places that make you think you've walked into a filming of "Happy Days." It's been around since 1948 and used to sell the milk and ice cream produced on John and Bernice Reig's dairy farm. Today, it's a popular eatery and old-fashioned soda fountain. Besides soaking up the old-fashioned atmosphere, you'll want to try the cheeseburgers. Topped with crispy slabs of fried cheese, they look a little like UFOs. Cheese fanciers can get an order of fried cheese on the side. Then try the ice cream or a soda fountain creation such as a sundae or soda.

Peachy Keen Factoid

Every day there are about twenty-five ice cream flavors from which to choose. Popular flavors such as chocolate chip are always on the menu, while flavors such as mincemeat or cranberry ice cream rotate with the seasons. Things get really hectic and crowded at Shady Glen because it's something of a Manchester tradition, but the tables turn over quickly, so be patient and wait. Open Monday through Saturday, 8:00 A.M. to 10:00 P.M., Sunday, 11:00 A.M. to 7:00 P.M. Call (860) 649–4245. There's a second Shady Glen at 360 West Middle Turnpike; (860) 643–0511.

If you visit Shady Glen with kids, we suggest you let them run off their sugar high from the Glen's wonderful ice cream concoctions, with a visit to a museum that's not the least bit staid and gives them lots of wonderful hands-on things to do. So many museums are off-putting for children; if the security guards don't intimidate them, then the adult-size exhibits bore then into heavy-eyed sleepiness or into restless bad behavior. The **Lutz Children's Museum,** 247 South Main Street, Manchester, is scaled for and built for children. The emphasis here is on "please touch" science and natural history exhibits. The museum sponsors several excellent programs throughout the year. Open Tuesday and Wednesday, 2:00 P.M. to 5:00 P.M.; Thursday and Friday, 9:30 A.M. to 5:00 P.M.; Saturday and Sunday, noon to 5:00 P.M. Admission. Call (860) 643–0949

The **Rocky Hill–Glastonbury Ferry,** spanning the Connecticut River and linking one part of Route 160 (Ferry Lane) to the other, has been in operation since 1655. That makes it the oldest continuously operating ferry in America. It's also a good place to cross the river, if you want to avoid the usually heavy traffic around Hartford's bridges. Service is provided by a tug called the *Cumberland* and by a three-car barge called the *Hollister.* The ferry operates May 1 to mid-November. Hours are 7:00 A.M. to 6:45 P.M. Monday through Friday; 10:30 A.M. to 5:00 P.M., Saturday and Sunday. Prices are almost insignificant. For more information call (860) 594–2000.

Central Connecticut

New Britain got its manufacturing start making sleigh bells. From these modest beginnings the city gradually branched out after

THE HEARTLAND

New Britain Trivia

The Copernicus Planetarium at Central Connecticut State University in New Britain houses the second largest publicly available telescope in the United States.

1800 into the manufacture of other hardware products, until it eventually came to be known as the "Hardware City." With the expansion of industry came waves of new immigrants seeking jobs in the tool works. The Irish came first, then the Germans and Swedes, then the Italians. The biggest waves, though, consisted of Eastern Europeans, including Lithuanians, Ukrainians, and Armenians. Probably the largest group in this wave were the Poles. Even after the hardware industry moved abroad, Polish immigrants continued to come to New Britain. Today the city's population of first- and second-generation Poles is greater than that of many cities in Poland. They have contributed their music, their language, and their food to the city.

The center of the Polish community is a Broad Street business district where Polish is spoken almost as freely as English.

You can taste the wonders of Polish food at **Cracovia** at 60 Broad Street. Our Polish friends swear by its food. The decor here is dominated by the Polish falcon, and announcements about upcoming community events are printed in Polish only. Thankfully the menu is in English, and the waitresses are good at explaining menu choices to non-Poles. The food is Central and Eastern European, bounteous, and cheap. The *pierogi* are excellent. So are the *golombki* (tender, tasty cabbage rolls stuffed with beef and rice, braised in a slightly sweet tomato sauce). Most of the entrees are served with true mashed potatoes, with the happy little lumps that mark them as the real thing instead of the instant variety. The homemade soups are served in bathtub-sized portions; the white borscht and the dill pickle soups get high marks. Open 8:00 A.M. to 8:00 P.M. daily (only until 6:00 P.M. on Sunday). Call (860) 223–4443.

To create at home some of the Polish specialties you enjoyed at Cracovia, make a stop at **Podlasie,** 95 Broad Street. It's like visiting a marketplace in Eastern Europe. You'll find Polish mineral water, dark dense bread, newspapers, ingredients for Polish cooking, and some very intriguing Polish chocolates on the shelves. The back of the store is given over to a dairy case (great country butter), a pastry case full of some elegant looking tortes and cakes, and a case for cheeses, herring, fresh meats, and cold cuts, many made in the store. Most of the shoppers are Polish, so Polish is the common tongue. There's usually at least one English-speaker in the store who is happy to help you translate. If not, we've gotten by quite nicely by pointing, smiling, and nodding. Open Tuesday through Thursday, 9:00 A.M. to 6:00 P.M.; Friday, 9:00 A.M. to 7:00 P.M.; Saturday, 8:00 A.M. to 5:00 P.M. Call (860) 224–8467.

Like Rodney Dangerfield, New Britain gets no respect. But it should. At least for its *New Britain Museum of American Art* (56 Lexington Street). Established in 1903, this is the oldest museum in the United States devoted solely to American art. Its 3,000 holdings include portraits by Cassatt, Stuart, Copley, and Sargent and the western bronzes of Solon Borglum, as well as works by the likes of O'Keeffe, Noguchi, and Wyeth. Its collection of American impressionists is second to none. There are landscapes by Hassam, Inness, Bierstadt, Cole, and Church, among others. Most impressive of all are the *Arts of Life in America* murals by Thomas Hart Benton. These murals must have been reproduced in half the American history textbooks published in the past thirty years, and most people are familiar with them, but it's only when you look up at the full-size originals that the power of Benton's work really manifests itself. Open Tuesday, Thursday, Friday, and Sunday from 1:00 P.M. to 5:00 P.M.; Wednesday from noon to 7:00 P.M.; Saturday from 10:00 A.M. to 5:00 P.M.; closed Sunday. Gift shop. Admission is $5.00 for adults, $4.00 for seniors, $3.00 for students, and free for children under twelve. Free admission on Saturday mornings from 10:00 A.M. to noon. Call (860) 229–0257.

New Britain is also home to the *Copernican Space Science Center,* a small planetarium, observatory, and space museum located on the campus of Central Connecticut State University. The planetarium presents programs every Friday and Saturday at 8:30 P.M., and the observatory is open at the same time. The latter facility boasts the largest public telescope in New England, a monster with a 16-inch reflector, and visitors are encouraged to step up to the device and view the moon, planets, and stars. In fact, a visit to the observatory is free when you attend a show at the planetarium. There is a modest admission for presentations or for visiting the observatory. Call (860) 827–7419.

Before hardware meant things like CPUs and printers, New Britain was Connecticut's (maybe the world's) Hardware City. That history is commemorated in the *New Britain Industrial Museum,* 185 Main Street. It's a small but choice museum, put together by people who genuinely love New Britain and its industrial past. You can trace New Britain's past and see its future as you view of history of the companies that put New Britain on the map: Stanley Works, Fafnir Bearing, and American Hardware. Open Monday through Friday, 2:00 P.M. to 5:00 P.M. Free. Call (860) 832–8654.

Got cannoli? When LiVecchi's Pastry Shop on Franklin Avenue in Hartford moved to Wethersfield, we were desolate—where would we ever find such heavenly cannolis? And then we had an epiphany, which came as it tends to do to most travel writers: we got lost and while lost we found *Giovanni's Bakery and Pastry Shop,* 488 New Britain Avenue,

Pop Culture

*W*e grew up calling that fizzy, sweet stuff that came in bottles "pop"; we didn't learn to call it "soda" until we moved to Connecticut. Had we moved farther north to Massachusetts, we'd call it "tonic." Whatever you call it, soda pop was one of the quintessential memories of our youth. About twice a summer, our fathers would load up the kids in the station wagons and drive down to the local bottling plant where we'd pick up a case of pop—clear glass bottles of neon-colored liquid, all nestled nicely in a wooden carrying case. Somehow picking up a six-pack of cans at the convenience store doesn't carry the same aura of romance.

That's why we make a pilgrimage each summer to **Avery's Beverages,** 520 Corbin Avenue. It's the wonderful Aladdin's cave of jewel-colored soda and mysterious Rube Goldberg machinery we remember from childhood. At Avery's they bottle soda the way we remember it, wooden carrying cases and all. The family has been bottling soda in the same red barn in New Britain since 1904. You can choose from among twenty-six different flavors of soda or go for what we do, the mixed case. If you call ahead, you can arrange a tour of the bottling works. Call (860) 224–0830 for hours and tour information.

Newington. Not only are the cannoli delightful, but the cookies, cakes, and all those other wonderful Italian pastries—the ones with names we can never pronounce—are equally toothsome. And it doesn't hurt that the guy who bakes up most of the pastries is something of a hunk (in a pony-tailed, Steven-Seagalish way) himself! Giovanni's also dishes up great Italian ice, making it a refreshing stop on a blistering central Connecticut summer Sunday. Closed Monday. Open Tuesday through Saturday from 7:30 A.M. to 7:00 P.M. and Sunday from 7:30 A.M. to 5 P.M.

Several "hams" of our acquaintance took us to task for not including the **American Radio Relay League,** 225 Main Street, Newington, in previous editions. To assuage hurt feelings and because we think it's a cool place, here's the skinny on the ARRL. Founded in 1914, the 163,000-member ARRL is not only Mecca for ham radio operators but also the official voice of Amateur Radio. In these days of computers, e-mail, telecommunications, and cell phones, you may think of ham radio as merely an interesting hobby. During natural disasters, however, ham radios help to rescue people and provide vital information. Our favorite ham operator, Bill Blackwell, once provided a "find shelter now" warning to a lady in the Caribbean during a hurricane that probably saved her life. Beside the administrative offices of the AARL, you'll find W1AW, the league's amateur radio station. Visitors can tour the station, listen to radio calls, try their hand at tapping out code, or view some of the artifacts of the league's history. By the way, there's no one story as to why operators are called hams. Some people say it's because the radio gives operators a chance to "ham it up," others say it comes from the ham-fisted way early operators pounded their code keys. The most likely story is that "ham" is derived from "am," a contraction of "amateur." Call (860) 594–0200 for information about tours, special programs, or membership in the league, or visit them on the web at www.arrl.org.

As you drive down Route 9 between New Britain and Farmington, you'll pass a hauntingly familiar sculpture of some American marines raising a flag. This is the *Iwo Jima Survivors' Memorial Park and Monument.* It is dedicated to 6,821 Americans who, during World War II, gave their lives in the desperate fighting for the Pacific island of Iwo Jima, the place where it was said that "uncommon valour" was a "common virtue." The monument's sculpture recreates the famous flag-raising by American troops atop Mount Suribachi. This is the only such monument in the United States dedicated to America's Iwo Jima dead. On special days, such as Veterans' Day, the monument is decorated with an avenue of American flags. Open daily from 9:00 A.M. to sunset.

Back in the eighteenth century, *Route 10* was the major thoroughfare passing through Plainville. It was down this road that Rochambeau's French army marched on its way to join Washington at Yorktown and win the decisive battle of the American Revolution (the location of one of the French campgrounds is marked by a small plaque next to a gas station on Route 6 in Farmington). French armies notwithstanding, the road was less traveled in that century, and trips had to be planned more carefully. To aid the traveler the route was marked with milestones indicating the distance to Hartford. Today, at three places along the east side of Route 10 (at the corner of Betsy Road, at the junction of Route 372, and in front of Woodmore Village), you can still see the old milestones.

Just south of Main Street on Route 10, you can also see the *Old East Street Burying Grounds.* First used in 1766, this cemetery is noted for its remarkable headstones. It is also known for a curious effect of Plainville's geography. The water table lies very near the surface here, so special poles had to be employed to hold the coffins of the departed in their graves. The cemetery went out of use in 1856 and is closed today. Each Memorial Day, however, after the parade, the cemetery holds an open house; you can also get a guided tour by calling (860) 747–6577 for an appointment.

Recently renovated to the tune of $35 million, Bristol's *Lake Compounce Amusement Park,* 822 Lake Avenue, is the country's oldest continuously running amusement park. The roller coaster, the dreaded Zoomerang, is properly frightening, and the river raft ride is fun on a hot day. But we like Lake Compounce for its old-fashioned carousel. You'll find horses carved by Looff, Carmel, and Stein & Goldstein. There are forty-nine horses (twenty-seven jumpers and twenty-two standers), a goat, and two chariots. The original Wurlitzer organ still grinds out tunes for riders. Admission. Open daily, except Tuesdays, from about Memorial Day until Labor Day and weekends from Labor Day until the end of September. During Halloween, Lake Compounce sponsors a scary haunted house attraction with some way scary admission prices. Call (860) 583–3300 for operating hours and schedule. Web address: www.lakecompounce.com.

Ever since we started writing *Connecticut: Off the Beaten Path*, **Dick's Antiques** has been subject of much discussion between the authors. It goes something like this: (Deborah) "Gee, Dick's is so great we have to include it in this edition of the book." (David) "No, no, Dick's stuff is too good. I don't want to tell people about Dick's." Well, guess who finally won! So without further ado, here's all about Dick's Antiques. Located not far from Lake Compounce, Dick's Antiques, 670 Lake Avenue, is a treasure trove of great antiques, especially oak, Arts and Crafts, and Mission. We love visiting Dick (yes, there really is a Dick at Dick's Antiques); he's always got something new and nifty to show us. Almost as much as we like his American oak, we love listening to Dick spin yarns about his adventures in antiquing. Dick's quite a raconteur in the time-honored spirit of Yankee peddler of yesteryear. Hours at Dick's are as eccentric as the owner, especially in summer, so call ahead to make sure he's around. Open Monday and Friday, 10:00 A.M. to 6:00 P.M.; Saturday and Sunday, noon to 5:00 P.M.; closed Tuesday. Call (860) 584–2566 for information and hours.

About the middle of the nineteenth century, Bristol was the center of clock- and watchmaking in the Northeast. At one time the town supported 280 clockmakers, and in 1860 they turned out a total of 200,000 clocks. Today the great clockworks are only a memory preserved in the town's **American Clock & Watch Museum,** which is located in a big white clapboard house at 100 Maple Street.

Within the walls of the 1801-vintage Miles Lewis House and two modern additions, the museum manages to display a collection of 3,000 clocks and watches, including many of local manufacture. This vast assemblage is organized by types and eras, so that as you move from room to room, you can observe how the styles of clock cases changed to match furniture styles. Tours are entirely self-guided, but the exhibits are well marked,

Halloween Spooktaculars

*N*ew England and Halloween go together hand and glove. Maybe it's the scudding clouds posed against a full harvest moon. Maybe it's the whirling wisps of ground fog whipped along by a shuddering wind. Maybe it's the weight of all those years of history. We're not sure what it is, but we enjoy Halloween in New England a lot. While the Witch's Dungeon is our all-time favorite Halloween celebration, Connecticut really goes all out for Halloween.

We've always been partial to old cemeteries. In fact, we decided to get married while walking in an old cemetery in Pennsylvania, so we're really in our glory with Connecticut's ancient boneyards to roam in. Several old cemeteries offer walking tours, great places to explore our state's history or atmospheric places for a fall walk.

- **Old Norwichtown Burial Ground,** Old Cemetery Lane (off Town Street) in Norwich. Located near the town green, the cemetery is open every day until dusk. Brochures are available at the cemetery entrance for self-guided tours. For more information, call the Norwich Tourism Office at (860) 886–4683.

- **Cedar Hill Cemetery,** 453 Fairfield Avenue, Hartford, offers self-guided walking tours with free brochures available at the cemetery and free guided tours on most weekends throughout the summer. For a

schedule of tours, call the cemetery office at (860) 956–3311.

- The **Wethersfield Historical Society** offers tours of the Village Cemetery at certain times of the year. The tours begin at the cemetery behind the First Church of Christ, 250 Main Street. Admission. The society also sells a booklet for self-guided tours, which is available by calling (860) 529–7656.

- The **Middlesex County Historical Society** offers a graveyard tour each year on the Sunday before Halloween. Admission. For more information, call (860) 346–0756.

Other Halloween Spook-Fests

- The **Haunted Graveyard** at **Lyman Orchards** in Middlefield isn't a proper cemetery, but rather a fundraiser (and hair-raiser) for juvenile diabetes. The event consists of several outdoor areas, including haunted castles, bizarre mazes (the scariest part for us), and the pièce de résistance, the graveyard. There's no guide on your tour, just stumble along from site to site, getting the bejeebers scared out of you. This place is so scary we recommend you leave little kids at home. The haunted graveyard usually opens on weekends sometime after Columbus Day and stays open through Halloween. Admission. Call Lyman Orchards at (860) 280–3399 for hours and more information.

and the logical organization aids comprehension. Among the more interesting items are some oak clock cases from the 1920s and 1930s, which are exhibited together with the metal rollers that pressed the intricate designs into the wood. There are also some lovely "tall" clocks, including some made by Eli Terry. There's even one clock whose workings are carved entirely from wood. The American Clock & Watch Museum is open daily, from April to November 30; 10:00 A.M. to 5:00 P.M. Open during the winter by appointment only. Admission. Call (860) 583–6070.

Clocks and watches aren't the only items collected in Bristol. Housed in a restored turn-of-the-century factory building at 95 Riverside Avenue, the *New England Carousel Museum* contains some of the best examples of antique carousel art in existence, more than 300 pieces in all. Featured items include a collection of band organs, the entire carousel from Santa's Land, in Putnam Vermont, and a gorgeous pair of 1915 carved chariots, each encrusted with 1,500 glass jewels. During the hard winter of 1993–94, the museum also sheltered the horses from the carousel at nearby Lake Compounce amusement park and may do so again in the future. This was the first museum of its kind on the East Coast, and many preservationists still consider it the best.

The main museum occupies the building's ground floor. Wood-carvers and painters perform restorations on the second floor, and if you happen to be there while they are working, you can go upstairs and watch. Open Monday through Saturday 10:00 A.M. to 5:00 P.M., Sunday noon to 5:00 P.M. You can also reserve the museum for special events, with youth group sleepovers (called "Painted Pony Pajama Parties") and weddings being hot tickets in this part of the state. Admission. Call (860) 585–5411.

New England Carousel Museum

Connecticut's Friendliest Antiquing Village

Woodbury may boast of having Connecticut's "Antique Avenue" and Putnam might wear the laurels for being a whole town of antique shops, but for our money, the prize for the friendliest antiquing destination in the state goes, hands-down, to the Plantsville section of Southington (exit 30 off I–84).

When we first visited Plantsville, we assumed its name came from its proximity to Cheshire, the "Plant Bedding Capital of Connecticut." The owners of the Plantsville Station Antique Shoppes quickly set us straight. Plantsville is named for its founder, Robert Plant. (Unfortunately, not the Robert Plant of Led Zep fame.)

Throughout the year Plantsville keeps a busy calendar of special events such as a Halloween festival and a winter holiday celebration. Call the Central Connecticut Tourism District at (860) 225–3901 for more information. Visit them on the Web at www.centralct.org or e-mail at info@centralct.org.

The village is pretty compact; we recommend you park your car on Main Street and just start exploring. To get you started, here are a few of our favorites:

Plantsville Station Antique Shops, 75 West Main Street. This group shop carries lots of nice old linens, oak furniture, and collectibles. Owners Robert and Kathleen Celetano are very friendly and helpful—just don't ask them when the next train leaves. The building in which the shop makes its home only looks like a train station. In previous incarnations it housed a

machine shop and other light industry—never a train station. Even so, the Celetanos frequently field phone calls from people wanting a train schedule. Open Wednesday through Saturday, 10:00 A.M. to 5:00 P.M. and Sunday from noon to 5:00 P.M. Call (860) 628–8918.

Dayle's Antiques, 53 West Main Street, is quite a nice little shop, beautifully and imaginatively decorated. We like the owner, who is a friendly and gregarious sort, always happy to entertain with antiquing war stories and tales of the "great find that got away." Makes amateur antiquers feel a little better knowing the pros sometimes get skunked, too. Dayle's is a wonderful place to browse for linens, china, and collectibles. Open Wednesday to Saturday, 10:00 A.M. to 5:00 P.M. and Sunday, noon to 5:00 P.M. Call (860) 378–0290.

Victoria Rose, 35 West Main Street, doesn't sell antiques. It's a charmingly decorated little jewel box of a store brimming with Victoriana. Just about anything you might covet from the pages of Victoria magazine, you can find at Victoria Rose—collectibles, cards, wrapping paper and gift bags, decorative items, and wonderful replica, ornate Victorian jewelry. Definitely worth a visit. Open Monday to Saturday, 10:00 A.M. to 5:00 P.M. and Sunday, noon to 4:00 P.M. Call (860) 621–0935 for more information.

Nothing's New, 69 West Main Street, is a cool place for people who like old vacuum-tube radios. The owners, John and Corrine Watts, specialize in the sale and service of vintage radios. It's a fun shop to poke around and an *interesting experience for kids. Try explaining a vacuum-tube radio to kids raised on computers. Open Wednesday to Saturday, 10:00 A.M.* *to 4:00 P.M. and Sunday, 1:00 to 5:00 P.M. Call (860) 276–0143 for more information.*

One of the best attractions in Bristol is one that you are unlikely to stumble across unless you're a native Nutmegger and you happen to be around at Halloween time. For many years now, Bristol artist Cortland Hull has been re-creating some of the world's classiest horrors in a museum that he operates only during the last two weekends in October. This seasonal extravaganza pays loving tribute to all those cinematic monsters (and the geniuses behind them doing the makeup and special effects) that made our hearts pound and our palms sweat and caused a few of us to spend our childhoods wearing necklaces strung with garlic cloves. Hull's **Witch's Dungeon** on Battle Street is a labyrinth of room-sized scenes from famous Hollywood chillers, complete in every visual and aural detail. Imagine standing before a realistic Egyptian tomb and seeing Karnak, the mummy, slowly rise from his sarcophagus, or watching Dracula wither to dust after being impaled by Dr. Van Helsing. The Witch's Dungeon is a fine place to celebrate All Hallows' Eve by getting scared out of a few years' growth, but be cautioned, this place is not for younger children. Admission. Open the last two weekends in October, 7:00 to 10:00 P.M. Call (860) 583–8306. For information on special events year round, go to www.witchesdungeon.org.

Saint's on Route 10 in Southington has a simple philosophy: use top-quality ingredients and don't tinker with success. The philosophy must work because the eatery's been dishing up its famous hot dogs to popular acclaim since 1967. Since then, they've used the same mustard, the same relish, and the same chili sauce recipe. *Yankee* magazine gave Saint's an honorable mention when it rated "Best Hot Dogs of New England," and some chili dog connoisseurs swear these dogs are the best in the state. Saint's is something of a local hangout with an easy camaraderie shared with the customers and the staff. Open daily from 6:00 A.M. to 8:30 P.M. Call (860) 747–0566.

The Tobacco Valley

ocated off Route 20 in East Granby, **Old New-Gate Prison and Copper Mine** was originally chartered as the first copper mine in America in 1707. By 1773 further mining proved uneconomical, and in December of that year, the Simsbury copper mine was turned into the Connecticut Colony's chief place of confinement for various classes of thieves and counterfeiters. The new facility was named for London's notorious Newgate prison, whose evil reputation it eventually came to share. New-Gate became the nation's first state prison in 1776, when the colonies severed their ties with the British Crown. In 1827 the prison was abandoned, and its inmates were transferred to a newly completed prison in Weathersfield; in keeping with the prison's lurid history, an inmate died the night before the transfer while trying to escape. During its half century of operation, New-Gate was widely known as "the worst hell-hole in North America." While the prison did include a substantial complex of above-ground buildings, the prisoners were confined 50 feet below ground in the dank passageways of the old mine. Disease claimed many. Others committed suicide or went insane.

One of the prison's most famous inmates was one William "Big Bad Bill" Stuart of Wilton, the leader of what was, in the second decade of the nineteenth century, the most infamous criminal gang in New England. From his early teens, when he was expelled from school for (among other things) tarring and feathering the schoolmaster's cow, Bill had been raising Cain; before entering New-Gate he blasted his way out of a seemingly secure stone-walled jail in Albany and had escaped from numerous other jails. New-Gate was his greatest challenge; in fact, Stuart made two unsuccessful attempts to escape from the prison, the second of which, in 1817, resulted in a prison riot during which Big Bad Bill was bayonetted three times in addition to being shot in the groin and sabered across the head. Stuart healed and was finally released in 1825 to disappear into the Litchfield Hills. The riot that he started, however, sparked an investigation that ended the worst practices at New-Gate and ultimately contributed to its being shut down.

The ruins of New-Gate are picturesque, the view of the surrounding countryside is magnificent, and there are picnic facilities available outside the walls. The real fun, though, is the underground tour of the mine itself. Be sure not to miss it. The gift shop sells some neat replicas of jailer's warrants and wanted posters and cute "I Escaped from Old New-Gate Prison" T-shirts. Open Wednesday through Sunday, 10:00 A.M. to 4:30 P.M., from mid-May through October. Bring sneakers or walking shoes and a sweater or jacket if you intend to go underground; the mine is damp, and subterranean temperatures average in the forties. Gift shop. Admission. Call (860) 653–3563.

If you are a lover of attractions of the biggest, smallest, first, and oldest variety, take a minute in Granby to visit the **Granby Oak** on Day Street, off Route 20. This 300-year-old white oak has been a source of inspiration to more artists and photographers than we can shake a stick at. And it's Granby's town seal, appearing on everything from official stationary to town vehicles. In the fall, it's especially attractive and worthy of a photograph.

The antiques shops at **Salmon Brook Shops,** 563 Salmon Brook in Granby, may be hard to find, but it's definitely worth the drive. When we first set out to find it, we drove and drove and drove on Salmon Brook (Route 10), and, finally, after seeing signs alerting us the Massachusetts border was just minutes away, we gave up and went home. Fortunately, we decided to try again. It's definitely worth the drive, so just hang in there and keep driving. Salmon Brook Antique is a cozy group shop, with lot of cutie-pie stuff. While you won't find eighteenth-century Newport desks, you will find lots of nice kitchen items and a plethora of ephemera (postcards, movie posters, and advertising art). A frame shop shares quarters with the antiques shop, so when you find the perfect old movie poster, framing it is as easy as pie. We've found the people who staff the place as charming as the objects they carry. Call (860) 653–6587 for hours, information, and directions.

For anyone interested in the history of aviation, the **New England Air Museum** in Windsor Locks is a must. This is one of only four large museums of aviation history in the United States, and one of only two in the East. The oldest of its seventy-five aircraft (a beautiful wood-and-canvas Bleriot XI monoplane) dates from 1909. There is also an extensive collection of World War II vintage fighters and bombers and quite a number of modern jet aircraft, including an F–100A Super Sabre, a Vietnam-era F–105 ("Thud"), and some early Eastern bloc jet fighters. The exhibits seem to be split about equally between military and commercial craft. The fifty aircraft housed indoors are in excellent condition, most having been more or less completely restored. The mostly larger items kept outside are less complete, and some of them are still being restored.

In addition to the aircraft themselves, there are numerous smaller items of interest strewn about the museum's hangarlike main building, including a variety of engines, some cockpit simulators, a couple of fairly slick video presentations, and a collection of flight memorabilia. Many of these smaller items in the museum were acquired from area aerospace companies and can't be seen anywhere else.

The New England Air Museum is located off Route 75, within hailing distance of Bradley International Airport. Just follow the signs, and try to ignore the fact that you seem to be driving through a tangled wilderness right out of *Sleeping Beauty.* Open daily, 10:00 A.M. to 5:00 P.M. Gift shop. Admission. Call (860) 623–3305. Web address: www.neam.org.

A few miles up Route 75 from the New England Air Museum is another museum commemorating a quite different era. The restored 1764-vintage home at 232 South Main Street (Route 75) in Suffield is now the **King House Museum.** The building's interesting architectural features include seven original fireplaces (one with a beehive oven) and a unique shell-carved corner cupboard. Among the period furnishings is a four-poster bed that formerly graced the Jonathan Trumbull house in Lebanon. Displays include an assortment of Bennington pottery, a tin-ware collection, and, appropriately enough for the Tobacco Valley, a collection of cigar and tobacco memorabilia. The King House Museum is open May through September on Wednesdays and Saturdays from 11:00 A.M. to 4:00 P.M. Admission. Call (860) 668–5286.

The **Connecticut Fire Museum** at 58 North Road (Route 140) in East Windsor is one of two unrelated museums in Hartford County that attempt to trace the history of fire fighting. It has a collection of about twenty fire trucks built between 1850 and 1950. It also includes some models and displays on the history of fire fighting. Open April through August, weekdays, 10:00 A.M. to 4:00 P.M.; Saturday and Sunday, noon to 5:00 P.M. Open September and October on Saturday from 10:00 A.M. to 5:00 P.M. and on Sunday from noon to 5:00 P.M. Admission. Call (860) 623–4732.

The **Connecticut Trolley Museum,** at the same location as the Connecticut Fire Museum, is one of two unrelated trolley museums in the state. This one, run by the nonprofit Connecticut Electric Railway Association, has a collection of more than thirty trolley cars made between 1892 and 1947 plus steam and electrical locomotives and various historic railroad equipment. While most of the trolleys are from New

England and Canada, there are some from as far away as Illinois and Ohio and one from Rio de Janeiro. The museum offers a carbarn tour and, on selected weekends, a 3-mile trolley ride. Special events are held throughout the year. The most interesting are a Halloween Festival, called Rails to the Dark Side, and the annual Winterfest in December. For Winterfest the association offers nightly (until 9:00 P.M.) leisurely rides along a 1½-mile route decorated with twinkling colored lights.

Walking and Hiking Hints

*C*onnecticut offers miles of wonderful walking and hiking on state trails and in state and municipal parks. We want you to enjoy your hike and stay in the best of health, so please take a few precautions:

• Wear appropriate clothing for the season. Wear footgear that protects your feet and ankles from injury and, even in the hottest weather, don't forget to wear socks.

• Bring a hat, sunscreen, insect repellent, and a first-aid kit.

• Don't get dehydrated. Bring along extra water, no matter what the season.

• If you're hiking in a park with park ranger services, always check in and tell park authorities where you'll be hiking.

• Before walking or hiking, take the time to learn more about the prevention of Lyme disease by talking with your physician or a staffer with the local public health department.

• Lyme disease, a bacterial infection transmitted through a deer tick bite, is a problem in Connecticut. Symptoms of Lyme disease include: rash, flu-like symptoms (such as fever, joint aches), headaches, stiffness, stiff neck, and occasional forgetfulness and mental confusion. By taking a few simple precautions you can avoid contracting Lyme disease:

• If there are furred animals around, then it's a good bet, ticks are around, too. Make it a habit to check your dog for ticks after each walk. Learn how to distinguish the deer ticks from "dog ticks." Deer ticks in the adult form are reddish brown; dog ticks are larger and darker than deer ticks. Dog ticks are not believed to carry Lyme disease.

• Wear protective light-colored clothing and brush your clothes carefully before going indoors. Tick repellent spray can be effective, but follow manufacturers directions carefully. Take a thorough shower after a walk or a hike and check yourself carefully.

• If a tick is attached to you, carefully remove it by tugging gently with fine-nosed tweezers. Do not burn it off or cover it with an ointment such as Vaseline because this can increase your risk of infection. When you've removed the tick, save it in a small empty bottle (an empty prescription bottle is ideal) for identification, if needed.

Open April through December, Saturday 10:00 A.M. to 5:00 P.M., and Sunday, noon to 5:00 P.M. Hours vary in the off-season but are pretty much restricted to weekend and holiday afternoons. There is a modest charge to ride the trolleys. Call (860) 627–6540.

Once upon a time, every town had a **Bart's Drive-In,** 55 Palisado Avenue, Windsor. Today, they are as scarce as hen's teeth. Once you find a place like Bart's, you become a customer for life—it's just that kind of place. Bart's started as a hot-dog stand and eventually expanded to include an indoor dining area. One counter serves cold sandwiches—that's the counter in the eat-in area. The walls are lined with newspaper clippings, telegrams, and letters from folks. The grill and ice cream fountain counter is the more popular counter. Even with indoor seating, lots of folks continue to eat in their cars or at the picnic tables that over-look the river. You can usually spot anglers fishing from the shore or in boats, so after a meal it's fun to sit awhile and watch, or stroll down the sidewalk that runs along the river. On Wednesday nights in the summer Bart's hosts Cruise Nights. Tuesday is Family Night with games and contests that are family oriented, like hula hooping. Bart's has a customer service that many Fortune 500 companies might adopt: Treat customers like they are your own best friends. That's true whether you're a lifelong customer or a first-time walk-in.

The grill menu features the hot dogs, hamburgers, award-winning chili-dogs (regular or spicy), French fries, onion rings, fried fish filets, whole bellied clams, etc. The full-meal menu changes daily; offerings include homey dishes like meatloaf, shepherd's pie, yankee pot roast, and pasta dishes. Old-fashioned milkshakes in vanilla, chocolate, coffee, straw-berry, and peanut butter (better than it sounds) are available at the foun-tain. For 25 cents more, you can request an old-fashioned malted milk shake. The staff keeps the eat-in area pretty clean, but sometimes the traf-fic is so heavy that you may need to brush off a table before you sit down. Call (860) 688–9035 for hours and information about special events.

Settled on October 4, 1633, Windsor claims to be the "oldest English settlement in Connecticut." Wethersfield disputes this claim. Windsor is also home to the annual **Shad Derby Festival,** a distinction dis-puted by absolutely no one.

The Connecticut River shad is a fat but bony, blue-green-and-silver rela-tive of the herring. Each spring the shad migrate to northern waters to spawn, and one of their favorite spawning grounds is in the Connecticut River near Windsor. This means Windsor gets the best of the shad world, both fish and roe.

As a comestible shad has both its partisans and its detractors. Some natives feel spring isn't spring in Connecticut without a dish of broiled shad roe with bacon or shad baked on a plank. Others maintain that you should throw away the shad and eat the plank.

In Windsor they've been celebrating the shad as part of the town's annual rite of spring for more than four decades. The shad season lasts for about six weeks, but most of the shad festivities happen during the first two weeks of May. That's when you'll find everything from the Shad Derby (biggest shad caught) to the crowning of the Shad Queen, with a golf tournament and road race thrown in just to make things interesting. On Derby Day Windsor pretty much closes up shop to honor the shad with a townwide festival on Broad Street, where you'll find many food booths featuring the shad and its roe.

Shad mania aside, Windsor is known for a small but interesting museum that documents the early days of European settlement in Connecticut. The Windsor Historical Society's **Wilson Museum** at 96 Palisado Avenue documents the town's history. The society's library includes, among other things, old journals and maps, an 1800 highway survey, and an original payroll list of the Windsor residents who answered the rebel alarm in Boston in spring 1775. The museum also contains a variety of Indian relics and a display of Americana that includes a rare Hadley Chest.

Next door to the museum and connected to it by a breezeway is the **Lieutenant Walter Fyler House,** deeded in 1640 to Lieutenant Fyler in recognition for his services in the Pequot War (1637). The old house has been partially restored to its original condition, complete with interior shutters and original paneling.

The society offers guided tours and a slide show on Windsor. The museum is open Tuesday through Saturday, 10:00 A.M. to 4:00 P.M. Also open by appointment. Adult admission. Call (860) 688–3813.

For the agrarian minded, the **Farm Implement Museum** (434 Tunxis Avenue Extension; Route 189 north) in Bloomfield features exhibits of hand tools and farm implements dating from 1790. There is also a small petting zoo on the premises. Open daily from 9:00 A.M. to about 5:00 P.M. Admission. Call (860) 242–1130.

Also in Bloomfield, you'll find one of the best places in Hartford County for a leisurely walk: the campus of the CIGNA Corporation at 900 Cottage Grove Road. You can roam over 280 acres of roads and trails that pass through woodlands and by ponds, and lush plantings as well as sculptures by Isamo Noguchi. Open daily dawn to dusk.

Bloomfield is a far piece from the shore, but it's home to one of the best, most underrated seafood restaurants in the state. ***Bloomfield Seafood,*** 8 Mountain Avenue. Many years ago when we first started eating at Bloomfield Seafood it was hidden behind an auto repair shop. After that location burned, it moved to its current home, tucked into a very pedestrian shopping center. In fact, the location is so uninspiring you might be tempted to bus right past it. Don't—it offers some of the best and freshest fish and seafood in Hartford County at very good prices. We like the seafood chowders or stews; the oyster stew is especially comforting on a blustery day. We've made a tradition of having a bowl of their oyster stew for Christmas Eve supper. We prefer our fish simply prepared, so we love their sautéed sole. You can't go wrong ordering from the regular menu offerings or the daily specials. Don't leave without sampling their key lime pie. The service is knowledgeable, warm, and friendly. You'll find the staff knows how to treat kids well. The servers have the knack of turning the biggest "fish-frowning" kid into a fish-eating fan. And did we mention that the prices are very moderate for the quality of food and service? Open for lunch, Tuesday through Saturday, 11:00 A.M. to 2:00 P.M.; early bird dinners, Tuesday through Saturday, 4:00 TO 5:00 P.M.; dinner, Tuesday through Saturday, 5:00 to 8:00 P.M. Call (860) 242–3474 for more information.

The Farmington Valley

*H*ill-Stead Museum (35 Mountain Road) is so Farmington that it is almost impossible to imagine it existing anywhere else. Housed in a white clapboard 1901 replica of a neocolonial house built in an eighteenth-century English farm-style is an amazing collection of French impressionist paintings, prints, antique furniture, porcelain, textiles, and clocks!

Hill-Stead was originally home to Cleveland iron mogul Alfred Atmore Pope. In keeping with his wealth and pretensions, Pope made sure that when it was time for daughter Theodate to go away to school, his child was entrusted to a proper Eastern institution: Miss Porter's School in Farmington. Upon graduation Theodate persuaded Daddy to forsake the Buckeye State and move east to the Nutmeg State. She also talked him into springing for a new house designed by then trendy architect Stanford White with a sunken garden designed by landscape architect Beatrix Farrand. And, since Theodate had an abiding interest in architecture, nothing would do but that the young lady should assist White in designing the new family manse. White was either a very good business-man or he was truly impressed with Theodate's work, because he cut his fee by $25,000 in appreciation for her help. Miss Pope went on to become the first woman licensed to practice architecture in the United States.

Like so many American captains of industry, Pope was a collector. This was an age in which America's newly rich raided the homes and galleries of Europe for furnishings, often buying art and antiques in wholesale lots. The Popes were fairly typical in this regard, and their tastes were certainly eclectic. Chippendale furniture, fine porcelain, contemporary bronzes, and pre-Columbian statuary all jostled for space in the Pope home. On the walls hung a Degas, a Manet, a Cassatt, and no less than three Monets. The piano was a custom-designed Steinway. It was all glo-riously excessive. And it is all still there, just as it was when Theodate died, leaving behind fifty pages of instructions for the house to be turned into a museum and maintained just as she left it.

Hill-Stead Museum is open Tuesday through Sunday, 10:00 A.M. to 5:00 P.M., with the last tour leaving at 4:00 P.M. each day. Hill-Stead has a wonderful gift shop, which includes prints of works exclusive to it, such as Monet's *Haystacks* and Degas's *Dancers in Pink*. Admission. Call (860) 677–4787. For tour information, call (860) 677–9064.

At 37 High Street in Farmington, just around the corner from the Hill-Stead Museum, is the **Stanley-Whitman House,** a beautifully restored 1720 colonial homestead. The original house, built to a typical early eighteenth-century standard, has a central chimney flanked by two chambers on each of two floors; it was later expanded by the addition of a lean-to that gives it a saltbox shape. The wood-sided exterior was originally painted with a mixture of ox blood and buttermilk; the restoration has not gone to quite that extreme, but otherwise it seems authentic. Hinged access panels inside the house let you see details of the original construction and restoration. The house is filled with period furnishings and is surrounded by herb and flower gardens. May through October, open Wednesday through Sunday, noon to 4:00 P.M. November through April, open Saturday and Sunday noon to 4:00 P.M. The gift shop sells some wonderful hand-painted wooden boxes of the house and the neighboring First Church of Christ as well as some beau-tiful hand-sewn baby blankets. Admission. Call (860) 677–9222.

The neighborhood around the Stanley-Whitman House includes a large number of eighteenth-century (and some nineteenth-century) homes and buildings, all of them still in use by modern residents. These can be seen to best advantage from Route 10, where, in less than a mile,

The Amistad Revolt

*T*hanks to a couple of recent books and a Spielberg movie (filmed in part at Mystic Seaport), the Amistad revolt now has its rightful place in American history. If you don't know the story, here's a vest-pocket synopsis. In spring 1839, people of the Mendi culture were abducted from their home in Africa by slave traders and transported to Cuba, where they were sold into slavery and boarded the schooner Amistad. Once aboard, the Mendi, led by Sengbe Pieh (later called Joseph Cinque), rebelled against their captors and staged a successful mutiny. The Mendi attempted to steer the boat back to Africa, but instead the Amistad floated off Long Island Sound and eventually was brought into New London. The Mendi were arrested and tried, spending more than a year in jail in New Haven. Former President John Quincy Adams successfully argued their case for freedom to the United States Supreme Court. But what happened to the Mendi after they won their freedom forever linked Farmington to the Amistad story. In March 1841, thirty-eight Mendi traveled to Farmington, where they lived and were educated for nine months while the village raised funds for their passage home. With a population of little more than 2,000, rural Farmington was such a stronghold of abolitionist sentiment that it was known as the "Grand Central Station" of the Underground Railroad. In November 1841, thirty-seven Mendi (one, a man named Foone, drowned in the Farmington Canal) left Farmington and

started the long journey home to Africa, arriving in January 1842.

Today you can visit several sites in Farmington associated with the Amistad revolt. Most places are within easy walking distance in Old Farmington on Main and Garden Streets. The First Church of Christ Congregational, 75 Main Street, (860–677–2601), was designed by boatbuilder-architect Judah Woodruff in 1771. During the Mendis' stay, the Reverend Noah Porter, father of Sarah Porter, founder of Miss Porter's School, led the congregation. Union Hall, also known as the Farmington Art Guild, was once a meeting place—oddly—for both the pro-slavery and abolitionists factions. Riverside Cemetery, 160 Garden Street, (860–674–0280), is the final resting place of Foone, the Mendi who drowned in the Farmington Canal. Outside of Farmington center, the Barney House, 11 Mountain Springs Road, was built by John Treadwell Norton, who served as mentor to Mendi leader Joseph Cinque.

The Farmington Historical Society, 71 Main Street, (860–678–1645), publishes a pamphlet featuring a map of Amistad-related sites with a short history of each. For more information call or write the Farmington Valley Visitors Association, P. O. Box 1015, Simsbury, CT 06070; (800) 4–WELCOME. For a fee, the Farmington Historical Society offers group (ten or more persons preferred) tours of Farmington sites on the Freedom Trail. Call (860) 678–1645 for more information.

you can view a 1772 Congregational meeting house, a renovated 1650 gristmill, a colonial-era graveyard, and the remains of the Farmington Canal. Also on Route 10, a couple of hundred yards from the intersection of Route 4, is Miss Porter's School, known for turning out such graduates as Jacqueline Bouvier Kennedy Onassis.

The old saying "Can't see the forest for the trees" is particularly well suited to the MDC's (Metropolitan District Commission) *Demonstration Forest Trail,* Farmington Avenue (Route 4) on the Farmington-West Hartford border, near MDC Reservoir 1 (the West Hartford Reservoir). On this ³/₄-mile trail you can find many points of interest that illustrate just how interconnected and complex our ecosystem is—worlds within worlds. At the trail head, pick up a booklet describing the trail's twenty eight points of interest. As you walk the trail, you'll see the environment not from your point of view but from the point of view of the animals and plants that inhabit the ecosystem. It's a wonderful way to teach kids how trees depend on birds, and how the insects on the forest's floor live in their own little universe. The booklet also includes some interesting tidbits about the plants and animals that make their home in the Demonstration Forest area. This is an excellent field trip for school classes, Cub Scouts or Brownies, or an Earth Day celebration with your own kids. The MDC Demonstration trail is open year-around from 7:00 A.M. to dusk. There's ample free parking. Call (860) 278–7850, ext. 3104 or (860) 379–0916, ext. 3104 for more information.

Heading into Farmington on Route 4 west, you'll see off to your right, as you come down the hill a small plaza, which houses the *Epicure Market* (838 Main Street). We love heading west on Route 4 to the Litchfield Hills, but on some days of the week the whole Litchfield Hills region can feel as though it's wearing a big CLOSED sign. That's why we usually stop at the Epicure, the Farmington Valley's version of Dean and Deluca, for picnic fixings. You'll find wonderful takeout at the deli, from entire meals to hearty sandwiches. In fact, our cat Vlad is addicted to their meat loaf. The market carries the awesome LaBreu handcrafted breads, perfect with a deli salad sampler or a selection from the cheese case. To wash down your picnic, you can choose from their selection of microbrews or Norwalk's own SoBe soda. Open seven days, from 8:00 A.M. to around 7:00 P.M.; longer evening hours on Fridays and shorter hours on the weekend. Call (860) 677–1601 for hours and information.

Should you be in Farmington over a weekend and find yourself with a little time on your hands, stay on Route 4 west through Farmington Center, cross the bridge over the Farmington River, and turn right onto

Mini-Golf

*E*ven though two of our houses have backed up onto golf courses, we've managed to resist the lure of serious adult golf with its attendant rules and, in our humble opinions, emphasis on loud polyester clothes. But miniature golf with all its goofy charm is a different story. Connecticut abounds with mini-golf courses with settings ranging from pretty and pastoral to Disney-ish. Here are some of our favorites:

Riverfront Miniature Golf and Ice Cream, *218 River Road, Farmington,* fronts Antiques on the Farmington, so parents can drop the kids off for a round of mini-golf while they leisurely browse through the antiques shop. Unlike most mini-golf courses, Riverfront doesn't rely on kitsch, but rather has constructed a course with hazards and holes made up of rocks taken from the nearby Farmington River. It's one of the prettiest mini-golf courses we've seen and one adult enough that older kids will enjoy it without thinking it's "duh." A word of warning: The course runs along the Farmington River, so keep an eagle eye on young golfers, who might tend, as our niece Elise does, to invent their own rules involving throwing balls and golf clubs into the river. There's a cute ice cream shop attached to the golf course, where parched duffers and their families can refresh themselves. Birthday parties and other special occasions a specialty.

Open daily from around Memorial Day to Labor Day; open weekends from Labor Day through around Halloween. Call (860) 675–4653.

Safari Golf, *2340 Berlin Turnpike, Berlin.* Safari Golf is probably Connecticut's most famous mini-golf course. Playing the course is a lot like taking a safari; you'll find lots of life-sized jungle animals lying in wait for you, waterfalls to traverse, and lots of waving, ominous junglelike landscaping. The replicas of lions, tigers, and other critters give the course a sense of wonderful silliness and the water hazards make it difficult enough that older kids and adults won't get bored. Open daily in the summer, with shorter hours in fall and spring. Ice cream and other snack stuff available. The folks at Safari Golf know how to make kids' birthday parties an occasion. Call (860) 828–9800.

Hidden Valley, *2060 West Street, Southington.* Like Riverfront Mini-golf, Hidden Valley relies on pretty rather than cute. It's a challenging course for older kids and adults with lots of waterfalls and other traps. Batting cages and snack foods available. Available for birthday parties and other special occasions. Open daily in summer, with shorter hours in spring and fall. Call (860) 621–1630 for information.

Town Farm Road. You'll pass a monster, forty-five-hole golf course called ***Tunxis Plantation Country Club and Golf Course,*** Town Farm Road; (860) 678–7128. How Tunxis Plantation Country Club came into being is something of a local legend. Denied membership in one of Farmington's snootier golf clubs, a local developer simply built his own. Golfers of our acquaintance highly recommend the place, especially for autumn golfing. Tunxis Plantation usually opens around Easter and closes mid-November.

About 2 miles past Tunxis Plantation you'll happen upon the **Fisher Old Farms,** 199 Town Farm Road; (860) 676–1281. This is one of the oldest family farms in Connecticut, and the only organic dairy farm left in the Farmington Valley. Be sure to see the rolling meadows in this gentle valley. They are marked by glacial mounds left by the last Ice Age. During spring and fall you can often see a rafter of wild turkeys grazing in the fields. Yes, rafter is the term for a flock of turkeys. The farm's vegetable stand is open from tomato and corn season through pumpkin season. You'll also find wonderful tiny nubbin new potatoes, squash, some herbs, and colorful bouquets of old-fashioned kitchen garden flowers.

Crossing into Avon, follow the road to its end. If you turn left, you travel the narrow, winding roads past **Avon Old Farms School.** This private school for boys was designed by Theodate Pope Riddle of Hill-Stead Museum fame. The buildings are modeled after cottages in Great Britain's Cotswolds.

In 1997, Connecticut produced 9,000 gallons of maple syrup. It takes forty gallons of sweet sap from the sugar maple tree to make one gallon of maple syrup. Maple syrup comes in grades with Fancy being the lightest in color and the most delicate. As you move from Grade A Medium Amber to Grade B the syrup's color gets darker and the flavor stronger. Real maple fanciers might want to check out the Annual Hebron Maple Festival, which is usually held the second weekend in March. It's a good place to enjoy sugar on snow, a taffy-like candy made by pouring boiling hot maple syrup on clean snow. Call (860) 228–9503 for more information.

There are no tours of the campus for the public, but you can drive through the school to look at the buildings. By the way, Old Farms Road can be tricky; it's full of full of sharp curves, twists, and narrow bridges, so drive carefully and obey the speed limits.

If you had turned right instead of left, you would have quickly happened upon Fisher Meadows Conservation Area, a wonderful little park for hiking and walking. The green trail around Spring Lake pond measures a little over a mile and is a good, flat walk. For a more strenuous hike, take the 2-plus-mile red trail, which follows the Farmington River. The red trail offers lots of up and down walking, so it's not a good walk for small kids or tots in strollers. In the spring and summer, both trails offer great opportunities to spot wildflowers such as the Virginia waterleaf, a declining species numbering less than twelve populations in Connecticut. Due to fallout from the town council's Dog War of 1998, dogs are no longer permitted to run off-leash.

Farmington Antiques Weekend

*T*ravel about 1½ miles on Town Farm Road to the verdant pastures of the **Farmington Polo Grounds,** 152 Town Farm Road, (860) 677–8427. Most weekends between Mother's Day and Columbus Day, this spot hops with activity from various shows. In early June and over the Labor Day weekend, the Polo Grounds hosts the Farmington Antiques Weekend, (508) 839–9735, one of the most prestigious (and colossal) antiques shows in the country. Such style-setters such as Martha Stewart and Ralph Lauren are regulars, and Steven Spielberg and Barbra Streisand have also attended. The quin-tessential Farmington Antiques Show story is the one about the dealer who asked Robert Redford to show his dri-ver's license before accepting his check.

We're not style-setters, but we are vet-eran show-goers, and we're happy to share with you our hints for successful antiquing. Other events at the Polo Grounds include: two huge craft fairs, held over Mother's Day and Columbus Day weekends (craft fair information line 860–871–7914), folk-art shows, chili cook-offs, and horse shows. No matter whether you attend in the spring or fall, the Farmington Antiques Weekend is one mammoth show. Here's how to make the most of the show:

• Don't dress to kill. Yeah, it's a kind of chi-chi show with an upscale crowd, but wear comfortable clothes and shoes. Don't forget your hat, sun-glasses, and sunblock.

• Stormy weather. It's more likely the spring show will be washed out, but Labor Day is smack dab in the middle of hurricane season, so be prepared. Umbrellas are OK, but a rain hat and poncho or foldable raincoat is better.

• Hands free. Forget the designer leather bags. Bring a fanny pack or, better yet, a backpack for money and personal things. A folding tote bag for carrying small breakable stuff is also helpful.

• Bring folding green. Forget charge cards and even checks. You'll get the best deal if you pay in cash. Many dealers and the food vendors can't break large bills (and many are suspicious of counterfeit $50s and $100s) so bring along small bills.

• Nix the early admission. Unless you're a dealer or have a long or very

Back out on Route 4 west, you'll encounter, tucked away in a converted trolley barn, a top-flight restaurant called **Apricots** that serves an eclectic cuisine based on French, nouvelle American, and country cooking. The downstairs is a comfortable bar and lower-priced pub-style restaurant, popular, noisy, and crowded. Upstairs is an elegant, white-tablecloth eatery, occupying several rambling windowed rooms overlooking the Farmington River. The service here is impeccable. The menu changes throughout the year, but there's always a pasta and chicken dish of the specific hit list, don't pay the early buyers fee ($20 per person for admission between 7:00 and 10:00 A.M.), but do arrive as close to the 10:00 A.M. general public show opening as you can.

- Bring extra water. Various service clubs sell beverages and food at the show, but we usually tote along some extra water. The field gets dusty, so pack some Wash & Dry towelettes or a damp washcloth for mopping up. The food at the show is just OK, so bring a snack and eat elsewhere after the show.

- Leave tiny tots and dogs at home. Neither will have a good time. It's hot, crowded, dusty, and full of boring, big-people stuff. And the tents are chockablock with fragile, very expensive pretties that tempt tiny hands and wagging tails.

- Use the porters. It doesn't cost much to have them haul your treasures to your car.

- It's easy to get lost. Set up a meeting place like the main food tent or the ATM machine for reunions. Also, it's a good idea to decide who stays put and who hunts if someone wanders off.

- Use your program to mark dealers and to take notes. Trust us, by the end of the show, you'll never remember where you saw the perfect Roseville vase at 10:00 A.M.

- If you snooze, you lose. When you find the absolutely perfect whatever, snag it. Prices are relatively high at the Farmington show, but if you ask, most dealers will do a little better on the price. Nonetheless, the discounts might not be as generous as you're accustomed to. The closer you get to the end of the show, the easier it is to dicker.

- Be prepared. Bring a notepad, pen, and measuring tape. Bring measurements of any space at home you want to fill.

day, as well as several fish and seafood entrees. Among memorable dishes are pork tenderloin in sour cherry sauce and the apricot dessert sampler full of everything apricot from gelato to chocolate-apricot truffles. Open daily for lunch (11:30 A.M. to 2:30 P.M.) and dinner (6:00 P.M. to 10:00 P.M.) and Sunday for dinner (5:30 P.M. to 9:00 P.M. Call (860) 673–5405.

About 5 miles east of the center of Farmington along Route 4 is the Unionville section of the township. During the late eighteenth and early nineteenth centuries, this area was a minor industrial center. It made flints for Washington's army and guns for the War of 1812. It also manufactured the pikes that Torrington native John Brown took with him to Harper's Ferry (and that he intended to use to arm the Southern slaves whom he planned to induce to revolt). The **Unionville Museum** at 15 School Street displays many of these items of local manufacture. The museum is open Wednesday, Saturday, and Sunday from 2:00 to 4:00 P.M. Call (860) 673–2231.

How Do You Like Your Cider?

Early cider is sweet. Mid-season cider is tart. And sweet comes around again with late cider because the apples are riper and have more sugar.

Located in a converted gristmill at 218 River Road in Farmington's Unionville section is *Antiques on the Farmington,* a multidealer shop. The antique furniture and appointments are displayed to advantage in room settings, and considering the quality, prices are quite reasonable. Call (860) 673–9205.

LaMothe's Sugar House at 89 Stone Road in Burlington is one of just a handful of real old-fashioned sugar houses left in Connecticut. Here, during February and March, visitors can tour a working house and see the whole process of "sugaring off." There's a big old sap boiler that cooks maple sap into syrup, which you can then see blended with cream and butter and poured into molds to make creamy shaped candies (like Santas or maple leafs), or mixed with other ingredients to make maple taffy. The sugar house sells syrup, maple candy of all persuasions, and maple fudge. Visitors always get a sample of some type of maple sweet. In Connecticut, the peak season for sugaring off is late February or early March, but LaMothe's is open year-round. In addition to the sweet treats, LaMothe's also keeps several bunnies, just right for petting, and their golden retrievers are always around to provide a neighborly escort to the sugar house. Open year-round, noon to 7:00 P.M., Monday through Thursday; noon to 5:00 P.M., Friday to Sunday. See syrup made mid-February through mid-March on weekends. Call (860) 582–6135 for more information.

About ¼ mile south on Route 10 (Waterville Road) from Avon Old Farms is the *Avon Cider Mill.* Armando Lattizori built the mill back in 1919, and the present generation of Lattizoris still make cider the old-fashioned way. When Armando opened his cider mill, he bought a used

Seeing Connecticut's Fall Foliage

*H*ere are some of our suggestions for places to see the best and the brightest in Connecticut's fall colors.

• Avon. A walk, either on the green or red trails, around Spring Lake in Fisher Meadows Conservation Area. See pages 44–45 for a description of Fisher Meadows.

• Burlington. A hike along the Blue Trail's Mile of Ledges. Not for the beginning hiker, this rough trail starts off Greer Road, which is off West Chippens Hill Road.

• Farmington. A ride west on Route 6 is a good starting off place for fall foliage.

cider press; today that more-than-200-year-old press is still making cider. During cider season, the press runs six or seven days a week and produces 35,000 to 60,000 gallons of cider. Avon Cider Mill also sells produce, lots of local apples, crafts, home-baked goods, pumpkins galore, and Christmas trees. Between Columbus Day and Christmas Eve, you can get hot fritters and doughnuts on weekends. The mill shuts down after Christmas and opens again in the spring to sell bedding plants. In season, open daily, 9:00 A.M. to 5:00 P.M. Call (860) 677–0343.

If you continue west on Route 44, you'll pass *Old Avon Village* on East Main Street in Avon. When we do book or library talks, someone always asks us about the giant rocking chair on display in the front of the shopping complex. The huge Hitchcock-style rocking chair is something of a local landmark. People give directions based on proximity to the rocker and rival high school students often "chair-nap" it to celebrate a football victory. Unfortunately the story behind the big rocker doesn't exactly sing with romance. When a furniture dealer in New Britain went out of business, managers of the shopping center moved the chair to Old Avon Village as a marketing ploy. For information about Old Avon Village shopping or special events, call (860) 678–0469.

As the theme song for *Cheers* goes, everybody needs a place where they know your name, and for us that place is *Fabiola's Bistro,* 195 West Main Street in Avon. Like many of the places we seem to gravitate to, Fabiola's is a bit hard to find. Look for it in the Tweeter's Plaza, sort of tucked around the corner from The Dormitory. Fabiola's is a no-frills, family-run kind of place. Don't look for decorated plates or tricky dishes. Do look for big bowls of wonderful, from-scratch soups, such as lobster or crab bisque, roasted tomato or corn chowder. Fabiola's has a knack of making vegetarian sandwiches taste every bit as savory as those with meat. (We always cringe when our vegetarian friends call it flesh.) We like the Beatrice Veggie, which consists of heaps of seasonal veggies stir fried with a lively teriyaki sauce, then topped with a rich mix of three cheeses and served on a crusty grinder roll. On days when we're being bad and eating meat, you can't beat Fabiola's burgers. Portions are generous, and prices are low for the quality of food served. Open for lunch only, Monday through Saturday from around 11:00 A.M. to 3:00 P.M. Call (860) 674–9113.

Farther west on Route 44, you'll find the *Avon Congregational Church* at the intersection of Routes 10 and 44. The Congregational church in Litchfield may be the most photographed church in New England, but to our mind, this classically simple, 178-year-old, white church is one of the most beautiful we've ever seen. From its weathervane to its crisp white curtains, this church exemplifies the religious life of New England. Services and church school are held on Sundays at 10:30 A.M. Call (860) 678–0488.

The West Avon Congregational Church, 280 Country Club Road, is another picture-perfect, classic New England church. It's been around since 1751 and gets prettier every year. Call (860) 673–3996.

Heading north past Avon Old Farms along Nod Road, you'll eventually come to the **Pickin' Patch,** at number 276. The land here has been farmed since 1666. This family friendly farm stand and pick-your-own place is one of our favorites in Connecticut. During pick-your-own strawberry season, the Pickin' Patch looks like the Grand Central Station of strawberry patches. We find their strawberries incredibly sweet and fragrant; in fact, on a hot day, just inhaling the concentrated strawberry aroma can be an intoxicating experience. In addition to produce, raspberries, and blueberries, Christmas trees, wreaths, and holiday

Praise the Lord and Pass the Donuts

*W*hen we bought our new house in West Avon, some friends accused us of buying it only to be within a brisk Saturday walk of **Luke's Donut Shop,** 395 West Avon Road. That's a foul canard, although we did exchange high-fives when we realized proximity to Luke's was a benefit of living in "old" Avon. Luke's is a rarity these days—an old-time, nonfranchised donut shop, where everything is made fresh by the owner and his family. And we're not alone in our opinion, in the 1980s, Yankee Magazine named Luke's as one of the top six doughnut places in New England. We like the plain cake and maple doughnuts, but certainly wouldn't turn down one of Luke's cinnamon rolls, crullers, or cream-filled delights. And Luke's is one of the few places these days you can get what our dads called a "cup of Joe,"

no fancy flavorings, no special Seattle roast, just fresh-brewed all-American coffee.

Almost more important than the donuts and coffee is the sense of community Luke's gives Avon. Avon is basically a bedroom community without a real center or much of an identity, unless you count the town council's silly Dog War of 1998. Regulars have been coming to Luke's for years, and if you want the skinny on what's happening in Avon or what the hot-button issues are, just hop on a stool and listen a while. Be careful where you sit because, depending on the time of day, seating around the counter at Luke's is a hard-won privilege of the regulars. Open Monday to Saturday, from 6:00 A.M. to 2:00 P.M. and Sunday from 6:00 A.M. to 1:00 P.M. Call (860) 673–0622.

flowers are sold. The farm stand opens when the pansies start to bloom and stays open until Christmas Eve. Between Christmas Eve and spring, you'll find it open only by chance. On October weekends, you can take a hayride with the Pumpkin Lady to the pumpkin patch. Call (860) 677–9552 to find out what's available for picking.

Just west of the junction of Route 44 and Route 10 north is Avon Park North. Turn into this complex on Ensign Drive, then turn onto Bunker Lane. At numbers 25 and 27, in a historic stone-walled building that used to be an explosives plant, is the *Farmington Valley Arts Center.* This picturesque structure is home to the Fisher Gallery and Shop and to about twenty artists' studios. Pottery, basket weaving, printing, painting, leather working, and silversmithing are all represented. Studios are open at the discretion of the individual artists, but Saturday afternoon is when most of the artists are available. The shop and gallery are open Wednesday through Saturday (daily during November and December), 11:00 A.M. to 4:00 P.M.; they are closed for major holidays. Call (860) 678–1867.

The *Governor's Horse Guards* (West Avon Road; Route 167) is the oldest cavalry unit in continuous service in the United States, tracing its lineage back to 1658, when the Connecticut Colony founded a troop of mounted guards. In 1758, the Horse Guards were reformed as a company of Light Dragoons, modeled on the Royal Regiment of Horse Guards in England. When Connecticut joined the Revolution against the British Crown, the new state took over the Horse Guards. In those days the unit's main function was to escort and protect visiting dignitaries, and it acted as an honor guard to President Washington when he visited Wethersfield in 1789.

Talking Turkey

Gobble, Gobble. Gobble. *You probably won't be watching the Horse Guards practice when the winter holidays roll around, so stick a bookmark here to remind you to seek out the farm next to the Horse Guards headquarters:* **Miller Foods, Inc.,** *308 Arch Street. This place grows some of the best gobblers in the region, but fresh birds are only available during the fall and winter holidays. At Thanksgiving Miller's pitches its "turkey tent," an outdoor bazaar full of lots of special goodies for your holiday table. The turkeys sell like hotcakes, so call ahead to order. Outside the holiday season, Miller Foods sells other meats such as hams and smoked turkeys. Call (860) 673–3256. Web address: www.choicemall.com/millerfoods.*

The unit saw somewhat more dangerous service as a mounted unit in the War of 1812 and the Spanish-American War. In 1916 it patrolled the Mexican border during operations against Pancho Villa. Dismounted and reorganized as a machine gun battalion, it served in seven major engagements in France during World War I. At the end of the war, the Horse Guards were remounted as the 122nd Cavalry Regiment of the Connecticut National Guard; four days after Pearl Harbor they became the 208th Coast Artillery and served as an antiaircraft unit in the South Pacific.

Today the Horse Guards' duties are once again mainly ceremonial. The company makes appearances at presidential and gubernatorial inaugurations. It consists of thirty riders and thirty-two horses. All horses are donated, and they include just about every breed except Clydesdales. Most Thursdays, from 7:30 to 9:30 A.M., the public is invited to watch the unit practice its drills (at which time you can also tour the stable). These consist of intricate, beautifully choreographed precision maneuvers, often accompanied by music. Call the Governor's Horse Guards, (860) 673–3525 for information on drills. The Horse Guards host two horse shows each year; one in late June and one in early October. The Second Company of the Governor's Horse Guards holds its summer practices in Newtown; see page 000 for details.

Once a large dairy farm, **Riverdale Farms Shopping** on Route 10 north of Avon is now the site of one of the more interesting shopping centers in the area. This complex occupies several low hills under the eye of the Heublein Tower, atop Talcott Mountain to the north and east. Eleven renovated farm buildings along with six new buildings now house around fifty offices, stores, and boutiques. Most of the stores are crafts, gift, or fashion stores, but Riverdale Farms is also home to the Farmington Valley outpost of Harry's Pizza of West Hartford and a sushi bar.

West of Avon is Canton, which like so many Connecticut towns, has a ghost. This one is supposedly the shade of a Revolutionary War messenger who disappeared in the vicinity while conveying a payroll from Hartford patriots to French officers aiding the Americans. After a bleached skeleton was found under the Canton Tavern, where the man was last seen alive, stories began circulating that the innkeeper had murdered the hapless messenger and stolen the money. Shortly thereafter, people started seeing a headless horseman, presumed to be the ghost of the paymaster, riding west along the Albany Turnpike (Route 44) toward Saratoga. They still do. So if you're down by the Canton Golf Course some dark and foggy night, and you notice that your headlights

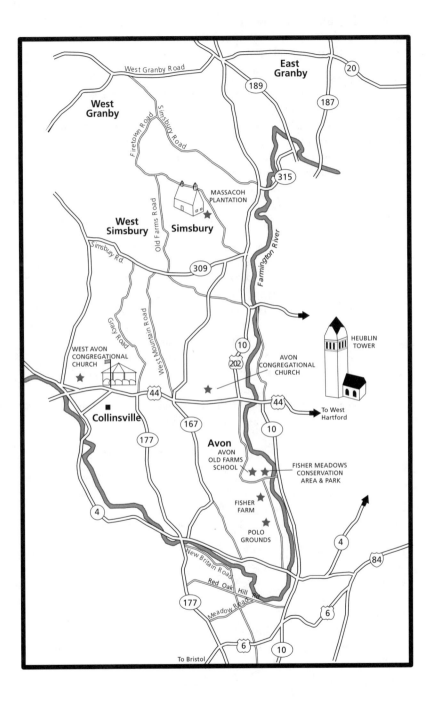

are shining through a ghostly horseman and his steed to illuminate the road beyond, don't pay it any mind. It's just the Headless Horseman of Canton on his perpetual journey.

The headless horseman isn't the only antique in Canton. In fact, from Canton west to the state line, the Albany Turnpike (Route 44) is dotted with dozens of antiques shops, flea markets, and just plain junk stores filled with antiques, collectibles, and vintage items. Some of the best are in Canton itself, including **Antiques at Canton Village** in the Canton Village Shopping Center and **Balcony Antiques** at 81 Albany Turnpike. Both are multidealer shops, and Balcony is the oldest such shop in the state. Both are open Monday through Saturday, 10:00 A.M. to 5:00 P.M. Balcony is also open Sunday, noon to 5:00 P.M. Call (860) 693–2715 (Antiques at Canton Village) or (860) 693–6440 (Balcony Antiques).

One of the best ways to learn about antiques or to just up some good furniture at bargain prices is to go to an auction. For our money the best auction is held at **Canton Barn Auction Gallery,** 75 Old Canton Road, Canton. Auctioneer Richard Wacht keeps the auction zipping right along. You never know what you'll find—Arts & Crafts one week, Country Victorian the next. It's all good fun even if you go home empty-handed. Almost as much of a draw as the auction are the powerhouse pies made by Susan Wacht, the co-owner. We favor the chocolate pecan, which is sinfully delicious, but every flavor of pie has something special. Be warned, however the pies go at the speed of light. Here's the drill: grab your pie, reserve your seat (nothing fancy, just slap a Post-it note on your chosen seat), and then preview the auction. Auctions are usually held on Thursdays with previews a couple of hours before the 7:00 P.M. start, but call (860) 693–0601 for auction and preview times.

In recent years, Route 44 has become the Farmington Valley's Restaurant Row. From Avon to Canton, there are more restaurants of different types and ethnicity than we can describe in this book. Here's the lowdown on four of our favorites that you might not find on your own.

The Bamboo Grill at 50 Albany Turnpike (Route 44) in Canton is a wonderful Vietnamese restaurant with tasty, inexpensive, and healthy food. You can't go wrong ordering any of the bun dishes. *Bun* is sort of Vietnam's fast food; it consists of rice noodles topped with grilled meat or chicken, shredded lettuce and carrots, caramelized shallots, chopped peanuts, and a wonderful sweet-hot-tangy sauce. Open for dinner only, Tuesday through Sunday, from 5:00 to 9:00 P.M., later hours on weekends. Call (860) 693–4144 for hours and reservations (a good idea on weekends).

Maria's Italian Restaurant at 140 Albany Turnpike (Route 44) in Canton is probably a place you wouldn't find unless you're a local. Nothing splashy, just an unassuming place tucked into a strip mall, but once you taste the bread, you'll repeatedly find your way back. The bread, baked there, comes to the table golden brown, with a good chewy crust, firm texture, and a just-baked aroma. This signature bread gives a special touch to a broad selection of sandwiches; we especially like the pepper and egg grinder. The menu consists of Italian favorites, prepared with care, and daily specials that highlight the chef's take on traditional and contemporary Italian cuisine. The atmosphere here is comfortable and friendly, and we've never seen a visitor, either newcomer or regular, enter or leave without a friendly word. In fact, the owners make it a point to circulate through the dining room and talk with each customer. Open Tuesday and Wednesday, 11:00 A.M. to 8 P.M.; Thursday, Friday, and Saturday, 11 A.M. to 9 P.M.; closed Sunday and Monday. Call (860) 693–8022.

We were having dinner at Maria's Italian Resturant and discovered ***Maggie Dailey's Fine Celtic Wares.*** We said, "Great, someone else cashing in on the Celtic craze with tourist stuff." Well, after our first visit we ate our words. Not only is the merchandise quality imports, but the welcome you receive from the owner, Bobbi Marquis, could not be warmer. You'll find lots of crystal and china in stock, but for our money, the best thing in the store is the Nicholas Mosse pottery, which has quickly become highly collectible. We love the farm animal motifs as well as the flower patterns. Among the featured selections are lovely replicas of Celtic artifacts that are perfect as wall art or in a garden. You'll find lots of wearing apparel—from shawls to kilts for tiny tots—as well as favorite foods from Ireland and Scotland. You'll love the Celtic design gold and silver jewelry. Recently, the store has started to carry fine wares from Scotland. Throughout the year, the store sponsors concerts, classes on playing Celtic instruments, and lecture and discussion groups, which can be pretty lively. Open Tuesday, Wednesday, and Friday from 10:00 A.M. to 5:00 P.M.; Thursday from 10:00 A.M. to 8:00 P.M.; Saturday from 10:00 A.M. to 5:00 P.M., and Sunday from noon to 5:00 P.M. Call (860) 693–4577 for information on concerts or e-mail at info@maggiedaileys.com. Visit Maggie Daileys on the Web at www.maggiedaileys.com.

Under various names, **Junior's,** Route 44, Canton, has been delighting hot dog and burger lovers since the fifties. It's one of those places that's been around forever. Mainstays on the menu include very good chili dogs (called "Michigan dogs" at Junior's), excellent burgers, good, crispy fries, and thick shakes. Our favorite menu item is the chocolate coconut Mounds shake, which tastes just like the candy bar. Junior's is open seven days, but hours vary depending on the season. You'll usually find them open from lunchtime through dinner. Winter hours are curtailed, so call ahead before paying a winter visit. Call (860) 693–8838.

Probably one of the best-kept secrets on the Farmington Valley foodie scene is **Hibachi** at 33 East Main Street (Route 44) in Avon. It's nestled way in the back of Old Avon Village shopping center. Specializing in perfectly wonderful, "pick-up Japanese cuisine," nearly everything on the menu is cooked on the smoking hot grills that dominate the front room of the two-room restaurant. On the menu, you'll find grilled food such as ginger chicken, Japanese dumplings *(gyoza),* and sushi. While you can buy a soda to wash down your lunch, we suggest the soothing green tea. You can take your food away, or eat at one of the two tables in the tiny, austerely elegant dining room. Monday through Thursday, 11:00 A.M. to 7:00 P.M.; Fridays and Saturdays, 11:00 A.M. to 8:00 P.M. Call (860) 674–1266.

Of late, Route 44 has begun to look like strip-mall city, but the **Trading Post,** 221 Albany Turnpike, (Route 44), Canton, still sits by the side of the road, looking much like it did in the 1970s. We love taking our nieces and nephews—who view us as charming antiques of the hippie culture—here to relive the days of our long-gone youth. Happily, the hippie gene seems to have stuck with a few of the nieces and nephews, so they find the place way cool. The interior looks much as it did in our crunchy-granola days, full of imported clothing and dangling earrings and ear cuffs, bedspreads, incense and tie-dyed t-shirts. Beside all the other accoutrements of latter-day hippie life, you'll find good buys on used books, especially science fiction and horror, and tapes and CDs. Make sure to visit **Eastern Accents**, next door to the Trading Post, for lots of decorative objects from Asia and beyond. Call (860) 693–4679 for more information.

South of the town of Canton on Route 179 is the village of Collinsville, formerly home of the Collins Company, an eighteenth- and nineteenth-century manufacturer of axes and machetes that were sold around the world. The old brick factory building at 1 Main Street along the Farmington River is now home to the **Collinsville Antiques Co.,** an operation representing fifty dealers. Open Wednesday through Sunday, 10:00 A.M. to 5:00 P.M. Call (860) 693–2658.

The story of the Collins Company is recounted in a series of exhibits in the **Canton Historical Museum** at 11 Front Street. This small museum houses one of the largest collections of Victoriana in the United States. There is also a striking 2,000-square-foot railway diorama accurately showing Collinsville and Canton as they appeared circa 1900. Open April 1 to Thanksgiving, Tuesday through Thursday, noon to 4:00 P.M., and Sunday, 2:00 to 5:00 P.M. Admission. Call (860) 693–2793.

Simsbury was settled in 1648 by a group of Windsor families who acquired the land from the Massacoe Indians. They called their new settlement **Massacoe Plantation,** a name that was eventually changed to Simsbury when the town was incorporated by the Connecticut General Court in 1670. In March 1676, when King Philip's War began to heat up, the entire village of about forty dwellings was destroyed by Wampanoag Indians. The Wampanoag uprising was over by August, but it was two years before reconstruction began. Once it did, Simsbury quickly became an important factor in Connecticut's economy and politics. The first copper coins in America were struck here in 1737, and the first steel mill in America was built here in 1744. Hundreds of residents fought in the American Revolution, including Major General Noah Phelps, who, as America's first spy (he was just a captain then), entered Fort Ticonderoga in disguise to gather information for Ethan Allen; Allen then proceeded to capture the fort. By the 1820s the town was a major stop on the Farmington Canal, which ran along the route of today's Hopmeadow Street (Route 10).

Simsbury's Charthouse Restaurant, junction of Routes 202 and 309, is one of the valley's oldest steak houses. The bill of fare isn't fancy or revolutionary, but they do know how to grill a mean steak, and the salads and potato dishes are always good and savory. Berthed in a mellow yellow colonial building, the decor is as fancy as the menu is simple. You'll find lots of lavish wood carvings and vast fireplaces. The big draw, though, is the restaurant's resident ghost who has been known to give diners a friendly pat or poke now and again. The Charthouse ghost is a Farmington Valley tradition, with radio disk jockeys often spending All Hallows' Eve at the restaurant reporting on ghostly doings. Whoever the ghost is, she appears to be friendly, usually making appearances only when the restaurant decides to renovate or redecorate. Call (860) 658–1118.

Massacoh Plantation at 800 Hopmeadow Street in the center of Simsbury is a cluster of a dozen eighteenth-century buildings containing artifacts and exhibits that re-create life in Simsbury over a period of a hundred years. The site includes, among other things, an art gallery, a Victorian carriage house, an icehouse, a 1740 schoolhouse, a barn, a carriage shed, and a 1795 cottage. There's also the 1771 Elisha Phelps House, built by the brother of Noah Phelps (of Ticonderoga fame). The plantation's First Meeting House is the only replica at the site. The original building was constructed in 1683 by Thomas Barber, who had stood atop his roof beating a drum to sound the alarm on the day of the Wampanoag attack. Town witch Debby Griffin is supposed to have entered and left that building through the keyhole. Make a stop at the gift shop before you leave. There's a nice stock of old-fashioned penny candy and old-fashioned toys for the kids, and the handsome woven cotton blanket depicting some of Simsbury's historic buildings makes a nice souvenir. Massacoh Plantation is open Tuesday through Saturday. Guided tours lasting about one hour are available from noon to 4:00 P.M. The last tour starts at 3:00 P.M. Admission. Call (860) 658–2500.

You might be tempted to zip past *One-Way Fare* at 4 Railroad Street, thinking, as we did for years, "former railroad station turned restaurant. Nah, way too cute." One-Way Fare is more than a cutie-pie place full of railroad memorabilia. To us, it seems like an extension of Simsbury's town hall, a place where longtime residents meet to talk about the burning and not-so-burning issues of the day. It's popular, too, with the members of the Thomas the Tank Engine set, who enjoy inspecting all the cool train stuff in the restaurant and the adjoining railroad cars. Big people can take comfort in the eatery's signature station burgers, a tower of hamburger patties, Canadian bacon, sautéed onions, and cheese on an English muffin and a nice cold beer. As with Luke's in Avon, seating at the bar is a hard-won right. Newcomers who hop up on the bar stools can expect, at the very least, a stern look from the regulars. Remember that One-Way Fare is a bar-cum-restaurant, so expect smoking in the main room. There is a nonsmoking section, down the basement, sort of in the restaurant's Siberia. From May through October, it's pleasant to eat outside on the front porch. Call (860) 658–4477 for hours and for information on daily specials.

The rambling, comfortable *Simsbury 1820 House,* 3 blocks down from Massacoh Plantation at number 731, is one of those country inns just made for winter celebration dinners. The house, built in 1820, was the home of Gifford Pinchot, the man who raised America's consciousness about conservation. Today the restored inn looks much like it did in its heyday with shining oak floors and glorious leaded glass windows. All the rooms are comfortably furnished with antiques and high-quality reproductions. The dining room serves a menu that's probably best described as contemporary American, with an emphasis on seasonal foods. The desserts are excellent; we highly recommend the chocolate terrine with raspberries. Open all year. The dining room serves dinner from 5:00 to 8:00 P.M., Monday through Thursday. Call (860) 658–7658 or (800) TRY–1820.

For much of Simsbury's early history, *Talcott Mountain* cut the region off from the meadowlands of the Connecticut River Valley to the east. This isolation ended when the Albany Turnpike was hacked across the mountain, but the state of mind engendered by that knife-edge of rock looming dramatically over the landscape remains. Though separated by only a mile from the towns of Hartford's meadowlands, Simsbury, Avon, and even Farmington, to the south, have far more in common with the small towns to their west than they do with the suburbs east of the mountain.

There has been a tower atop Talcott Mountain for most of the past 180 years. The first was built in 1810 and was the inspiration for John Greenleaf Whittier's poem *Monte Video*. It was blown down in a windstorm in 1840. Others followed until finally, in 1914, businessman Gilbert Heublein built a fourth tower atop the mountain, a grand white 165-foot-high edifice of steel and concrete anchored in the rock. For twenty years this so-called Heublein Tower was the Heublein family home. Today the mountain and its tower are all part of *Talcott Mountain State Park.* Four states are visible from the top of the tower, but first you have to get there. The main public access route is off Route 185. A road leads part way up the mountain to a parking area, from which you can hike the $1\frac{1}{4}$-mile trail to the top. The early part of the climb is fairly steep, but there are benches for resting. Once you reach the tower, you'll have to make another climb up the stairs to the top; there are no elevators.

The park is open year-round. Heublein Tower is open Thursday through Sunday, 10:00 A.M. to 5:00 P.M., April 1 through Labor Day, and daily, 10:00 A.M. to 5:00 P.M., Labor Day through October. Call (860) 566–2304 or (860) 677–0662. Web address: www.connecticut.com/parks/parks/talcott.html.

When leaving Talcott Mountain, turn left on Route 185 and drive west toward Route 10. A mile or so west of the access road you'll come to an old iron bridge. On your right is a huge, bare, witchy-looking tree whose branches loom over the road like some spectral presence. This is the Pinchot Sycamore, reputedly the oldest tree in Connecticut. The small meadow in which it grows is open to the public and has some picnic tables and benches if you care to sit a spell.

Cyber-travelers might want to check out other tall trees in Connecticut. The **Connecticut Notable Trees Project** maintains a Web site that lists the tallest and biggest trees in the state. Besides a city-by-city list of notable trees, you'll find information on how to measure and report the big trees you spot on your travels or in your front yard. Web address: www.conn coll.edu/ccrec/greennet/ct.trees/notable1.html.

Merrywood, a cozy B&B, located at 100 Hartford Road (Route 185) in Simsbury, has some notable trees of its own. Set off among tall pines on five secluded acres, it's hard to believe this quiet and elegant Colonial Revival B&B is just minutes away from Route 44 and some of the Farmington Valley's best shops and restaurants. The interior of the house is furnished with what the owners, Mike and Gerlinde Marti, call "an eclectic mix of period antiques, oriental carpets, and original artwork." Many of the decorative elements are souvenirs from the couple's world travels.

**Heublein Tower,
Talcott Mountain State Park**

Merrywood offers two double rooms and two suites, all with private bath. Unlike many B&Bs where decorating is more important than the guest's comfort, the beautifully decorated guest rooms contain lots of amenities targeted for maximum comfort. Afternoon tea, consisting of dainty sandwiches and sweets, is served for guests. Merrywood's breakfast menu is one of the most ambitious we've seen at a B&B with offerings like eggs Benedict, eggs hussard, pancakes, and some special Swiss breakfast dishes, such as eggs scrambled with toast cubes, potatoes, tomatoes, onions, and two cheeses. For the quality of the accommodations and service, the rates are very moderate. Merrywood is open all year. No smoking; no pets; no children. E-mail: mfmarti@compuserve.com. Call (860) 651–1785; fax: (860) 651–8273.

Don't Miss

Attractions

Vintage Radio & Communications Museum of Connecticut, 1231 Main Street, East Hartford; (860) 675–9916. At this little gem of a museum, you'll find displayed the history of electronic communication from the 1920s through today. The sound effects room is a real kid pleaser. Open Thursday and every other Friday, 10:00 A.M. to 2:00 P.M.; Saturday, 11:00 A.M. to 4:00 P.M.; Sunday, 1:00 to 4:00 P.M. Admission.

Rose's Berry Farm, 295 Matson Hill Road, South Glastonbury, and 1200 Hebron Avenue, Glastonbury; (860) 633–7467. A great place to pick your own strawberries, raspberries, blueberries, and pumpkins. The farm shop features berry jams, pies, and other fruit-flavored gifts. Hours are changeable, so call head for hours and directions.

Luddy/Taylor Connecticut Valley Tobacco Museum, Northwest Park, 135 Lang Road, Windsor; (860) 285–1888. Baby boomers may

think they discovered cigars, but in Connecticut's Tobacco Valley, growing wrapper tobacco for cigars has long been a way of life. This small museum gives you a chance to see part of Connecticut's historical link to the cigar-making industry. Open Tuesday through Thursday, and Saturday from noon to 4:00 P.M. Open other hours by appointment.

Shopping

The Bird House Antiques, 244 Main Street (Route 10), Farmington; (860) 666 –4623. Tucked behind the barn-red Farmington Crafts Common, this tiny shop sells lots of collectibles and cutie-pie things. Their furniture is displayed in the much larger space of the Farmington Crafts Common. The owners gladly confess that their own antiquing habits got out of control, so they opened the shop to take care of the overflow. It's a neat shop to browse in, made even nicer by its Lilliputian size and the charm of its owners. Open Tuesday through Thursday, noon to 5:30 P.M.; Friday and Sunday, 11:00 A.M. to 5:30 P.M.

Town Farm Dairy, 73 Wolcott Road, Simsbury; (860) 658–5362. You'll find milk in wonderful, old-fashioned glass bottles and the heaviest cream imaginable—all from the dairy's herd of Jersey cows. The farm also sells yogurt, cottage cheese, sour cream, free-range eggs, and organic vegetables. Call for hours and more information.

Tulmeadow Dairy Farm, Inc., 255 Farms Village Road (Route 309), Simsbury; (860) 658–1430. There's no greater pleasure in the summer or fall than sitting on a hay bale at Tulmeadow Farm and sampling the made-there ice cream. The farm store also sells vegetables, bedding plants, perennials, herbs, pumpkins, maple syrup, and Christmas tress. Farm store open April through December. Call for more information.

Antiq's, 1839 New Britain Avenue, Farmington, is another shop that's a bit hard to find, but worth the trip. (Exit 38 off I–84, take a left at the fifth light. Antiq's is at the corner of Hyde Road.) The store specializes in early and Victorian antiques, but we go there for the architectural treasures the owner salvages from old houses. Depending on when you visit, you may find gorgeous old doors, stained-glass windows, and other architectural gems. Also in stock are wonderful old mechanical banks and nice estate jewelry. Say "howdy" to Newf, the shop dog if he's around. Open from Wednesday to Sunday, 11:00 A.M. to 4:00 P.M. On the Web at: antiqs.com; e-mail: info@antiqs.com.

The Vintage Shop,
61 Arch Street, New Britain. This snug little group shop offers great prices on kitchenware, collectibles, and china. We've also found some wonderful old lamps and accessories here. The owners are very pleasant and can often give you tips on upcoming estate and yard sales. When you visit, take a minute to stop by the Vintage Shop's neighbor, the Thrift Shop for the Hospital for Special Care, where you can often find good buys on vintage clothes and costume jewelry.

Garden of Light, 394 West
Main Street, Avon, (860) 409-2196. A welcome oasis for vegetarians, vegans, people who rely on homeopathic remedies and supplements, and people like your authors who buy organic produce and enjoy an occasional vegetarian meal. Check out the bakery for wonderful breads and pastries. We think their semolina-sesame bread makes the best toast ever! The deli stocks lots of vegetarian and vegan treats like savory samoas (crusty, Indian veggie–filled turnovers) with chutney and vegan spring rolls. The daily hot buffet features hearty vegetarian meals and fresh-tasting, made-there soups. At the juice bar you can quench your thirst on freshly squeezed orange juice or power up with freshly-pressed wheatgrass juice. For dessert, try their vegan carrot cake or snack on some of Paul Newman's latest treat—Dark-Chocolate-covered Peanut-Butter-Cups. Open Monday through Friday, 9:30 A.M. to 8 P.M.; Saturday from 9:30 A.M. to 7 P.M.; and Sunday from 11 A.M. to 5 P.M. Check out their Web site for the daily specials at the deli or buffet and for recipes: www.gardenoflight.net.

RESTAURANTS

Brookside Bagels,
563 Hopmeadow Street, Simsbury; (860) 651–1492. When we first moved to Connecticut, bagels ran a distant third to muffins and doughnuts as breakfast breads of choice. Today, due to several bagel bakeries making fresh New York–style bagels, bagels are quickly becoming Connecticut's choice for breakfast. Brookside Bagels is one of the places we love to find for you because unless you're local you probably won't happen upon it on your own. It's a pleasant, sunny little bakery-deli with a handful of tables and some of the best bagels into which you've ever sunk a tooth. You'll find all the typical flavors of bagels along with a few unexpected ones. We like the cheddar bagel, with its slightly uneven shape, chewiness, and tangy taste of sharp cheddar. Brookside also bakes some interesting bagels du jour, ranging in flavors from sun-dried tomato and parmesan to pumpkin. Add a cup of the Green Mountain Coffer Roasters java du jour and one of Fresh Samantha's freshly squeezed juices such as Raspberry Dream, and you've got a grand way to start the day. Open Monday through Friday, 6:00 A.M. to 6:00 P.M.; Saturday, 7:00 A.M. to 3:00 P.M.; Sunday, 7:00 A.M. to 1:00 P.M.

Cottage Restaurant,
427 Farmington Avenue, Plainville; (860) 793–8888. Many Connecticut foodies of our acquaintance call the Cottage the best restaurant in the state. We agree it's beyond wonderful, and the menus always surprise us with their originality and zest. Owner Patty Queen,

the Johnson and Wales-educated chef, who has cooked at Restaurant Jasper in Boston, Peppercorns Grill and Max on Main in Hartford, and the Bistro at Maison de Ville in New Orleans, is a lady who knows how to cook to impress. Patty's brother Dave is co-chef and together they cook up a storm of flavor.

The cooking style is contemporary American, and it's hard to tell you what to order because the menu changes almost daily. You'll find Southwestern touches, Asian influences, and Creole seasoning on practically every menu. We've had an amazing salmon cheesecake, beautiful salads, and wonderful grilled steaks with sauteed potatoes and crispy, frizzled onions. Desserts, while not quite as elegant as those at Woodbury's Good News Cafe, are still remarkable, from a perfect crème brûlée to a homey bread pudding. Reservations are a must, especially on weekends. Here's our tip: Try lunch; it's cheaper and easier to get into. Smoke-free; handicapped accessible. Open 11:30 A.M. to 2:30 P.M. for lunch, Monday through Friday and 5:00 to 8:30 P.M. for dinner, Monday through Thursday; 5:00 to 10:00 P.M. Friday and Saturday.

First & Last Tavern,

26 West Main Street (Route 44), Avon; (860) 676–2000. The original convivial tavern on Maple Avenue got its name from being the last eatery in West Hartford and the first restaurant in Hartford. We usually go to the Farmington Valley outpost in Avon. You can't beat their old-fashioned spaghetti and meatballs, served with a side salad on the same plate. There are some good new-fashioned offerings such as the mesclun salad with goat cheese and the herb-spangled focaccia. We love the home-baked cream pies, especially the chocolate cream, made by one of the owners' moms. Open Monday through Thursday, 11:30 A.M. to 10:00 P.M.; Friday and Saturday, 11:30 A.M. to 11:00 P.M.; Sunday, 4:00 to 9:00 P.M.

Carville's Ranch House,

27 Windsor Avenue, Windsor; (860) 522–2266. This place reminds us more of the dog and burger places of our Pennsylvania-Ohio youth than of a restaurant in staid Windsor, Connecticut. We don't know how such a treasure managed to wind up in Windsor, but we're glad it did. From the neon cowboy on the roof to the crowd at the counter, Carville's is home to some of the best dogs and burgers in the state. We love their hot dogs, plain or with the works (called "a junkyard dog"), which includes cheese, peppers, sauerkraut, chili, and cole slaw. Any of the burger concoctions are equally splendid. The french fries are the real McCoy, piping hot and crisp. Open Monday to Saturday, 11:00 A.M. to 9:00 P.M.

LODGING

Charles R. Hart House,

1046 Windsor Avenue, Windsor; (860) 688–5555. We love Victorian Painted Ladies and this B&B with its gables, tower, and wraparound veranda, is a good one. Here you'll find all the embellishments and ornamentation so dear to the hearts of the Victorians, including Eastlake-style newel posts, gorgeous Lincrusta wall coverings, and a colorful ceramic-tiled fireplace. The owners, Bob and Dorothy McAllister, have fully restored the house and furnished it with period and high-quality reproduction furniture. It's worth a visit just to see their collection of clocks. The Hart House has four guest rooms, each with private bath. Full breakfast served, often with homemade breakfast breads or muffins. No pets; no smoking; no small children. Moderate. You can tour the inn at the McAllister's Web site: www.ntplx.net/ ~harthous/; e-mail: harthous@ntplx.net.

Butternut Farm,
1654 Main Street,
Glastonbury;
(860) 633–7179.
You might be tempted to
call this comfortable B&B
"Animal Farm" due to the
number and types of ani-
mals the inn's owner, Don
Reid, keeps around the
place. Not to worry; this is
not *Green Acres,* with
Arnold the Pig wandering
through the house. You
will, however, find ducks, a
llama, goats, Sophie the
parrot, some elegantly
beautiful Abyssinian cats,
and a bunch of those way-
cool chickens with punk-
rocker hairdos. Even if
you're not an Animal
Planet fan, come for the
food. Don Reid's fabulous
cooking has been profiled
in *Yankee Magazine.*
(Often on the breakfast
menu are egg dishes
made from contributions
from Reid's own hens.)
The inn boasts five guest
rooms, one apartment,
and two suites, all with
private baths and all
decorated perfectly in
keeping with the colonial
character of the house.
The grounds are beauti-
fully landscaped and the
herb garden could turn
Martha Stewart green
with envy. Moderate.

The Litchfield Hills

West of Hartford is Litchfield County, an area largely synonymous with Connecticut's western uplands. As one moves north and west through Litchfield, one moves deeper into the Litchfield Hills, a forested spur of the Berkshires that typifies what comes to most people's minds when they think of New England. Steepled white churches, romantic old inns, quaint antiques shops, and small establishments run by Yankee craftspeople still abound. In recent years, though, the Litchfield Hills have become home to many of the rich and famous: Susan Saint James in Litchfield, Arthur Miller and Dustin Hoffman in Roxbury, Henry Kissinger in Warren, and Meryl Streep in Salisbury, to name but a few. Their onslaught has brought with it upscale shops and nouvelle restaurants that give the area an intriguing flavor of cosmopolitanism. The southern portion of this hill mass merges into the region's "Alpine Lake" country, an area of cool, forest-shrouded lakes, and meadows reminiscent of Switzerland. This region is home to some of the state's best inns. Cutting between the Litchfield Hills and New York's Taconic Mountains from the extreme northwestern corner of Connecticut all the way to Stratford, on the coast, is the Housatonic River, in its northern reaches a wild freshet that is surely one of the prettiest rivers in New England. Litchfield County is bordered by Massachusetts on the north and New York on the west. To the south of the lake country are the populous counties of Fairfield and New Haven.

The Albany Turnpike

In the days before railroads and superhighways, Hartford and Albany, New York, were linked by a rutted roadway called the Albany Turnpike. This highway of sorts was the main route through the rugged northwestern uplands, and its location determined the patterns of settlement in this part of the state. Today the successor to the old turnpike is a gleaming asphalt ribbon dubbed Route 44, and any traveler through this part of Connecticut must pass over it.

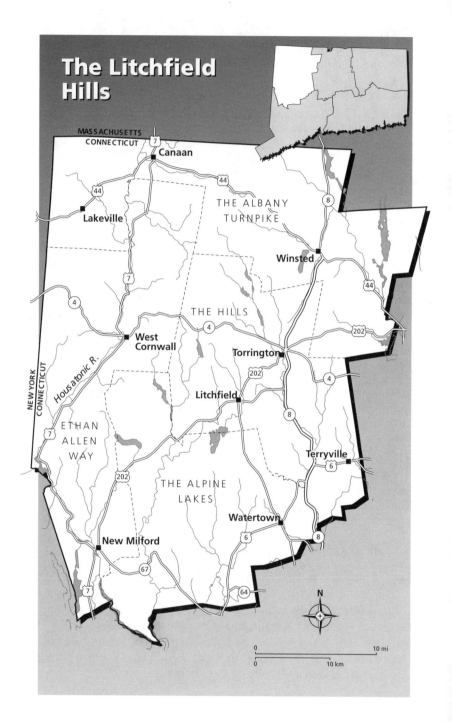

The Litchfield Hills

MASSACHUSETTS
CONNECTICUT

Canaan

44

THE ALBANY
TURNPIKE

44

8

Lakeville

Winsted

7

44

4

THE HILLS

202

West
Cornwall

4

Torrington

202

4

Litchfield

NEW YORK
CONNECTICUT

Housatonic R.

7

ETHAN
ALLEN
WAY

8

Terryville

6

202

THE ALPINE
LAKES

Watertown

New Milford

6

8

67

7

64

N

0   10 mi
0   10 km

The easternmost township along the Litchfield portion of Route 44 is New Hartford. New Hartford is divided into four sections, of which **Satan's Kingdom** and Pine Meadow are the best known. Satan's Kingdom is named for the bandits who used to hide out in the rugged, wooded countryside flanking the turnpike to ambush and rob the Hartford–Albany stagecoach. Today a company called **North American Canoe Tours, Inc.** will rent you an inflated rubber river tube in which you can float down the Farmington past the gorges where the robbers made their homes. Trips take two to three hours and cover 2 miles and three sets of rapids, ending up in Canton. The company picks you up and returns you to your starting point by bus. The service operates from Memorial Day through Labor Day. Call (860) 693–6465.

Blue Sky Foods, 431 Main St. (Route 44) in New Hartford likes to call itself a blend of Key West and Nantucket. We call it lots of good eating and good times. Two words describe the ambiance of this charming roadside eatery—Jimmy Buffett (whose music also dominates the sound system). The décor is simple but manages to communicate the laid-back sensibilities of the tropics with vibrant colors (vivid sky blue dominates), shells scattered around the tables, and of course, plenty of pink flamingos. Blue Sky is the unofficial home away from home for area parrot heads. Service is friendly but somewhat minimal. You order at the counter, choosing from the menu, the blackboard specials, or whatever looks good in the cold case, grab a table, and pretty soon a member of the wait staff zips your food to the table. You won't find lots of tricky, trendy food, but you will find what one of our friends calls "the food real people eat." The fried whole-belly clams or fried oysters (which sell out at lightning speed) are almost as good as those at Johnny Ad's, and we like their New England take on a Cuban sandwich (grilled ham and cheese, pickles, mustard, and mayo). Blue Sky pays homage to Mr. Buffett with their Cheeseburger in Paradise, and it is a heavenly burger. The Couch Potatoes (fries topped with chili, cheese, and onions) make a light lunch or quite a hefty side. Desserts change with the seasons; you might find mango crisp in summer and gingerbread in winter. If pressed to make a dessert decision, you can't miss with their key lime pie—the perfect blend of creamy, tart, sweet and tangy, topped with a cloud of real whipped cream. Patio dining starts around Memorial Day and ends around Columbus Day. From May through mid-October, open Wednesday and Thursday 11:00 A.M. to 8:00 P.M.; Friday and Saturday from 11:00 A.M. to 8:30 P.M. and Sunday from 11:00 A.M. to 7:00 P.M. Winter hours are curtailed, so call before going. (860) 379-0000. E-mail: blueskyfood@earthlink.net.

If you're in New Hartford at sugaring-off time (February and March), you might want to visit the **Kasulaitis Farm and Sugarhouse,** (69 Goose Green Road) to watch the process and buy some tasty maple products. If you miss sugaring-off by a few weeks, stop by anyway and waste a few minutes watching the lambs frisk and frolic in the spring pasture. Such things are good for the soul, and you can justify the time spent by telling yourself that you just came to look for a souvenir. The Kasulaitis family sells beautifully spun yarns and blankets woven from their very own wool, and these make terrific and useful remembrances of your visit to this part of Connecticut. Please call ahead before visiting: (860) 379–8787.

North of New Hartford, Route 44 loops through Barkhamsted. This township's combination of sparse population, winding roads, heavy forest, and large lakes makes it one of the most dramatic parts of Connecticut for the popular custom of leaf peeping: driving through the rural countryside and letting the sunshine, blue skies, and fall colors wash away all cares.

One of the best leaf-peeping jaunts through Barkhamsted starts north of the town at the junction of Routes 20 and 181 in Hartland. If you approach this intersection from the east on Route 20, you'll pass through West Hartland on the way. Don't let this confuse you; with typical Yankee contrariness, *West* Hartland is actually *east* of Hartland, so keep driving for another mile. At the intersection in Hartland, take Route 181 south. This road runs between the Barkhamsted Reservoir and the Farmington River, for much of the way under the eves of the lovely Peoples State Forest. At the tip of the reservoir, Route 181 meets Route 318. Take 318 east to the Saville Dam, separating Barkhamsted and Compensating Reservoirs. There's parking nearby and even on the dam itself; this is a great spot to stop for pictures or for an informal picnic. From the dam, continue east to Route 219. From there you can either drive south to pick up Route 44, return west for more leaf peeping, or loop back up to Route 20 in Granby.

If you loop south you'll pass the **Compensating Reservoir** on your right. Also known as Lake McDonough, this body of water is a major state recreational area, with facilities for boating, swimming, picnicking, hiking, and fishing. Boating is allowed from mid-April through September; both rowboats and paddleboats can be rented. Fishing is allowed mid-April through November. Open weekdays, 10:00 A.M. to 8:00 P.M., weekends and holidays, 8:00 A.M. to 8:00 P.M. No admission; parking fee. Call (860) 379–3036 or (860) 278–7850.

If, after reaching Saville Dam, you're still in the mood for more fall

THE LITCHFIELD HILLS

FAVORITE PLACES IN THE
LITCHFIELD HILLS

1. *Lorenz Studios*
2. *Carole Peck's Good News Cafe*
3. *Action Wildlife Foundation*
4. *Blue Sky Foods*
5. *The Last Post*

color, head back west on Route 318 for ½ mile beyond the intersection of Route 181. Turn right on East River Road. This will take you directly through **Peoples State Forest** along the banks of the West Branch of the Farmington. It is one of two roads that run along the riverbank. The other, West River Road, runs through the forest on the west bank, intersecting with Route 318 a few yards west of, and across the bridge from, East River Road. The two roads don't quite intersect several miles north of the bridge in the village of Riverton, home of the Hitchcock chair.

While other Connecticut entrepreneurs were experimenting with the use of interchangeable parts in the manufacture of rifles and clocks, Lambert Hitchcock set out in 1818 to mass produce furniture in a little factory at the junction of the Farmington and Still Rivers. A decade later, Hitchcock was turning out 15,000 chairs each year, and his factory employed a hundred people in the rapidly growing village of Hitchcocksville. The mass-produced Hitchcock chairs, selling for between 45 cents and $1.75, were an instant success. They were also extremely sturdy. Quality control consisted of dropping each assembled chair from a second-floor workshop into a waiting wagon; only those items that survived the drop unscathed were considered sufficiently sturdy to wear the Hitchcock label. Once the chairs were assembled, workers finished them by hand, often using multiple stencils that produced a colorful and distinctive look.

In the middle of the nineteenth century, Hitchcock's business foundered; in 1852 its owner died penniless. About the same time, the village that bore his name disappeared from the map. Tired of constantly being confused with nearby Hotchkissville, the residents of Hitchcocksville, in typically pragmatic Yankee fashion, changed the town's name to Riverton. Riverton, today, is a sleepy, picturesque village that owes its economic health almost equally to tourism and to the presence of the **Hitchcock Furniture Factory,** which reopened in 1946, roughly a century after it had closed.

If you like Mr. Hitchcock's splendid chairs (or are just interested in old furniture), visiting the **Hitchcock Chair Factory Store** down by the river in Lambert Hitchcock's original factory, and the **Buckingham Galleries** in the Lambert Hitchcock Home next door can occupy the better part of an afternoon. The Hitchcock Chair Factory Store and Buckingham Galleries stock traditional American furniture, including Hitchcock chairs.

Both are open Monday through Saturday, 9:30 A.M. to 6:00 P.M., and Sunday, noon to 6:00 P.M. Call (860) 379–4826.

When you're in Riverton, don't confine your visit to the various Hitchcock-related establishments. It's only a five-minute walk along Route 20 from the Riverton Grange Hall on the banks of Sandy Brook at the west end of town to the bridge across the Farmington River at the east end. But that stretch of road abounds with enticing stores and snack shops. You might, for example, wrap up your visit with a bite at the *Catnip Mouse Tea Room* or grab a deli sandwich and Moxie at the *Riverton General Store* and picnic along the river. Or you could just stroll along with one of the *Village Sweet Shop*'s quality ice-cream cones; if you like strange mix-ins, try the coconut ice cream with dark chocolate. Peek inside *Antiques and Herbs* for antique linens and quality linen reproductions, cards, silver, and a few large antiques. The *Thomaston Clock Company* next door has mantel, wall, grandfather, and travel clocks by Seth Thomas and others at decent prices.

Hitchcock Furniture Factory

Riverton has always been a delightful village to visit, but getting a really good meal has been problematic at best. The *Yellow Victorian,* 6 Riverton Road (Route 20), billeted in what else but an antique-filled, yellow Victorian house, offers a new dimension to dining in Riverton. Sided with one of their salads, any of the hearty chowders like their creamy New England clam chowder or the Asian-influenced spinach and mushroom soup make a meal. The salmon and crab cakes with lemon-garlic mayonnaise are great for lighter appetites. For a more substantial dinner, you can choose from a menu of offerings that leans heavily to the meat and potatoes side like the rack of lamb with port wine sauce. Desserts are homey as a mother's hug. We like the gingerbread, but if you visit in the fall, try the pumpkin pie baked in a gingersnap crust. Open for dinner, Friday through Sunday, 5:00 to 9:30 P.M.; Sunday brunch from 10:30 A.M. to 2:30 P.M. Lunch and afternoon tea, Wednesday through Saturday from noon to 2:30 P.M. Call (860) 379–7020 for more information or reservations.

THE LITCHFIELD HILLS

If you fish, mark your calendar for the first day of trout season (in April). That's when Riverton holds its annual *Fishing Derby* on the Farmington River. The Farmington was recently designated a National Wild and Scenic River, and probably offers the best flyfishing in Connecticut. Rainbow and brown trout don't exactly beg to be caught, but it's pretty easy to catch one. The contest starts at 6:00 A.M. and lasts about four hours, rain, sun, or snow. There's no entry fee; all you

Like much of America, we grew up with a Seth Thomas clock on the mantel. And, yes, Virginia, there really was a Seth Thomas and he really was a clockmaker. The town of Thomaston is named after him.

need is a Connecticut fishing license. Non-fishers are welcome to observe, and presumably applaud when a particularly promising catch gets landed. Kids under twelve can fish in a specially stocked area. For more information, call the Riverton General Store at (860) 379–0811, where you can also buy that all-important Connecticut fishing license.

If you intend to overnight in this part of Connecticut, we recommend the *Old Riverton Inn* on Route 20. Opened as the Ives Tavern, a stagecoach stop on the old Boston-to-Albany Turnpike (Route 44), this historic inn bills itself as offering "hospitality for the hungry, thirsty, and sleepy since 1796." And it retains its colonial charm to this day. Small, quaint, and friendly, the Old Riverton Inn is famous for the hospitality of its staff.

The floor of the enclosed Grindstone Terrace is made of grindstones quarried in Nova Scotia, sent by sailing ship to Long Island Sound, then dispatched upriver to Hartford and hauled by ox cart from Hartford to Collinsville, where they were used to grind axe heads and machetes in the Collinsville Axe Factory (now an antiques store). The inn's dining room is decorated with Riverton's famous Hitchcock chairs. The fare here is pretty good, although some dishes are regretably institutional, and includes tasty homemade soups.

Located on the west bank of the Farmington River, just across from the Hitchcock factory, the Old Riverton Inn is open year-round. The restaurant serves lunch from noon to 2:30 P.M., Friday and Saturday. Dinner runs from 5:00 to 8:30 P.M. Wednesday through Friday, 5:00 to 9:30 P.M. on Saturday, and noon to 7:30 P.M. on Sunday. The inn is closed on Mondays, Tuesdays, Christmas Day, and the first three weeks in January. Call (860) 379–8678.

Southwest of Riverton is another beautiful forest: the *American Legion State Forest* in Pleasant Valley. Even on the hottest day, the tall trees and pines keep the forest shady and glade cool, and at night, it's mouse quiet and real country dark. You can fish or tube on the

Farmington River, and there's good hiking all around. A moderate fee for campsites. Most state parks and state forests are open from 8:00 A.M. to sunset. For detailed information, including maps, on Connecticut's state parks and forests, contact the Bureau of Outdoor Recreation, State Parks Division, Connecticut Department of Environmental Protection, 79 Elm Street, Hartford, CT 06106–5127; (860) 424–3200. Web address: dep.state.ct.us.

You probably won't meet up with the *New York Times* food critic in the **Winsted Diner** at 496 Main Street (Route 44). Not his kind of place at all, and besides he probably couldn't manage to find it. We like it, though, and we bet that you will, too. Part restaurant, part local gathering place, the Winsted Diner has been a town institution since 1941. It's tiny and easy to miss because it's angled off from Main Street. But persevere. The atmosphere is friendly, and the pancakes and French toast are good. Or you might try the Ra-Doc-a-Doodle, a breakfast sandwich that is what Egg McMuffin only wishes it was. Call (860) 379–4429.

While you're in the Winsted area, you might want to head down Route 263 from Winsted to Winchester Center. The **Kerosene Lamp Museum** (100 Old Waterbury Turnpike; Route 263) is right on the green. It occupies the old post office building, which used to be the general store, which used to be the gristmill; thrifty New Englanders tend to reuse old buildings a lot. This small museum is actually a private collection of 500 lamps belonging to George and Ruth Sherwood, who live next door and act as curators, guides, housekeepers, researchers, and whatever else is required. George Sherwood also doubles as the village postmaster. The Sherwoods have been collecting lamps since 1949, and the result often seems more hobby than museum. Visiting this place has the feel of just dropping in to chat with the neighbors about their collection and maybe catch up on the news. It's kind of a nice atmosphere.

Inside, the museum is cluttered, nay crammed to bursting, with antique lamps. There are lamps everywhere, hanging from the ceiling, fixed to

Scenic Winter Drive

*T*ake Route 183 north from Winsted for a scenic drive. The road winds through Colebrook and passes the Colebrook Reservoir. You'll pass some wonderfully charming private homes and see some pretty countryside. Route 183 continues north to Massachusetts. It's a nice drive anytime of year, but we like it best in winter, when the reservoir has a splendid sense of desolation.

the walls, or just standing on any convenient surface. Most were manufactured between the 1850s (when the kerosene lamp first came into use, destroying the American whaling industry) and 1880 (the year after Thomas Alva Edison invented the incandescent lamp, destroying the kerosene lamp industry). The oldest item is a whale oil lamp manufactured in 1834. The museum also has copies of 4,089 American lamp patents issued in the nineteenth century.

Some of the holdings are delightfully odd. There are several "angle lamps," whose side-mounted, angled burners prevented spillage when the lamps were secured to the walls of railway coaches. There are also special innkeeper's lamps with burners designed to function just long enough to get the guest into bed, but not long enough to illuminate any other activity, thus saving the innkeeper the cost of the fuel that might otherwise have been burned by guests who liked to read in bed. It's comforting to know that human nature doesn't change all that much. Open daily, 9:30 A.M. to 4:00 P.M. Call (860) 379–2612.

On your way down the hill into Norfolk, make sure you stop to look at the route maker on the green (across from the library). It's a lovely piece of primitive folk art, decorated with deer, bunnies, and other woodsy creatures. Definitely worth a photograph.

Located at the junction of Routes 44, 272, and 182 and with **Campbell Falls** and **Haystack Mountain State Park** just north of the town center, Norfolk is a crossroads of tourism in northwest Connecticut. While outdoor recreation is popular, the activity for which the town is famous is the **Norfolk Chamber Music Festival.** Think of this annual summer event as a little Tanglewood without so much of the crush of humanity. The Norfolk Chamber Music Festival and the **Yale Summer School of Music** perform summer concerts in the brown-shingled Music Shed on the grounds of the Ellen Battell Stoeckel Estate on Route 44, west of the Norfolk Green. The concert schedule varies from year to year, but the New York Woodwind Quintet, the New York Brass Quartet, and the Tokyo String Quartet have all appeared in the past. There are Friday and Saturday evening performances throughout June, July, and August. Call (203) 432–1966.

Norfolk has what many people consider the prettiest green in the state. What better way to see the sights of charming and historic Norfolk than in a horse-drawn carriage? The **Horse and Carriage Livery Service** (P.O. Box 264, Loon Meadow Drive, off Route 44) offers a horse-drawn tour of the town or horse-drawn hayrides with bonfires afterward. In winter (snow permitting) you can arrange for a private sleigh ride for two or for a larger sled that can handle groups on a romantic sleigh ride through snow-hushed woods. Warm up afterwards with a cup of mulled cider in the wood stove–heated barn. Open daily, 9:00 A.M. to 10:00 P.M. Reservations required; call (860) 542–6085; Web address: loonmeadowfarm.com.

Located just off the Norfolk green in a castlelike brownstone building adorned with stained-glass windows and turrets is *The Pub.* The decor is laid back and includes posters, memorabilia, and one very cool chair made from antlers. The wine list is notable not only for its 150 beers, mostly microbrews, but also for its microbrewed *root beers.* The food stretches beyond pub grub, with the vegetable pancakes (little patties of shredded veggies with a dipping sauce and a dollop of onion marmalade); good, filling soups like the baked potato soup; very good burgers; and salads like the chicken, apple, and walnuts over baby greens. Desserts tend to the chocolate side, for example, tri-chocolate mousse (white, milk, and bittersweet chocolate mousses layered together) or chocolate brownies topped with ice cream and chocolate sauce. Prices are very reasonable; without a doubt, this place offers one of the best deals on meals in the Litchfield Hills. Open: Tuesday through Thursday, 11:30 A.M. to 9:00 P.M., Friday and Saturday, 11:30 A.M. to 10:00 P.M., Sunday, 11:00 A.M. to 8:30 P.M. Throughout the year, the pub cooks up various special dinners, for example, an Octoberfest German dinner. When things get quiet in the winter, pub hours change, so call ahead. Call (860) 542–5716 for information about special dinners and reservations.

Just outside of town, at 105 Greenwoods Road East, is an unassuming bed and breakfast called *Greenwoods Gate. Yankee Magazine* has called it the "most romantic [B & B] in New England," and our readers seem to agree. A couple from New Jersey wrote us that their twenty-fifth anniversary at Greenwoods Gate was their most romantic ever. The pineapple, the colonial symbol of hospitality, greets you as you enter the white clapboard structure, a 1797 restored colonial with three opulent suites. Each suite has its own entrance, assuring you of maximum privacy. The three-level Levi Thompson suite has its own living room and a bathroom with a large whirlpool that would be the envy of many spas. Guests are encouraged to make the public rooms, living room, and family room their own. The owner serves splendid gourmet breakfasts on weekends and less elaborate country continental breakfasts on weekdays, but only for guests. Call (860) 542–5439; Web address: greenwoodsgate.com.

Way up in the farthest northwest corner of Connecticut is the *Mount Riga* area, a system of peaks that marches north and west from Salisbury to the New York and Massachusetts borders. The Appalachian

Trail crosses the region, running over **Bear Mountain,** at 2,316 feet the highest peak in the state. The highest *point* in the state is a shoulder of **Mount Frissel** that rises to 2,380 feet in the northwesternmost corner of Connecticut. According to tourist brochures, you can stand on that mountain and (assuming that you are reasonably limber) place one foot in Connecticut and one foot in Massachusetts and bend over and put both hands in New York. Very near this summit is Crying Child Rock, which, they say, makes a soft crying sound just like an infant whenever the wind is right. For detailed information on this area, call the state office of parks and recreation; (860) 566–2304. You can check out Connecticut's highest point and get hiking information at the Connecticut High Points Web site: www.cris.com/~Mfedor/cthp/ct.shtml.

If you plan to overnight in the Mount Riga area, you can't beat **Under Mountain Inn,** on Under Mountain Road (Route 41) about 4 miles north of Salisbury. This restored eighteenth-century farmhouse seems designed as a haven for Anglophiles. So much so that you almost expect Miss Jane Marple to totter into the dining room and declare that so-and-so reminds her of someone in St. Mary Mead. In keeping with British tradition, owners Marged and Peter Higginson share their colonial-style establishment not only with their guests but with a pair of inn dogs and a companion pair of inn cats.

The seven guest rooms are spacious and comfortable and come complete with sherry and mints and one or two stuffed animals from Marged's extensive collection. The terrace and grounds are beautiful in any season, but especially so in summer. The thorned locust in the yard is said to be the oldest in Connecticut.

The inn has three public dining rooms and one private one. It serves a full breakfast and dinner for its houseguests, with dinner available for inn guests midweek at 7:00 P.M. The menu is a tempting mix of American classics and British cooking and changes with the season. We recommend choosing from the British side of the menu; the steak-and-kidney pie is superb, as is the trifle. Breakfasts are hearty and British, tending toward eggs and sausage. And don't forget to snag a copy of the *Manchester Guardian* to read while you enjoy a proper cuppa (brewed tea, not that tea-bag stuff). Children over six welcome; no pets. Call (860) 435–0242.

Chaiwalla means tea-maker in Hindi. So what else could a place named **Chaiwalla** be but a teahouse? Located at 1 Main Street in Salisbury, this establishment somehow fits the town (you should pardon the expression) to a T. Salisbury has always been a simple, pastoral village, with a small measure of sophistication and a lot of country charm. In recent years, these qualities have made it a popular destination for weekending New Yorkers. The combination of a rustic setting and a sophisticated audience made this a perfect place for tea lover and importer Mary O'Brien to set up shop.

Chaiwalla serves light lunches and teas. The lunches are quite good, but high tea is what is done best. This is not your simple tea and a bun, but rather a bounty of scones and lemon curd and a selection of desserts. The kitchen really shines when it comes to desserts. Fruit tarts glistening with fresh fruit on crisp, ultralight pastry are always a good choice, as are the butter cakes and a rich whisky cake bursting with coconut and raisins. Chaiwalla serves nineteen different teas, all of which are blended at the restaurant. The tea is proper tea, of course, not bag tea. Freshly brewed, it's available in half or full pots. In addition to conventional blends, tea enthusiasts can choose from such rare and exotic brews as *banarshi,* brewed with vanilla and cardamom, and Moroccan mint tea, made with—what else?—crushed mint leaves. Open Wednesday to Sunday 10:00 A.M. to 6:00 P.M. Call (860) 435–9758.

It must be something in the water because Salisbury is also home to **Harney & Sons Tea,** 23 Brook Street. We don't know if Connecticut appoints ambassadors, but if they do, then John Harney is a natural for ambassador of tea. He is so charming and persuasive, we bet he could turn Pacific Northwest coffee drinkers into tea fanatics without breaking a sweat. Naturally, you can buy any of Harney's teas at the shop, but even better, you can sample the teas in a tasting room. We like the decaf teas and the fruit teas for iced tea. The shop sells other accouterments dear to the heart of tea fans such as cozies, pots, spoons, spreaders, biscuits, and jams. Tea tastings are open to the public, 10:00 A.M. to 5:00 P.M., Monday through Saturday; Sunday, noon to 5:00 P.M. Call (800) TEATIME for more information or to request their mail-order catalog. You can also find them on the Internet at www.harney.com.

West of Salisbury on Route 44 you'll come across Lakeville where you'll find the *1768 Holley-Williams House.* By now, your eyes are probably glazing over when you see the words "restored house," but hang in there. The Holley House is worth a look for several reasons. First, it's just about the purest example of classic revival architecture we've seen. More important, however, the house tour is something special. Instead of the usual dry mix of trivial facts and obscure decorating information, this place offers living, breathing history. Using diaries, letters, and the household accounts of the Holley family, the tour presents a spirited portrayal of what life was like in the eighteenth and nineteenth centuries. Tours are given by a costumed guide playing the role of Maria Holley Williams. Maria led a remarkable life for a woman in the nineteenth century; among other things, she negotiated a prenuptial agreement, which saved her from penury when she divorced her husband. After the tour, be sure to spend some time in the 1844 Heritage Garden, which includes specimens of antique flowers and plants. Open Memorial Day through September, Saturday and Sunday from 1:00 to 5:00 P.M. or by appointment. Call (860) 435–9649 for tour information and special events.

The Hills

No one driving past 192 Main Street in Torrington can possibly ignore the awe-inspiring symphony in Roman brick and rosy-red slate that occupies the property. At first, all you see is the big, round, three-story corner tower. Then the eye begins to jump from dormer to porch to porte cochere, taking in the Victorian carvings, the intricate sashes, the many small details that speak of another age, when decoration for its own sake was a common element of American home-building.

The magnificent sixteen-room *Hotchkiss-Fyler House* is now the headquarters of the Torrington Historical Society. It still displays the original mahogany paneling, hand stenciling, and parquet floors that made it such an opulent example of Victorian excess when it was built by Orsamus Roman Fyler back in 1900. The original furnishings, on display here, are almost as extravagant as the house itself. Several of the rooms feature wonderful little collections of art objects, including gold Fabergé spoons, Sevres porcelain, Victorian art glass, and Dresden and Meissen figurines.

The Hotchkiss-Fyler House and an adjacent museum devoted to local history are open Tuesday through Friday from 10:00 A.M. to 4:00 P.M. and Saturday and Sunday from noon to 4:00 P.M. Both are closed during November and January through March. Call (860) 482–8260.

One of the nicest places to take a leisurely fall hike is located in *Burr Pond State Park,* Route 8 in Torrington. The circuit around the 88-acre pond in the park is a pleasant walk. There's history in the park, too; it was the site of Borden's first American condensed milk factory. The 436-acre park offers swiming, hiking, fishing, camping, and picnicking. Admission (lower on weekdays than weekends). Call (860) 424–3200 for more information.

Torrington Trivia

Torrington was once known by the rather odd moniker of "Mast Swamp."

In 1856 Gail Borden of Torrington created a way to preserve milk. His creation, condensed milk, was called the "milk that won the Civil War."

As you bump west through Torrington along Route 4, you'll turn left past a diminutive flat-topped building at Lawrence Square (the corner of North Elm and Main Streets.) If the place is open, stop. This impossibly small restaurant is **Skee's Diner,** and it is actually a genuine wood-sided 1920s-era diner built into an old train car. Thought to have originally occupied a site in Old Saybrook, Skee's is also probably Connecticut's oldest diner. Its dollhouse exterior, original frosted windows, and white block lettering makes it a Torrington landmark. The interior still has its original mahogany woodwork, black marble countertop, and white enamel stools. And the pancakes and sausage-and-pepper omelets are outstanding. Open Tuesday through Sunday from 5:00 A.M. to 2:00 P.M. Call (860) 496–0166.

They say that at one time, travelers passing through the Bridgeport area during the spring were shocked to see elephants plowing nearby fields; they were rented to local farmers by circus impresario P. T. Barnum. If you catch sight of an elephant nonchalantly strolling through a field along Route 4, it won't be plowing. In fact, it—and the other assorted circus animals on the property—are on vacation. You see, that field located just across Route 4 from the Village Marketplace belongs to **R. W. Commerford & Sons Circus Animals.** This place is sort of a home away from home for animals on hiatus from the circus. Alas, the animals there really are "resting" (as it's called in the business), and you can't tour Commerford's. But, at any given time, a fair number of the residents will be exercising and thus visible from the road.

Nodine's Smokehouse on Route 63, just north of the Goshen rotary and on your left as you leave town, is one of the two or three best smoke-houses in New England. It's also something of a Connecticut institution. Nodine's (it's pronounced *no-DINES*) carries more than eighty specialty items, ranging from smoked hams, turkeys, and chickens to more exotic smoked pheasants, shrimp, and venison sausage. If you hunt or hike and have had your fill of trail mix, try the beef jerky; it keeps forever and makes a satisfying meal that you can eat on your feet. The bacon and many other meats can be purchased with or without nitrites, and the non-nitrited variety will change your whole concept of how bacon should taste. If you like the flavor of game animals but you don't want them smoked, the freezer case includes such items as buffalo, quail, pheasant, and venison (including packages of stewing meat that are perfect for venison chili).

Nodine's more common meats can be had in made-to-order sandwiches. The bread is an import from Canada that comes frozen in huge loaves; it is grainy and chewy, a perfect match for the tender tasty meats. You can also get some very good sausage and bacon-and-spinach rolls and similar items for a cold-weather picnic; they'll be heated up for you on the spot. Open Monday through Saturday, 9:00 A.M. to 5:00 P.M.; Sunday, 10:00 A.M. to 4:00 P.M. If you see something you like, but don't want to drag it along for the rest of your trip, never fear; they have a mail-order operation. Call (860) 491–4009.

The *Litchfield Green,* which was laid out in the 1770s, is probably the best known location in this part of Connecticut. The stark white Congregational church with the towering spire on the green's north side is almost certainly the most photographed church in New England. Opposite the church, on West Street, there's a row of upscale shops and restaurants, behind which you'll find Cobble Court, an easily overlooked nineteenth-century cobblestone courtyard, around which several merchants have set up shop in rustic settings.

The Wild Life in Goshen

*J*ust before you get to the rotary in Goshen, you'll see several large, intriguing stone cairns, surrounded by stout stone fences. You've reached the home of the 115-acre **Action Wildlife Foundation,** Route 4 west. This former dairy-farm-turned-game-park is home to about one hundred exotic creatures from around the world. Some, like the zebra, you may be familiar with; others, such as the scimitar oryx, the yak, and the aoudad (wild sheep), may be new to you. The aoudad live in one of the cairns called "Aoudad Mountain" and share quarters with fainting goats. Yep, when under stress, the goats go stiff and fall over in a faint just like a proper Victorian maiden. Visitors can tour the various animal areas on foot by walking paths throughout the thirty-five acres of the park that are open to the public or on tractor-drawn wagons. If you are visiting with very small children, take the wagon tour as the paths can get a little steep and the footing difficult. In addition to the exotic animals, the foundation has a picnic area and a petting zoo in the farm's former dairy. Plans are also in the works for a museum that will house mounted animals shot by the owner and other hunters in South Africa, Siberia, Tanzania, and New Zealand as well as other places around the globe. Admission. Open April through November, Thursday to Sunday, 10:00 A.M. to 5:00 P.M. Hayrides on fall weekends only. For information, call (860) 482–4465.

For moderately fancy fare, Litchfield's chic **West Street Grill** (43 West Street, on the green) is the place. In just a few years, the West Street Grill has become such a part of the Litchfield landscape that its changes in management and chefs make front-page news in the local newspaper. The frequent upheavals in the kitchen haven't hurt the food, which seems to get better with each passing chef. Right now, the food has a country-house Irish feel, with dishes such as grilled pork chops with pan-seared polenta, roasted tomato, and apple chutney. By the time you visit, that may have changed. You can't go wrong by taking the easy way out with one of the daily specials or any of the pastas from the set menu. And take a minute to check out the wine list. We've found some unusual wines at moderate prices. Reservations are a must, and you may need to call far in advance to get a table on a peak fall weekend. Call (860) 567–3885 for reservations and operating hours. Web address: www.litchfield cty.com/dining/wsgrill.html.

The heart of historic Litchfield consists of a block or two of North Street and the few blocks of South Street (Route 63) immediately off the common. There you'll find the 1760 home of Benjamin Tallmadge, once an

Congregational church on Litchfield Common

aide to George Washington, and the house where Harriet Beecher Stowe was born. There's also the 1760 Sheldon Tavern, where George Washington really did sleep (he visited town five times), and the 1792 Pierce Academy, the first academy for girls in America.

Much of Litchfield's historic heritage is summarized in an exhibit in the newly renovated **Litchfield Historical Society Museum,** at the corner of South and East Streets. Here you can trace the history of Litchfield from the first contact between Europeans and Indians back in the seventeenth-century to the end of the town's "Golden Age" in the middle of the nineteenth century. The museum also features a display of antique furniture and a gallery of eighteenth-century portraits, plus several galleries of changing exhibits. There's also a research library

A Highland Fling in Goshen

In the Highlands, they'd call it a Gathering. The time, usually after harvest, when Scots would get together to buy and sell their wares, swap some yarns, and play a few tunes on the bagpipes. These days, in Connecticut, we call such things folk festivals. Even if you're not a Scot—nobody's perfect, after all—you'll probably find something to amuse you at the Scottish Festival held at the Goshen Fairgrounds on Route 63, the first Saturday in October. Naturally, there's Celtic music and folk dancing, including periodic performances by half a dozen local pipe bands. Also Scottish games, most of which seem to involve big sweaty guys tossing around rocks and logs. If you're looking for a souvenir, there are dozens of booths flogging everything from custom-made kilts to clan badges. Other booths sell Scottish food, everything from shortbread to forfar bridies (meat pies). Sorry, no haggis. The booths in one section of the fairgrounds are given over to the clan associations. Probably our favorite part of the proceedings are the border

collie trials and demonstrations. If you've never actually seen the way an eagle-eyed, spirited sheltie or border collie operates, the sheep-herding demonstration is an eye-opener, and kids seem to be especially delighted by the duck-herding demonstration.

*There's a similar folk festival in the town of Scotland, but we like the Goshen venue better; the rolling, flame-clad October hills just seem to be a perfect background for this event. Even when it rains—and there have been plenty of "soft" days in recent years—early October is a fine time for being outdoors. If you go, try to be there for the stirring opening ceremony, with its massed pipes and evocative Calling of the Clans. And if you visit the clan tents, you can learn more about the different clans and maybe discover that you're a Scot, too. Admission. Usually held the first Saturday in October. For more information, write the **St. Andrew's Society of Connecticut,** P.O. Box 1195, Litchfield, 06759.*

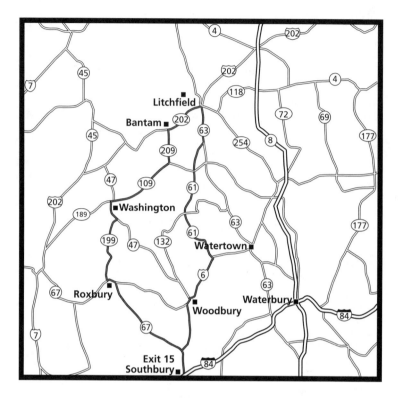

Litchfield Driving Tour

*O*ne of the best fall driving tours through Litchfield County gives you spectacular views of foliage and the chance for some antiquing as well. Start in Southbury on Route 6 (exit 15 from Interstate 84) and head north on Route 67 to Roxbury and north on Routes 199 and 47 to Washington. Along the way, you'll come across the Institute for American Indian Studies (page 94) and the Gunn Memorial Library (page 94).

Follow Route 47 to Route 109 north to Bantam (page 85), then take Route 209 north to Route 202 into Litchfield (page 77). Out of Litchfield follow Route 63 south to Route 61 and then south on Route 6 to Woodbury (page 87).

and gift shop. The museum is open between mid-April and the end of November, Tuesday through Saturday from 11:00 A.M. to 5:00 P.M. and Sunday from 1:00 to 5:00 P.M. The museum shop is open year round, weekdays from 10:00 A.M. to 5:00 P.M. Admission. Call (860) 567–4501.

A block south of the museum is the *Tapping Reeve House & Law School.* Founded in 1773, this was America's first law school. Here's a chance to tour the school that trained political conspirator and former vice president Aaron Burr. Of course, it also schooled the likes of John C. Calhoun and some 130 other congressmen and senators, not to mention three supreme court justices, six cabinet members, and a dozen governors. Today the Reeve House contains displays of period furnishings; open April through November, Tuesday through Saturday, 11:00 A.M. to 5:00 P.M. and Sunday 1:00 to 5:00 P.M. Admission. Call (860) 567–4501.

Farther out Route 202 is the *White Memorial Foundation and Conservation Center,* whose 4,000 acres constitute Connecticut's largest nature center and wildlife sanctuary. This privately owned facility is administered by a nonprofit corporation, the White Memorial Foundation. It contains numerous picnic areas, nine camps, two family campgrounds, a number of bird-watching platforms, 35 miles of riding and hiking trails (including a hiking trail for the blind with Braille signs), more than seventy acres of open water, and more than half of the Bantam Lake shoreline. The property is open year-round for fishing, canoeing, cross-country skiing, and similar activities.

The Conservation Center building is the focus for the White Memorial Foundation's work. The first floor features a gift shop and a variety of exhibits, including some stunning nature dioramas and a collection of more than 3,000 species of butterflies. The second floor contains the finest nature library in the state, with a special section for children. The center is open Monday through Saturday, 9:00 A.M. to 5:00 P.M. during the winter and 8:30 A.M. to 4:30 P.M. the rest of the year; also open Sunday, noon to 5:00 P.M., year-round. Admission. Call (860) 567–0857.

A mile past the Conservation Center, a right turn onto Maple Street will take you to the studio of glassmaker Tony Carretta. Carretta works out of the *Milton Barn* at number 513, about 3 miles down the road. Like other area craftsmen, he's open daily but doesn't necessarily adhere to a fixed schedule. In addition, much of Tony's work is custom designed by request and not available for sale. But you are more than welcome to visit the studio and watch the artist, and that is a visual treat because Tony Carretta is a wizard with glass. Using both traditional and modern techniques, he makes one-of-a-kind stained-glass windows, table lamps, hanging lamps, glass sculpture, and etched glass. It's all quite beautiful, and even when you see it done, you still wonder how it came out so right. Call (860) 567–4851.

A little more than 3 miles south of Litchfield center on Route 63 is **White Flower Farm,** an establishment comprising more than ten acres of cultivated plants and thirty acres of wildflowers, plus assorted greenhouses. There are flowers blooming here all summer: from mid-May to mid-June the Exbury azaleas and tree peonies are in flower; throughout June, you can see tall bearded iris and herbaceous peonies; and around the middle of the month, the Japanese irises take over; they last until the middle of July. The stars of the farm, though, are its tuberous begonias that bloom throughout July and August. These have to be seen to be believed; the pictures in the farm's catalogs (written under the pen name of "Amos Pettingill") just don't do them justice. White Flower Farm also has a great gardening store. Open daily mid-April through December, from 10:00 A.M. to 5:00 P.M. Call (860) 567–8789.

As you travel east from Litchfield on Route 118, just past the East Cemetery is the **Lourdes in Litchfield Shrine.** For thirty-two years, Montfort Missionaries have operated this thirty-five-acre shrine, which features a replica of the famous grotto at Lourdes, France. An outdoor Stations of the Cross path winds its way to a spectacular crucifixion scene at the top of the hill. The grounds are open year-round and include a picnic area and small gift shop. In addition, outdoor services are conducted throughout the pilgrimage season (May 1 to mid-October), and the Blessing of the Motorcycles occurs in mid-May. At the blessing, each person, biker or not, and his or her vehicle is blessed. On many years, the Blue Knights, a bike club, host a roast beef dinner in the Pilgrim Hall beyond the grotto. In recent years, more than 500 bikers from as far as Maine and New York have attended the celebrations. Even if you aren't a biker, it's worth a visit to see some really fine bikes, such as the faux-1950 HDs Heritage Softail Nostalgia, nicknamed the "Moo Glide" with Holstein hide inserts on the seats and saddlebags. Call (860) 567–1041 for schedule and details.

Located on Chestnut Hill Road, off Route 118, about a mile east of Litchfield, the **Haight Vineyard & Winery** may not be quite *haut médoc,* but it is really quite a nice place for a Saturday afternoon vineyard walk, winery tour, and wine tasting. With vines that were first planted in 1975, this is Connecticut's oldest continuously operating winery and the first in the state to make sparkling wine using the French *méthode champagne.*

Tours are free. You can view the wine-making operation and vineyards from an outdoor balcony and picnic on the grounds. There's also a gift shop on the premises. The professional staff is friendly, knowledgeable, and eager to answer questions. Open Monday through Saturday, 11:00 A.M. to 4:00 P.M.; Sunday, 1:00 to 4:00 P.M. Each June the winery is also the site of the annual Taste of Litchfield Hills festival, a sort of food-tasting fair and giant picnic that is a "don't miss" event for those who happen to be in the area. Call (860) 567–4045. There a second Haight Winery, but no vineyards, in Mystic (exit 90 off Interstate 95, watch for blue wine trail signs at intersection of Route 127 and Coogan Boulevard) at Old Mystic Village, Coogan Boulevard; (860) 572–1978.

Wisdom House Retreat Center, formerly a convent for the Sisters of Wisdom, 229 East Litchfield Road, is the scene of Connecticut's only outdoor labyrinth. Don't arrive thinking you'll find a high, boxwood maze like those in England or in Colonial Williamsburg. The low circular path is a symbol older than time and one which transcends religions. Walking the spiral path helps you to meditate and heighten your awareness. You'll find a helpful pamphlet at Wisdom House suggesting

Eagle Watching

*N*ot so long ago, your chances of seeing eagles hunting and soaring in the wild were somewhere between slim and none, and Slim was out to lunch. Today, thanks to the Endangered Species Act, the American eagle population is itself soaring. In winter Connecticut bald eagles find the Southbury area much to their taste. In fact it's such a popular place that their eagle buddies from as far away as Canada and Maine flock there, too. Connecticut Light and Power has developed an eagle observation area for visitors. The observation area is staffed by knowledgeable guides to coach you in observing these beautiful birds—some of whom have a wing-span of 7 feet—while they fish, hunt, and soar. To use a worn-out phrase, they take your breath away. Eagle observations are held Wednesdays, Saturdays, and Sundays from late December through March. Reservations, far in advance, are a must. To protect the eagles and maintain their habitat, details about the site are not released until you make your reservation. After making the reservation, you'll receive a reservation number, directions to the site, and an eagle fact sheet that describes what will happen during your visit. CL&P usually starts taking reservations in mid-December. Call (800) 368–8954 to reserve your spot. Visit the eagles on the Web at www.nu.com/eagles/eagles.htm.

By the way, bald eagles aren't really bald. In truth, they have a glorious head of white feathers. The bald part comes from the word piebald, which means white.

different meditative approaches to walking the labyrinth. We like entering the labyrinth in silence and keeping our eyes focused on the path until we reach the center, then retracing our steps in silence. Whichever approach you take, it's a peaceful way to get in touch with yourself, to find some peace in the silence, and to shed the cares of twenty-first-century life. Many visitors use the labyrinth for silent meditation, so it probably isn't a place to visit if you are accompanied by rowdy children. Call (860) 567–3163 for hours and more information about programs offered by Wisdom House. Web address: www.wisdomhouse.org.

East of Haight Vineyard on Buell Road (off East Litchfield Road) is **Topsmead,** an estate turned park that looks like it belongs in the British midlands. When Waterbury heiress Edith Chase came home from a European tour enchanted with English manor houses, she determined to build herself an authentic Cotswold cottage, complete with leaded-glass casement windows, hand-hewn beams, and buttery stucco exteriors. She found the right location in Litchfield, and there she built. The Cotswold cottage of her dreams was designed by architect Richard Dana, who shared Miss Edith's love for English cottage architecture.

Topsmead, however, was more than a building. It was also a vast garden and a working farm. Miss Edith was as fond of English country gardens as of English architecture, and she surrounded her home with formal manicured gardens and with cutting gardens full of the flowers most beloved by English gardeners, roses, sweet William, and phlox. Even in her late seventies, she reputedly walked a daily mile around these gardens, inspecting, issuing orders, and sipping from an ever-present glass of skim milk.

When Miss Edith died, she left her 511-acre estate to the state of Connecticut so that everyone could enjoy a touch of England in Litchfield. The Topsmead gardens and grounds are now Topsmead State Forest and are open all year for picnicking, sledding, cross-country skiing, and hiking. You can tour the house on the second and fourth weekends of each month from June to October. Call (860) 485–0226.

If it's not springtime when you pass the junction of Routes 118 and 254 just east of Litchfield, make a mental note to come back to visit **Morosani Farms** on Wigwam Road. Something of a local legend, the ten-acre farm grows twenty varieties of daffodils, and in late April it's like looking at fields of gold. Visitors from all over New England, starved for a bit of springtime, stop by for a visit as do local artists and photographers. Take 118 east from Litchfield and then Route 254 south. The farm is near the village of Northfield. Just look for a patch of spring, you can't miss it.

The town of Lakeside, in Morris, is one of those beautiful, manicured little uplands villages that seems absolutely Norman-Rockwell-normal. Right up until you come upon the white lady floating above a roadside field. Relax. It's not some Yankee haunt. You've just happened on the studio of glassblower-sculptor Lorenz Livolsi. *Lorenz Studios* (Route 109, Morris) rambles over ten acres near Lakeside, and in this place, the strange and unusual are the norm. Livolsi creates his often ethereal works of art in one of a pair of red barns that he uses as a workshop. The other barn is a showroom for items ranging from handsome but utilitarian metal-and-glass tables to imaginative abstract sculpture. Many of the glass pieces are inexpensive. The blown-glass teardrops, priced under five bucks, make a wonderful addition to any family's Christmas tree. The opalescent blown glass balls, also inexpensive, are terrific souvenirs or hostess gifts. Stephanie Kafka, Lorenz's wife, contributes to the art with her unusual and intricate hand-painted wooden furniture. The most interesting stuff, though, dots the cow pastures that Livolsi has turned into an outdoor gallery. We'll say no more; with an attraction like this, the delight is in the unexpected. Call (860) 567–4280; visitors are welcome, but you might want to call ahead.

On Route 209, just north of Morris and Lakeside, you'll find the *Bantam Cinema,* just south of Route 202. The Bantam Cinema is an old-fashioned movie theater that screens those offbeat, independent, or imported films that never seem to get much play at suburban theaters. Even though the screening rooms and sound systems are modern, it's a wonderfully intimate and kind of old-fashioned way to see a film. Besides the well-chosen films and the really great snacks, what makes the Bantam Cinema so much fun is the synergy of the audience. Just standing around in the lobby and eavesdropping on conversations is a lot like taking a film 101 class. From time to time, the cinema holds special programs with celebrities, such as Bridgewater's Mia Farrow, talking about their work and film. Call (860) 868–1949 or (860) 567–0006 for show times and film information. Web address: www. bantamcinema.com.

One of our online friends told us about the *Bantam Baking Company,* 853 Bantam Road (Route 202), and we're glad he did. This is the type of hearth-baked bread that people line up for in New York and Los Angeles. We like the Holiday Loaf, a plump, whole-wheat sourdough loaf packed with toasted walnuts, plump and tender golden raisins, and tart dried cherries. The shop also turns out a variety of other breads— sourdough semolina, rosemary-scented kalamata olive, sourdough raisin—plus biscotti, cookies, and memorable tarts, including a lemon-strawberry number that is to die for. Open Tuesday through Saturday, 8:00 A.M. to 5:30 P.M. and Sunday, 8:00 A.M. to 4:00 P.M.; closed Monday. Call (860) 567–2737.

You'll find a great spot for a pre- or post-movie lunch or dinner right next door to the Bantam Cinema. *Wood's Pit BBQ & Mexican Cafe,* 123 Bantam Lake Road (Route 209), may be somewhat incongruous amid the Litchfield Hills' studied country casual, but it's a good place for a casual meal of smoked stuff, and kids and families are treated well here. We like the shredded beef brisket, smoky, tender, and simmered with a jaunty BBQ sauce, but the pulled pork and ribs are good, too. On each table rests squeeze bottles of BBQ sauce: a traditional, hot, ketchup-based variety and a mustard-vinegar Carolina-style sauce, so you can doctor your 'cue to fit your taste. Don't expect much of the side dishes—cole slaw, baked beans, potato salad, or green salad—but the desserts, especially the silky-textured pecan pie, are good. Open Monday through Thursday, 11:30 A.M. to 9:00 P.M.; Friday and Saturday, 11:30 A.M. to 10:00 P.M.; Sunday, 11:30 A.M. to 9:00 P.M. The staff generally takes a break during the afternoon on Monday, so don't try a late lunch that day. Call (860) 567–9869.

As one would expect from the name, the *Lock Museum of America* at 130 Main Street (Route 6) in Terryville is all about locks. In fact, its two floors house a unique collection of 22,000 locks, keys, and related paraphernalia, tracing the development of the American lock industry back to its local beginnings; there were once forty lock companies in Terryville (which was known as the "Lock Town of America"), and the Eagle Lock Company formerly occupied the site of the shopping mall across the street.

This is the largest collection of locks and keys in the United States, and there are all manner of locks and lock-related items on display. The oldest is a 4,000-year-old Egyptian pin tumble lock, but there are also a number of colonial locks and many nineteenth-century items. There are big locks and little locks, plain locks and fancy locks, safe locks and padlocks. There are also mail locks, which were invented by former Eagle Lock Company employee Burton Andrus when he was superintendent of the U.S. Mail Service Department in Washington, D.C. Many of the locks are part of doorknob assemblies, and some of these are quite beautiful. The oddest item is a modern dog-collar lock. Open May through October, Tuesday through Sunday, noon to 5:00 P.M. Admission. Call (860) 589–6359.

If you want to truly get away from it all and do something really different at the same time, try floating over the Litchfield Hills in a hot-air balloon. In mid-October, when the fall-color change is at its peak and the clear blue skies are just starting to bluster their way toward November, that's when a balloon ride can make you a little giddy from sun and wind. Take a friend who's not too chatty; the best thing about the experience is that except for the sound of the wind, it's absolutely quiet up there.

Ballooning, both private and public, is quite popular in Connecticut, and there must be a score of operations in the state that offer passenger rides. Many of these, however, are seasonal or operate over the less scenic parts of the state. **Watershed Balloons** at 179 Gilbert Road in Watertown offers year-round flights lasting about an hour each, and the normal flight takes you directly over Litchfield into the heart of the hills.

Generally passenger operations charge a couple of hundred dollars per person per ride; Watershed Balloons is priced a little below average. Like most such operations, this one can normally accommodate two to four guests. If you have a larger party, pilot Tom Murphy can arrange for an extra balloon and pilot to handle the overflow. All balloon pilots are licensed by the FAA. Reservations are required. Call (860) 274–2010.

Woodbury was one of the first towns established in inland Connecticut. During the early eighteenth century, it was home to Moll Cramer, the best known of Connecticut's witches. Known as the "Witch of Wood-bury," Cramer resided in a hut she built on Good Hill and supported herself by begging. Good Hill got its name from the fact that while Moll lived there storms and high winds never seemed to cross Woodbury. After she disappeared from Good Hill without a trace, Woodbury was hit by a series of destructive storms. Even today, old-timers speak of needing a "Moll Cramer storm" after a summer dry spell. If you enter Woodbury from Roxbury on Route 317 (Good Hill Road) you'll pass over the crest of the hill near the township line.

Before you get ready to do battle on Woodbury's "Antique Avenue," you might want to prepare yourself with a dose of carbs at **Mrs. White's Tea Room,** 308 Sherman Hill Road. When we first moved to Connecticut, you could count the number of tearooms on the fingers of one hand and still have fingers left over. Tearooms are all the rage now, and Mrs. White's is one of the best. Fans of Jan Karon's Mitford books will feel right at home in this snug, low-flung white house. You'll find lots of yummy things to eat amid the chintz and china, including the "hot dishes," so popular in Mitford. For breakfast you can't go wrong with the Scotch toast, French toast filled with walnuts and cream cheese. Lunch offerings include a daily soup, sandwiches, and a hot dish and salad. We like the spinach salad with apples, walnuts, and bacon. We usually go light on the main course because we want to save room for dessert. All the desserts are excellent, but fans of British literature will draw a bead on the sticky toffee pudding, a date-nut bread pudding with hot caramel sauce and dripping with mounds of freshly whipped cream. Included in the price of your meal is lots of cosseting and comforting; the prices are beyond moderate. Mrs. White's serves breakfast, lunch, and tea on Tuesday through Sunday, from 9:00 A.M. to 4:30 P.M.

Today, Route 6 runs through the center of Woodbury past rows of eighteenth- and nineteenth-century houses, many of which have been converted into antiques and gift shops. In fact, in this neck of the woods, Woodbury's Main Street is nicknamed *"Antique Avenue."* Some travel guides we've seen create the impression that unless you roll up in a chauffeured Rolls, you won't get very good treatment at many of the antiques shops in Woodbury. We've never experienced anything like that. We showed up at the very flossy Mill House tired, jean-clad, and looking definitely declassé, but were treated with great kindness and interest. So don't let the other guidebooks put you off. Park and explore.

Mill House Antiques, 1068 Main Street North (Route 6); (203) 263–3446. It's a pleasure just to walk through this restored mill house with its imaginative displays of top quality English and French furniture. The Welsh dressers, armoires, and harvest tables are noteworthy. Open daily, except Tuesday, from 9:00 A.M. to 5:00 P.M.

The Woodbury Guild, 4 Main Street South; (203) 263–4828; Web site: woodburyguild.com. Owner Michael Bird calls himself a "twelfth generation Yankee and just as eccentric as anything." The owner may be eccentric, but his store is beautiful. You'll find lots of Americana primitives, beautiful bronzes, and some really lovely reproduction pottery. Though it may not be there when you visit, last time we were there, Bird had a magnificent bronze pig outside on his porch. Open Wednesday through Sunday from 10:00 A.M. to 5:00 P.M.

Des Jardins Oriental Rugs, 289 Main Street South. Old Kilim rugs are our weakness, and we love visiting Gale Des Jardins's shop. Des Jardins has a good eye and does her own buying, so the quality tends to be high. Prices, however, are quite reasonable. Today, with so many "modern antique" rugs on the market, buying antique rugs is almost more a science than an art. Des Jardins makes it easy even for novice buyers like ourselves. Aside from the tribal patterns we crave, she carries a wide variety of other Orientals and a few quilts and textiles. Call (203) 263–0095 for hours.

Merry-Go-Round of Fine Crafts, 319 Main Street South; (203) 263–2920. Housed in an 1837 home, the seven rooms of this high-quality craft center are brimming with fun and interesting crafts products. All are made in Connecticut, and the selection is wide enough so that even if dried flower wreaths make you twitch, you'll probably find something you like among the textiles or hand-crafted jewelry. The owner loves both dogs and cats, so canine- and feline-embellished crafts play starring roles, as do gifts for Spot and Fluffy. Open Sunday, Monday, Friday, and Saturday, 10:00 A.M. to 6:00 P.M.; Tuesday through Thursday, 10:00 A.M. to 5:00 P.M. The center usually holds a summer craft fest in early June and a big sale the Sunday before Thanksgiving.

Write to the Woodbury Antique Dealers Association, P.O. Box 496, Woodbury, 06798 for a complete directory of Woodbury antiques dealers.

For a taste of the Woodbury that antiquers rarely see, visit the ***Canfield Corner Pharmacy*** on North Main Street. It has an old-fashioned soda fountain and is crammed from floor to rafters with every nostrum and homemaker's convenience on the market. Also on Main Street (Route 6), ***Philips Diner*** serves such old-fashioned comfort food as chicken pot pies and cinnamon doughnuts. One of our online buddies swears

Good News in Woodbury

*R*oadfoodistas Jane and Michael Stern adore **Carole Peck's Good News Cafe,** 694 Main Street in Woodbury, as do other restaurant critics and celebrity diners-out. This gem of an eatery has been compared to Berkeley's Chez Panisse. For us, it's like going home, except the food is better and you don't have to clean your plate to get dessert. Carole Peck buys most of her produce and other foods from local suppliers, so everything you get is fresh and high quality, and the food is healthy without being grim or preachy. It's also some of the tastiest and most innovative food we've ever encountered. Special favorites: warm smashed potato salad with blue cheese and corn on a bed of greens, corned beef hash with frizzled leeks, rotisserie chicken with buttermilk mashed potatoes and wok-fried veggies. The desserts are as splendid as the entrees, with the standout being a delightful white chocolate banana cream pie. The truth is, no matter what you order, the food is great, and the service remarkable, the art wonderfully watchable, and the atmosphere comfortable. Open daily for lunch and dinner; closed Tuesday. Call (203) 266–GOOD.

Dustin Hoffman regularly bikes in from nearby Roxbury for breakfast. Call (203) 263–2516.

Although they are not antique pewter, the pewter plates, mugs, lamps, and other accessories at the **Woodbury Pewter Outlet,** 860 Main Street South, look very authentic with any antique you buy in Woodbury. Featured in *Victoria* magazine, Woodbury Pewter has been around since 1952 when it was a tiny shop tucked into a blacksmith's shop. Today it's a modern retail operation that features not only its own products but also the pewter work and jewelry of pewterers from across America. Be sure to look for the birthday flower pins, earrings, and lockets; they're great gifts at exceptional prices. Speaking of prices, those at the outlet are very good, with significant discounts over what you'll find in well-known department stores. Seconds, on a hit-or-miss, what's-available basis, are also for sale. The staff is friendly and professional and more than willing to help you pick out just the right purchase, whether it's

The Legend of Chief Waramaug and His Great Lodge

*A*bout the time settlers first arrived in northwestern Connecticut, the Native Americans who lived along the banks of the Housatonic River were led by a gread leader, Chief Waramaug. Waramaug lived in a lodge high above the west banks of the Housatonic, not far from the beautiful alpine lake that bears his name. The lodge was so majestic that it was called Waramaug's Palace and, in its time, was without a doubt the most elegant dwelling in Connecticut. According to legend, Waramaug's longhouse was 20 feet wide by 100 feet long. Native American artists from all over New England worked ceaselessly for months to create Waramaug's Palace. Using bark gathered from all over New England, they intricately painted the bark with sumptuous colors distilled from herbs and flowers. Although much of the decoration came from Waramaug's own people and from the Iroquois from

nearby New York, the Hurons, Delawares, and even the fearsome Mohawks all sent their greatest artisans to decorate Waramaug's great lodge.

The interior of the lodge was as magnificent as the outside. Waramaug's council chamber was decorated with portraits of the great chief, his family, and the elders and wise men of the tribe. Other rooms were alive with pictures of the animals who shared the forests with Waramaug and his people. According to legend, Chief Waramaug died peacefully in his great lodge and was buried nearby. For years after his death, passing warriors would add a stone to his gravesite as a gesture of respect for the great leader. The great chief's lodge is no more, but the elegant inns that ring Lake Waramaug carry on the tradition of graceful living by the beautiful lake.

an expensive lamp or a simple key chain; we once watched one sales associate spend a good half hour helping a little girl pick out just the right $5.00 pin for her grandmother's birthday. Open daily, from 9:00 A.M. to 5:00 P.M. Woodbury Pewter holds several very good sales throughout the year. Call (800) 648–2014 for more information or to request a catalog.

A "glebe" is the parcel of land granted to a clergyman during his tenure of office. The gambrel-roofed 1740 *Glebe House* on Hollow Road, off Route 6 in the center of town, has always had ecclesiastical connections. Mere weeks after the start of the American Revolution, a group of clergy secretly assembled in the house to elect the first American bishop of the Episcopal Church, the Reverend Dr. Samuel Seabury. His election broke the American connection with the Church of England and laid the foundation for the separation of church and state in America. Today the old farmhouse is used as a museum and kept much as it was. The original paneling remains, and the rooms are stuffed with period furnishings collected locally. The most interesting item, however, is outside, where you will find the only garden in America designed by renowned British horticulturist Gertrude Jekyll. The garden blooms with candytuft, iris, lavender, lamb's ear, and other flowers beloved by Jekyll. Open April through November, Wednesday through Sunday, 1:00 to 5:00 P.M. (other times by appointment). Donation requested. Call (203) 263–2855; Web site: ghmgjg@wtco.net.

Glebe House

During most of the year, Bethlehem is just another quiet, pretty New England country town. During the Christmas holiday season, however, all that changes, and for a few brief weeks, Bethlehem bustles with activity.

The reason, of course, is the name. The local post office increases its staff by 1,700 percent each December to accommodate the thousands of folks who want a Bethlehem postmark on their Christmas cards. If you're going to be passing through during early December, bring yours along and they'll be glad to add them to the bin. There's also a **Bethlehem Christmas Town Festival** in mid-December that draws a lot of people to listen to the music, ride hay wagons, and look at holiday arts and crafts and a small festival of lights; a far cry, you will agree, from the days when the Puritans who wrote the colony's stringent blue laws prescribed a five-shilling fine for "Christmas Keeping." For details, call the town clerk's office during the morning; (203) 266–7510.

Understandably, with so much traffic passing through town at Christmas, local businesses have sprung up to take advantage of the situation. The biggest of these is the **Christmas Shop in Bethlehem** at 18 East Street. This store does have gifts appropriate for year-round giving, but its main focus is, of course, Christmas. The huge shop occupies a converted barn filled to the rafters with by far the largest collection of Christmas paraphernalia we've ever seen under one roof. There are dolls and music boxes and trimmings and crèches and, well, just about everything that you'd expect from a Christmas store in a town called Bethlehem. The European glass ornaments hand blown from antique molds are especially beautiful. Open Tuesday through Saturday from 10:00 A.M. to 5:00 P.M.; noon to 5:00 P.M. on Sunday. Call (203) 266–7048.

South of Bethlehem, about 1½ miles down Flanders Road (off Route 61) is the **Abbey of Regina Laudis,** which operates a Little Art Shop offering for sale items hand-crafted on the premises by Benedictine nuns. Among crafts represented are printing, potting, and blacksmithing. You can also buy beauty products, honey, herbs, and postcards showing the abbey grounds. The Sisters of the Abbey have also produced their first CD, called *Women in Chant,* which is available at the gift store. The abbey's holiday decorations include a nativity scene composed of eighteenth-century Neapolitan figures. Open by appointment. Call ahead for hours and information on special events; (203) 266–7637.

Lake Waramaug, with its surrounding forests and hills, is often likened to Switzerland's Lake Lucerne, and the inns that ring its waters reflect the same alpine charm. Even though the lake is named for Chief Waramaug, the atmosphere and food at the inns are Swiss. One of the best ways to see the area, especially during leaf-peeping season, is to take the .9-mile drive around the lake. The burning autumn colors of the surrounding hardwoods, reflected by the cool, crystal-clear lake, make this a picture-postcard setting. Two outstanding inns grace this beautiful setting: *Hopkins Inn* and the *Boulders Inn*.

The food at the Hopkins Inn on Hopkins Road in New Preston is so stellar that people tend to recommend the inn solely for its cuisine and forget that it is a warm and comfortable hostelry in its own right, with nine guest rooms and a private apartment at reasonable rates. The outdoor patio, open for dining spring through fall, provides a spectacular view of the lake. In the past, the cuisine tended toward Austrian, complete with rich desserts smothered in *schlag* (lightly whipped heavy cream). Lately, we understand there are more American dishes on the menu. The inn is open April to December, during which time the restaurant serves lunch and dinner to the public (and breakfast to guests). It can be difficult to find, so call ahead for directions: (860) 868–7295. Website: www.thehopkinsinn.com.

Except for the name, there's no connection between the inn and the *Hopkins Vineyard* located at 25 Hopkins Road. But the dairy farm turned winery and the inn do share a spectacular view of Lake Waramaug and the surrounding countryside. The Hopkins family has farmed the land around the lake since the late 1700s but didn't plant its first grape vine until 1979. The vineyard produces a variety of wines, including a pretty good sparkler. Try their semi-hard cider as an ingredient for autumn recipes or as a celebratory drink before Thanksgiving. You'll find tastings, sales, and a gift shop in the winery's bright red barn. Open every day for sales and tastings. Open Monday through Saturday from 10:00 A.M. to 5:00 P.M., and on Sunday from 11:00 A.M. to 5:00 P.M. Closed Monday through Thursday in January and February, and Mondays and Tuesdays in March and April. Free guided tours available Saturday and Sunday at 2:00 P.M. Call (860) 868–7954. Web site: www.hopkinsvineyard.com.

The Boulders Inn on East Shore Road (Route 45) in New Preston takes its name from the large fieldstone boulders from which it was constructed. Some people say that it is the best inn in the "Alpine Lake" region. They could be right. Nestled below Pinnacle Mountain, the main inn building has five comfortable bedrooms with vaguely Victorian decor, but we like the eight cottages (with fireplaces) scattered around the grounds. Typical of the inn's comforts is the samovar in the living room that dispenses tea to guests in the late afternoon. The dining room serves a spare but enticing menu of New American cuisine with herbs and produce from its own gardens. The outdoor patio is open Memorial Day to Labor Day. There is also a private beach for swimming. If you like hiking, you can reach the top of Pinnacle Mountain from the inn's backyard; the reward, aside from all that healthful exercise, is a breathtaking view of three states.

The Boulders Inn is open year-round, with special rates (that include meals) available off-season. The restaurant is open for dinner daily except Tuesday during most of the year; closed Monday and Tuesday during the winter. Call (860) 868–0541 or (800) 552–6853 for prices and hours.

The crossroads village of New Preston at the southeast tip of Lake Waramaug contains several delightful little shops that are well worth a short stop, especially if you like antiques. *Black Swan Antiques* is always fun. Its specialty is seventeenth- and eighteenth-century English country furniture, but the store has also been known to carry Elizabethan, Queen Anne, and William and Mary pieces. *J. Seitz & Co.* handles both Southwestern antiques and reproductions, and the *Village Barn and Gallery* carries an eclectic selection of antiques and collectibles in a country-store atmosphere.

South of New Preston, on Curtis Road off Route 199 near the village of Washington, is the *Institute for American Indian Studies.* Splendid Indian craft exhibits and authentic recreations of Indian dwellings are among the features of this museum. The institute attempts, fairly successfully, to cover 10,000 years of Native American life; displays include a seventeenth-century Algonquian village and garden, a furnished longhouse, a simulated archaeological site, a prehistoric rock shelter, and a variety of nature trails. There's also a museum shop. The Institute holds several special events throughout the year. The museum is open Monday through Saturday, 10:00 A.M. to 5:00 P.M.; Sunday, noon to 5:00 P.M., with slightly reduced hours during the coldest winter months. Be sure to keep a sharp eye out for signs directing you to the museum, because they are easy to miss. Call (860) 868–0518 for help if you get lost.

The *Gunn Memorial Library and Museum,* 5 Wykeham Road in Washington, was named after Mr. and Mrs. Frederick Gunn, who founded the Gunnery school in Washington. The library was designed by architect and Washington resident E. K. Rossiter and features oak paneling and a beautiful stained-glass window. The ceiling mural, called the Mowbray mural, is exceptional. Donated by painter and muralist H. Siddons Mowbray in memory of his wife, it depicts Perse-phone's abduction to the underworld by Pluto and the world's ensuing four seasons. The Gunn Museum next to the library is stocked with heirlooms from the estates of town people.

Ethan Allen Way

Someone once estimated that the tiny village of Kent had one gallery for every 300 residents. One of the more interesting of these establishments resides in a red freight car beside the railroad tracks at Kent Station Square. This modest housing is home to Jacques Kaplan's *Paris–New York–Kent Gallery,* which exhibits an eclectic and ever-changing mix of local stuff and major pieces by world famous artists whose work is seldom seen outside of major metropolitan centers. Kaplan is the man who almost single-handedly started the gallery

Tall Tales of Ethan Allen

Being of a question-authority bent ourselves, Ethan Allen is our favorite Connecticut hero. Here are a couple of our favorite Ethan Allen stories.

Ethan Allen was a big guy (6 feet 6 inches) with a big thirst. According to one "tall" tale, on a hot August after-noon, Allen and his cousin, Remember Baker, having overindulged, repaired to a nearby shady woods to sleep it off. A besotted Remember was awakened by a strange noise, and he watched in horror as a rattlesnake bit his drink-befuddled cousin over and over. Before Remember could find a weapon to subdue the serpent, it moved away from Allen, gazed at Remember with a certain drunken stare, then wobbled its way into the bushes where it col-lapsed in a stupor. Allen awoke refreshed from his nap, except for com-plaints about "these eternal,

damnable, bloodsucking mosquitoes," which had disturbed his rest.

It stands to reason that Ethan Allen would marry a woman as formidable as himself. His wife Fanny was, by all accounts, his equal in temper and inde-pendence. The story is told that Allen's friends became concerned about his drinking and decided to frighten him into leading a more temperate life. They wrapped themselves in sheets and hid beneath the bridge Allen passed on his way home from his favorite tavern. Making the requisite booing, moan-ing, and keening sounds, they jumped out at their friend, only to scare his horse into rearing. Despite his snoz-zled state, Allen managed to control his mount and greeted the "appari-tions" by proclaiming, "If you are angels of light, I'm glad to meet you. And if you are devils, then come along home with me. I married your sister."

Ethan Allen Trivia

Litchfield-born Ethan Allen is one of the most colorful personalities in American history. We love the crusty old coot. You probably learned in fifth grade history that Allen ordered the British commander of Fort Ticonderoga to surrender by declaiming, "Surrender in the name of the great God Jehovah and the Continental Congress." What he really said was something like: "Come out of there, you goddam old billy goat." Spin doctors, even then.

boom in Kent. Usually open Wednesday through Sunday, but call ahead: (860) 927–3357.

Viewing all that art can work up quite an appetite, so it just makes sense to stop off at **Belgique Patisserie and Chocolatier** at the intersection of Routes 7 and 341 in Kent for a little treat to raise your blood sugar, purely for medicinal reasons. The tiny chocolate shop, owned by Belgium-born chocolatier, Pierre Gilissen and his wife, Susan, offers intricately shaped filled chocolates and amazing truffles. There's no seating in the chocolate shop, but the owners have thoughtfully placed some benches outside so you can rest your weary feet, enjoy a little chocolate, and sip hot or cold coffee and chocolate drinks. The separate patisserie is a jewel box of a place with pastries that sparkle like something from Tiffany's window. The variety is impressive with choices ranging from glazed fruit-topped cakes to fruit mousses to Madelines. In our opinion, best-in-show is the delightfully dark and rich chocolate ganache cake, which rivals Hartford's own David Glass Chocolate Mousse for top chocolate cake honors. At the time this edition went to press, the Gilissens planned to have a tearoom at the same address up and running sometime in 2002. Open Thursday through Saturday, 9:00 A.M. to 6:00 P.M. and Sunday from 10:00 A.M. to 5:00 P.M.; winter hours may be shortened, so call ahead before visiting. Call (860) 927–3682 for more information.

If you're looking for other attractions, Main Street (Route 7) is lined for several blocks with restaurants, antiques stores, craft shops, and the like. You'll also find interesting establishments on Maple Street and Railroad Street. **Kent Carved Signs,** for example, has on display a selection of more than thirty models of hand-carved wooden signs of the type that you see in front of homes and shops all over New England. There are other concerns we could talk about, but they come and go fairly frequently, so if you want to know what's there currently, you'll just have to visit.

A mile and a half north of North Kent on Route 7 (Ethan Allen Way) is **Kent Falls State Park.** The broad meadow and shaded picnic areas visible from the road are inviting enough, but you might be inclined to pass it by if you weren't specifically looking for a place to spread a picnic lunch. Don't. The best part of the park is a 250-foot waterfall that is easy to miss, especially when the foliage of high summer obscures it from view. If you like tramping through the woods, you can hike to the top of the falls; or, if

Macedonia Brook State Park in Kent is the largest state park in Connecticut.

you prefer less demanding pleasures, you can simply sit out on the rocks in the middle of the falls and dangle your toes in the torrent. Even though the water may be a tad cool for toe-dangling come autumn, we highly recommend visiting the park after the leaves have turned and the summer crowds have thinned.

About a mile north of Kent, you'll find a big maroon L-shaped barn set back a short distance from the west side of Route 7. The ground on which it sits used to be the Kent town dump, but all that changed back in the 1970s. At that time, New Britain's Stanley Tool Company was looking for a site for a museum to house a collection of American tools and implements collected by noted artist and author Eric Sloane. Stanley wanted the state of Connecticut to run the place, but the state would accept ownership only if the museum's site was somehow historically significant. As it turned out, down at the foot of the hill behind the town dump in Kent were the ruins of an old blast furnace that produced pig

Falling Waters

*K*ent Falls *is probably Connecticut's most spectacular waterfall. At 250 feet, it's certainly the largest, but other nearby parks offer equally beautiful, if somewhat more hard to find, waterfalls.*

At Campbell Falls *on Route 272 in Norfolk, you can see the Whiting River boil over rocks in a narrow gorge. You'll need to take a short hike to reach the falls; just follow the sounds of rushing water. The water drops in two levels, with a small pool in between and one at the bottom. The first level is a good place for a picnic among the weathered rock. Campbell Falls is off Norfolk Road, just south of Southfield, Massachusetts, just before Spaulding Road. If you are traveling from the other direction, it's about 5 miles north of Haystack Mountain, on Route 272 in Norfolk.*

You'll want to bring your camera with you to Southford Falls *in Southbury, where you'll find a lovely cascade of Eight Mile Brook as it rushes to meet the Housatonic River. The park also includes the remains of the Diamond Match factory, which was destroyed by fire in 1923. The ruins include an old steam engine foundation, a grinding stone, and some of the sluice pipe. The little covered bridge, built by carpenter Ed Palmer with the help of author/artist Eric Sloane, is based on an eighteenth-century arch design. There are picnic tables by the bridge, just the place for a romantic spring picnic, or perch on a rock by the falls and spend some time just listening to the water or reading. The park also includes a lookout tower, great for viewing fall foliage. Southford Falls State Park is located just south of Southbury on Route 188.*

iron during most of the nineteenth century. The presence of this jumble of stone made the dump suitably historical, so Stanley acquired the property and had Sloane design a building for his collection. Thus was born the **Sloane-Stanley Museum.**

The one thing to understand about this place is that it is not so much a museum of artifacts as it is a gallery of art objects. The tools collected here, some of which date from the seventeenth century, probably do have some historical interest as a link with everyday life in America's past; but Sloane vehemently rejected the image of himself as what he called "a nurturer of nostalgia." The contents of this museum are oddly beautiful. Sloane personally arranged and lighted the displays, and the resulting jumble of wooden bowls and woven baskets, yokes and mallets and pitchforks, axes and scythes, and weathered sawhorses has an internal order that is both pleasing and restful. It's as if each arrangement were a small work of art in itself.

In addition to the fine tool collection, the museum also contains a re-creation of Sloane's studio with some of his works on display. And don't forget that historic blast furnace; it's the tumbled pile of rocks surrounded by the split-rail fence down at the bottom of the hill behind the barn. Open May 15 to October 31, Wednesday through Sunday, 10:00 A.M. to 4:30 P.M. Adult admission. Call (860) 927–3849 or (860) 566–3005.

Located just off Route 7 about 4 miles south of Kent, **Bull's Bridge** is one of three remaining covered bridges in Connecticut and one of two that are still open to traffic (the other is in West Cornwall, also off Route 7 a few miles north). Bull's Bridge spans the Housatonic River between New York State and the small Connecticut town of Bull's Bridge on the river's eastern bank. George Washington didn't sleep here, but he did pass over the bridge, and he (or a member of his party) did manage to lose a horse in the Housatonic while so doing. If looking at the bridge gives you a sense of déjà vu, it's because it's probably been the source of more quaint New England covered bridge photographs on postcards and calendar covers than any other bridge in this part of the world.

After you cross the bridge, about 3 miles up the road on the **Schaghi-coke Indian Reservation,** you'll find an old cemetery with many timeworn headstones, including one commemorating the last resting place of a "Christian Indian Princess." We've never been able to find out the story behind this intriguing inscription. As with any visit to a cemetery, remember to show proper respect and not to take rubbings without permission.

The **National Audubon Society's Northeast Center** on Route 4 con-

Bull's Bridge

sists of 684 acres of woodlands, flower and herb gardens, and rural countryside. There are also a pond, a swamp, and a marsh, and the entire area is crisscrossed by trails and nature walks. Both guided and self-guided nature walks are available. A large house on the property contains exhibits, offices, a library, and a gift shop. The center offers programs for both children and adults.

The building is open Tuesday through Saturday, 9:00 A.M. to 5:00 P.M.; Sunday, 1:00 to 5:00 P.M.; closed major holidays. Trails open dawn to dusk. Admission. Call (860) 364–0520.

Up Route 7 from the Audubon Society's Northeast Center and only 1 mile south of the covered bridge at West Cornwall is another type of outdoor experience. *Clarke's Outdoors* is one of several outfitters along the Housatonic that offer kayaks, canoes, and rafts for those who want to try the river's white water. If you're not very experienced with a paddle, they'll teach you. If you're still a little shaky about going out on the river unsupervised, they'll take you. Look at the expressive anthropomorphic critters adorning Clarke's signs and vans. These are original Sandy Boynton paintings. Clarke's is open from March through December on Monday and Wednesday through Friday from 10:00 A.M. to 5:00 P.M. and on weekends from 9:00 A.M. to 6:00 P.M. Call (860) 672–6365.

On the west side of Route 7, a couple of hundred yards south of Cornwall Bridge, is something right out of an H. P. Lovecraft horror novel. There, jutting out from under a canopy of overhanging trees right along the side of the road, is a big rock painted to resemble a most lifelike giant frog whose leering mouth seems to be reaching for the occupants of the passenger side of the car. We don't know the story behind it, but every so often it gets refurbished with a coat of paint. Really, we're quite sure that there are no Marshes or Whateleys in the area; try Rhode Island.

About 6 miles north of Cornwall Bridge on Route 7, the largest and handsomest covered bridge in Connecticut spans the Housatonic at West Cornwall. Originally designed by Ithiel Town, the bridge has been in continuous service since 1837. Route 128 runs from Route 7 across the one-lane bridge to become the main street of West Cornwall.

Be sure to hit the *Cornwall Bridge Pottery Store.* Ever since Todd Piker started his pottery and store in 1972, this place has been selling world-class stoneware, much of it featuring a celadon glaze made from slag recovered from a local riverbed, where it was deposited by the iron-

White Water

*W*e've heard from several readers that they would like more outdoor activities. Well, we're sort of couch potatoes, so we called on a friend who thinks nothing of kayaking the Tarifville Gorge on the Farmington River for two hours before work. Here are some of his favorite places:

The **Small Boat Shop,** 144 Water Street, Norwalk, offers guided tours of the Norwalk Islands. You must make reservations in advance; the tours carry a fairly hefty per person price tag. Call (203) 854–5223 for more information.

Clarke's Outdoors offers guided tours on the Housatonic River, including a lovely trip under the covered bridge or a somewhat wilder white-water rafting trip down Bull's Bridge Gorge. The Bull's Bridge trip is usually offered only in spring. Reservations for the guided rafting trips are a must. Tip: Prices are lower during the week. Shuttle service available. Call (860) 672–6365 for more information.

North American Whitewater Expeditions in Madison takes you hearty outdoor types on rafting expeditions throughout Connecticut, including Bull's Bridge Gorge on the Housatonic in Kent, or a white-water raft trip on the Housatonic near Falls Village. For prices and more information, call (800) RAPIDS9.

Mountain Workshop, Inc., Ridgefield, offers a trip past Gillette Castle on the Connecticut River and a family canoe trip on the Croton River that winds through Croton Swamp. (Children must be at least six years old.) For prices and more information, call (203) 544–0555.

works that used to dominate the area's economy. None of the glazes, however, contain lead. Most items are decorated with simple blue or brown brushwork designs with an oriental flavor. The firing is done in a 40-foot, wood-fired kiln at Piker's pottery in Cornwall Bridge, and the flames give the finished pieces distinctive two-tone markings.

In addition to Piker's pottery, the Cornwall Bridge Pottery Store sells beautiful glassware by Vermont glassblower Simon Pearce and matted photographs by wildlife photographer William Ervin. Recently, the store opened a second-floor gallery featuring the work of local craftsfolk. Open Thursday and Friday, noon to 5:00 P.M.; weekends, 10:00 A.M. to 5:30 P.M. Call (860) 672–6545. Visit them on the Web at www.cbpots.com.

Housed in a rambling, high-ceilinged, gray clapboard house at the top of the hill is **Barbara Farnsworth, Bookseller.** This establishment can be a near-religious experience for bibliophiles and collectors of old prints and maps. The bottom floor of the shop contains nonfiction, cookbooks, reference books, and a variety of antique prints and ephemera. The top floor contains the bulk of the store's 50,000 volumes. Parking in West Cornwall can be tricky, especially during fall foliage season. Try the lot across the street from Farnsworth's, between the deli and the post office. Open Saturday, 9:00 A.M. to 5:00 P.M., and by chance or appointment. Call (860) 672–6571.

Up at the end of Dibble Road in West Cornwall there's a little piece of heaven. Set on a wooded hilltop and surrounded by stunningly land-scaped grounds, Everett Van Dorn's **Hilltop Haven** affords a view of the northwest hills that is hard to match. Each guest room in this inn's ele-gant country house has its own bath and a small sitting area overlook-ing the woods and the gardens (perfect for tea and a snack). The public rooms include a parlor with its own baby grand piano and a library whose fireside rockers beckon the browsing bibliophile to find a good story and sit a spell. Breakfast is served in the library or in the conser-vatory, which has a wonderful view of the Housatonic Valley. The grounds are open for strolling and the woods for hiking. These are fairly untamed woods, where you're likely to spot deer and many species of birds, including wild turkeys. No smoking; no pets; no gratuities; chil-dren over fourteen only. Call (860) 672–6871.

Go a little north from West Cornwall on Route 7 and west on Route 112 and you'll find **Lime Rock Park,** probably Connecticut's most famous sports-car race track. From time to time, you can see celebrities behind the wheel. Paul Newman is something of a regular at the track, and rac-ing buffs Walter Cronkite, Tom Brokaw, and Tom Cruise have also made appearances. For us un-famous people, it's a fun place to spend Memorial Day. The Dodge Dealers Grand Prix, held on Memorial Day, is one of the largest sports-car races in the country. Racing fans can get free race information and sign up for the free newsletter (800–RACE–LRP). Wanna-be drivers can learn the ropes at Skip Barber Racing and Driving School at Lime Rock.

East of West Cornwall is **Mohawk Mountain State Park.** The big draw here is skiing, but if that's not your thing, avoid the crowds and take a scenic 2½-mile stroll to the top of the 1,683-foot-high Mohawk Mountain instead. The view from the wooden observation tower is absolutely breathtaking. One of our favorite picnics is sandwiches from Nodine's

Cats in Retirement

*F*alls Village is also the site of one of the state's truly unique establishments, though not, perhaps, one that you would normally think of as a tourist attraction. Located on thirty-five rural acres off Route 126, **The Last Post** is a private animal sanctuary and no-kill shelter. It's also a retirement home for cats.

New York radio personality Pegeen Fitzgerald founded The Last Post in 1982 as a home for felines whose human companions had passed away. Since then, hundreds of cats have been willed to the place, along with bequests for their care. Depending on the provisions of the will, some live out their lives there, while others stay only until they are adopted. Over the years, these "retirees" have been joined by a legion of strays and drop-offs. Today, over 375 of the fattest, sassiest, friendliest cats we've ever seen live uncaged in two huge airy halls connected by a 100-foot-long sundeck which they can get to through cat doors and floor-level windows. There are cats of all shapes and sizes, ages, and appearances. They sprawl on couches, recline in stuffed chairs, and laze in tangled masses of fur on beds set next to the windows. Overhead, cats with swishing tails and mock feral eyes crouch on the exposed beams, while their somnolent cousins lounge under the skylights catching some rays. Others line the railing around the deck or prowl the five acres of fenced-in fields and trees set aside for their use. It's all very much like something out of Alfred Hitchcock's The Birds—only with cats.

The cat rooms are open to the public from 11:00 A.M. to 3:00 P.M. daily, including holidays, and The Last Post encourages visitors. So do the cats. In fact, if you sit down and hold still for even a moment, you'll find yourself bedecked with purring felines, all vying for your attention. Beware, though. It takes a hard heart to spend even a little time with these guys and not want to take one home. We know. One of our own fur companions, Magpie, joined us as a result of a petting spree at the Post. Call (860) 824–5469. Visit The Last Post on the Web at www.thing.net/~flux/lastpost.

Smokehouse in Goshen eaten at one of the handful of picnic tables atop Mohawk Mountain.

Although the festival in nearby Norfolk tends to be better known, the tiny community of Falls Village in Canaan also boasts an excellent summer musical program. From mid-June to mid-September the town is home to the *Music Mountain Chamber Music Festival,* the oldest continuous chamber music festival in the United States. During the season the Manhattan String Quartet plays weekend concerts at Music Mountain, off Route 7. On Saturday evenings there are folk, jazz, and baroque music performances. Call (860) 364–2084 for details.

Wanna take home a real slice of Connecticut? Well, south of West Cornwall is a small, family-run bakery called *Matthews 1812 House,* 250 Kent Road (Route 7) in Cornwall Bridge, housed in, what else, a vintage 1812 house. Stop by and sample the Lemon Rum Sunshine Cake. In an article in the *New York Times,* food writer Marian Burros called the Lemon Rum Sunshine Cake "moist and deliciously spirited." Lush with imported rum and zippy with lots of lemon, this old-fashioned poundcake is rich but still light enough to eat with a clear conscience. It really does taste like a piece of lemony sunshine. A small loaf-size cake sells for around $7.75. The bakery also cooks up several other types of loaf cake for sale or mail-order shipment. Open Monday through Friday, 9:00 A.M. to 5:00 P.M., Saturday, 10:00 A.M. to 5:00 P.M., Sunday, noon to 5:00 P.M. Call (800) 662–1812 for information or to request their mail-order catalog.

Originally built in 1872, Canaan's *Union Station* (located at the junction of Routes 7 and 44) is supposedly the oldest train station still in use in the United States, and it celebrates the fact with an annual Railroad Days festival (call 860–824–7580 for dates). It is also the main facility of the *Housatonic Railroad Company,* a tiny firm that operates a seasonal shortline across 17 miles of track between Canaan and Cornwall Bridge. Vice President Peter Lynch claims that his company's line is "one of the most scenic railroads east of the Mississippi," and we are inclined to agree. The 34-mile round-trip excursions that run down the Housatonic Valley and back pass through the most beautiful and unspoiled part of Connecticut. It's an area that is especially popular among fall-color fanciers, and business has been so brisk on peak color days that would-be riders have sometimes had to be turned away. The Housatonic Railroad Company's steam-powered trains operate daily from Memorial Day through the end of October. Call (860) 824–0339 for daily schedule and rates.

DON'T MISS

ATTRACTIONS

The Egg & I Farm,
355 Chestnut Land Road, New Milford; (860) 354–0820. A very good egg can be had at this farm as well as some bacon or sausage for alongside. Visitors are also welcome to visit the pigs in the barns. Other specialty items, such as country hams, kielbasa, and head cheese, are sold at the farm shop. Open daily 8:00 A.M. to 5:00 P.M. Visit them on the Web at www.nwvillage.com/porkfarm to sign up for the farm's free e-mail newsletter.

Cricket Hill Gardens,
670 Walnut Hill Road, Thomaston; (860) 283–1042. This beautiful spot is a wonderland of Chinese tree peonies. More than one hundred varieties are grown with most available for sale. We like the dark reddish-purple, almost black, variety, but it's a joy to stroll among the fragrant bushes. During the peony festival (mid-May to mid-June), the gardens are open to the public, Tuesday through Sunday, 10:00 A.M. to 4:00 P.M. Open other times by appointment. On the Web at www.treepeony.com/cricket2.html#.

Morris Historical Society Museum, Route 61, Morris; (860) 567–1776. Across from the firehouse in Morris, you'll find a nice small museum with a potpourri collection of artifacts such as horse-drawn carriages, antique ice-cutting tools, military memorabilia, and old-fashioned wares displayed in a peddler's wagon. It's a nice way to spend an hour or so and gives you a real sense of the character and substance of this quiet community. Donations welcome. Open Saturdays, 2:00 to 4:00 P.M., from June through September.

Hillside Gardens,
515 Litchfield Road, Norfolk; (860) 542–5345. Just a couple of miles south of the Norfolk green on Route 272, rambling stone walls encase a 1780s farmhouse and the stunning Hillside Gardens. Owner Frederick McGourty edited the Brooklyn Botanic Garden Handbook series for many years, so he knows whereof he speaks when it comes to flowers. You'll find much in bloom throughout the growing season, ranging from bleeding heart in May to asters in September. The gardens and nursery center are open from May 1 through September 15, from 9:00 A.M. to 5:00 P.M., daily except holidays. The garden tour, one of the few private residential gardens in America open to visitors on a regular basis, is free. The nursery center sells container perennials and small shrubs. Hillside offers several all-day workshops (admission and reservation only) throughout the summer. Frederick and Mary Ann McGourty suggest visitors take a minute to visit the tower at Dennis Hill State Park, adjacent to the gardens, for one of Connecticut's finest views. Limited handicapped accessibility.

The Silo, 44 Upland Road (off Route 202), New Milford; (800) 353–SILO. One of our ear-to-the-celebrity-grapevine, Litchfield County friends told us, "You want your readers to see celebrities, tell them to head for the Silo on Sunday." Evidently, full-time or part-time Litchfield County famous people head over to the Silo on slow Sundays to pick up cookware, a few gourmet goodies, or just cruise the aisles and socialize. Located on Ruth and Skitch Henderson's Hunt Hill Farm, the Silo is a long-time bastion of everything you need for cooking, dining, or collecting. From time to time, famous chefs hold cooking classes here (available by reservation only). From Halloween through Christmas, a huge, beautifully decorated tree holds sway over the gallery area. Open daily, 10:00 A.M. to 5:00 P.M.; shorter hours January through March; closed major holidays.

SHOPPING

Elephant's Trunk Flea Market, Route 7,
New Milford; (860) 355–1448. New England's largest outdoor flea market packs them in every Sunday from late March until after Christmas. This is truly one of those trash and treasure places. You'll never know what kitsch you'll see displayed, what gadget you suddenly decide you can't live without, or what treasure you want to haggle over. By the way, haggling is not only expected, vendors and customers seem to enjoy it. Get there early and bring a hat or sunscreen because there isn't a lot of shade. Rest rooms and food are available as is lots of free parking. Absolutely no pets allowed because of the recent rabies scare. Modest admission for anyone over fourteen. Open from 6:00 A.M. to 3:00 P.M.

RESTAURANTS

The Sheik Diner, 235 East
Elm, Torrington; (860) 489–5576. Not fancy, not elegant, but a food critic for the New York Daily News, Arthur Schwartz, loves their hot dogs. We do, too. Make sure you get your chili dog with the works and a chocolate shake alongside.

The Birches Inn, 233 West
Shore Road, New Preston; (860) 868–1735. Set on Lake Waramaug, this is a beautiful place for dinner in the summer. The view from the porch can't be beat, unless it's by the food. Not at all the stodgy country inn menu you might expect, but rather an exciting mix of tastes and textures. The roasted garlic custard with Portobello mushrooms and arugula is heavenly as is the grilled lamb with risotto and sautéed greens. Desserts range from delicious (fresh fruit tarts) to devastating (citrus crème brûlée). Open for dinner Thursday through Monday, 5:30 to 9:00 P.M. Reservations are a good idea.

The Cannery, 85 Main
Street, Canaan; (860) 824–7333. Inspired American cooking with dishes such as salmon en papiotte with gingered jasmine rice and roasted mushrooms or coriander-grilled black angus sirloin with garlic mashed potatoes. For lighter appetites, try the grilled Portobello mushrooms with Stilton and field greens. Desserts are updates on old classics such as the orange-scented pecan pie. It's a comfortable place with service that makes you feel very special. Open for dinner daily from 5:00 to 9:00 P.M. (10:00 P.M. on weekends). Reservations, especially during the chamber music festival in Norfolk, are essential.

Mayflower Inn,
118 Woodbury Rd, (Route 47), Washington; (860) 868–9466.
Dining in the main dining room at the Mayflower Inn can be a very heady experience. Everything is wonderful and ultra-deluxe, but not cheap. One way to enjoy the charm of the inn without the cost is lunch or dinner in their Tap Room. The menu is downscaled in both price and content and features some good down-to-earth foods such as burgers, salads, pastas, and some hot dishes, but it all comes out of the same superb kitchen and is served with the same charm and professionalism. Open daily for lunch and dinner.

LODGING

Curtis House, 506 Main
Street, Woodbury; (203) 263–2101. Connecticut's oldest inn (open since before 1736) is a bastion of old-fashioned Yankee cooking and hospitality. The Curtis House is open year-round and serves lunch and dinner Tuesday through Sunday, except Christmas. The inn's eighteen rooms often serve as a haven for Woodbury antique shoppers. Moderate.

Manor House, Maple
Avenue, Norfolk; (860) 542–5690. This lovely Victorian home, full of history,

is stuffed with glorious Tiffany and leaded-glass windows and lots of high Victorian touches. All guest rooms have private baths; some have balconies, a fireplace, or a Jacuzzi. Breakfast is hale and hearty, often with honey from the Manor House's own hives. Beautiful landscaping and gardens. Children over twelve welcome; no smoking; no pets, but boarding facilities are available close by. Moderate.

The Rose & Thistle,
24 Woodland, Barkhamsted; (860) 379–4744. Four rooms, all with private baths. Full breakfast. Located on ten hidden acres with trout pond, swimming, and paddleboat, this half-timbered cottage is the place to go to get away from its all. Good for hiking and cross-country skiing. Children welcome with limits; smoking permitted in designated areas; pets allowed

with limits. Handicap access. Moderate.

Tir'na nO'g Farm B&B,
261 Newton Road, Northfield;
(860) 283–9612.
Built in 1755, this B&B is charming and comfortable in a beautiful country setting. Catherine Weeks, the owner, is a gracious and knowledgeable host, who serves a mid-afternoon tea to her guests. A continental breakfast is included. Moderate.

Gateway to New England

For most of America, the coastal plain along Connecticut's southwestern shore is truly the Gateway to New England, the place where mid-Atlantic names, customs, and speech patterns begin to drop away and we Yankees start to quietly assert our personality. Most visitors to New England form their first impressions of our region from what they see in the busy towns and cities of the Gateway's populous Fairfield and New Haven Counties.

Geographically, the Gateway country is really just one long, lightly wooded coastal plain, with elevations ranging from sea level along the shore to 800 feet inland. The coastline of this low-lying plain is broken by many small bays and inlets and by the mouths of five rivers: the Mianus, Saugatuck, Mill, Housatonic, and Quinnipiac. A few miles inland, numerous lakes and ponds dot the countryside. The neighboring Long Island Sound helps regulate temperatures, making for pleasant summers and relatively mild winters, with plenty of rain but only moderate snowfall.

The southernmost of Fairfield County's towns (Greenwich) is only 28 miles from Times Square, and many of its residents commute daily to jobs in the banks, brokerage houses, and corporate headquarters of Manhattan. So do thousands of others in the southwestern towns. The wealth they bring back to the state combined with that generated by the dozens of corporations that have their headquarters here has helped earn this area the nickname of "the Gold Coast." As you move north and east, the tony quality of the Gold Coast gives way to the working-class atmosphere of cities such as Bridgeport. This transition is complete by the time you cross the line into New Haven County, the populous bridge between the commuter towns of the southwest and the outlying communities of Metro Hartford. New Haven, the easternmost city in the Gateway area, is a mixture of town and gown, famed as the site of Yale University, but also revered by the cognoscenti as the

Southbury Trivia

Kettledown State Park in Southbury gets its name from the story that settlers paid the Native Americans who originally lived on the spot one brass kettle for the land.

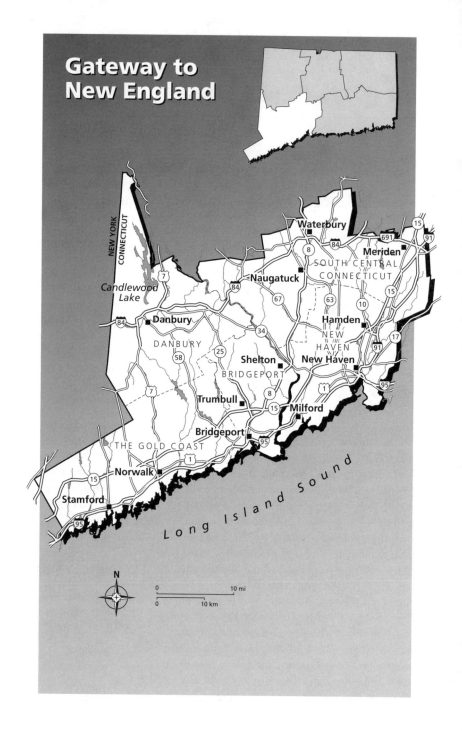

home of Louis' Lunch, birthplace of the American hamburger. Across the Quinnipiac River from New Haven, population density begins to fall away quickly as one moves east, and the eastern townships of New Haven County are really more typical of the Shore than of the populous southwestern part of the state.

The Gold Coast

As its mission statement proclaims, Greenwich's recently rebuilt *Bruce Museum* (One Museum Drive) "bridges the arts and sciences for people of all ages and cultures to foster learning and to preserve the past for the future." Sounds uplifting, to be sure. Fortunately it's also fun. For big people, the collection includes works by some of Connecticut's famed impressionists, including Childe Hassam, plus a wealth of art honoring diverse cultures. For the youngsters, there are scads of well-thought-out interactive exhibits and some special discovery boxes, full of neat things to touch. Open Tuesday through Saturday, 10:00 A.M. to 5:00 P.M.; Sunday, 1:00 to 5:00 P.M. Admission; free on Tuesday. Call (203) 869–0376 for information on special events and the museum's calendar of exhibits.

For a good big-city museum crawl without big-city crowds, noise, or prices, you might also try the *Whitney Museum of American Art at Champion.* Tucked away in the 15-story headquarters of Champion International Corporation at One Champion Plaza (corner of Atlantic Street and Tresser Boulevard) in Stamford, this cozy and charming mini-museum is the Connecticut branch of Manhattan's Whitney Museum of American Art; we think of it as the Whitney Lite. Funded by Champion, the museum mounts five free exhibitions a year, shutting down briefly after each one to get ready for the next. Intensive preparation is necessary because the staff goes to great lengths to educate visitors about each exhibit, offering lectures, guided tours, films, videos, and plenty of printed material. And if, after all this, you still don't get it, you can get some quick and intense tutoring from one of the permanent staff at the information desk. The Whitney has no permanent collection, but draws its exhibits from the renowned Whitney collection in the Big Apple. Since opening in 1981, it has featured works by Edward Hopper, Georgia O'Keeffe, Louise Nevelson, and George Segal, among others. Open Tuesday through Saturday, 11:00 A.M. to 5:00 P.M. Free. Free parking in the Champion garage on Tresser Boulevard. Call (203) 358–7630.

When you visit the *Stamford Cone* on Tresser Boulevard in downtown Stamford, you'll feel like you're standing inside a giant kaleidoscope.

Greenwich Trivia

This 46-foot-tall structure, commissioned by Warburg Dillon Read and designed by Brian Clarke, is made up of 204 panels of glorious stained glass. There's something magical about standing inside and watching the play of light and color. The Stamford Cone is open to the public from 9:00 A.M. to 6:00 P.M. After dark, the cone is lit inside until dawn. We love watching it on crisp winter evenings; it makes the season a little less bleak and desolate. For more information, call (203) 406–8800.

You can't miss *United House Wrecking Company* (535 Hope Street in Stamford). Just look for a rambling collection of buildings surrounded by a chain-link fence and guarded by a bunch of stone yard animals and lots of other junk.

Inside, there are more than five acres of every type of antique something or other you can (or can't) imagine. The main display area contains antique furniture, some salvaged from Gold Coast mansions, some from manor houses in England and France, others quality reproductions. There's so much of it that they organize it in sections; tables here, cabinets there, chairs over in that section. Everywhere, you'll find artifacts and structural elements removed from stately homes; for example, an entire room with nothing but mantels, some clearly intended for ox roasts. Several side rooms contain stained-glass windows, authentic Victorian gingerbread trim, antique lighting, doors, plumbing fixtures, clocks, collectibles, curiosities; and so it goes.

Though it may sound like an upscale junkyard, United House Wrecking is much more than that. It's a place where people come to recycle culture. That makes it an equally great spot to browse for bargains or ramble through history. Note though that the establishment's discovery by both Oprah Winfrey and Martha Stewart has caused the size of weekend crowds to balloon. If you really want to browse, go during off-peak hours. Open Monday through Saturday, 9:30 A.M. to 5:30 P.M.; Sunday, noon to 5:00 P.M. Call (203) 348–5371. Web address: www. united-antiques.com.

The *Stamford Museum and Nature Center* on High Ridge Road at the intersection of Scofieldtown Road is something of a hybrid. Part museum, part nature center, part concert venue, there's plenty here to appeal to a variety of tastes. For us, the animals are the main attraction. Aside from the barnyard run of oxen, sheep, pigs, and fowl, there's a variety of wildlife (including some adorable river otters) and a population of voracious ducks and geese. Most of the animal activity revolves

FAVORITE PLACES IN THE
GATEWAY TO NEW ENGLAND

1. *United House Wrecking
   Company*
2. *Bruce Museum*
3. *The Discovery Museum*
4. *Military Museum of
   Southern New England*
5. *Goulash Place*

around some gentle walking trails that feature enclosures where you can see native wildlife in near-natural surroundings. One of the neatest features is the live pond life exhibit, which includes a microscope/television system for viewing the mystery of pond life. If cuddly and furry isn't your bag, the gallery upstairs in the museum building houses a permanent collection of Native American artifacts. The special events schedule here includes ice-cutting and maple-sugaring, and there are concerts year-round, with those in summer held outdoors in the fountain area. Picnic tables overlook the river. For more information, call (203) 322–1646.

What kid doesn't like a swing? And what could be better than a single swing than a whole playground full of swings and playscapes. The ***Timbertown Swing Set Company*** of Stamford, 633 Hope Street, sets aside part of its facility as a giant indoor playscape open to the public. Kids can swing and play to their hearts' content, and it's not a bad way for a big kid to work off a little work-week stress. You'll find playhouses—actually more like play chateaus—pirate ships, complete portholes and planks for walking, and a super-charged tree house. Timbertown is a dandy spot for a kid's birthday party. There's an admission charge and reservations are encouraged. Call (203) 353–1222 for information and reservations. There's another Timbertown playscape in Milford at 65 Woodmont Road; (203) 876–5004. On the Web at www.timbert.com.

Fairfield isn't the most pastoral of Connecticut's counties, but smack dab in the middle are a couple of towns—Wilton and Weston—that have managed to preserve their bucolic atmosphere. Weston is especially pretty, thanks to tough zoning regulations and restrictions on development. According to folklore, old Mr. Scratch himself left some hoof prints on the rocks thereabouts. Uh huh. Anyway, Lucifer's purported stomping grounds are now the site of the ***Lucius Pond Ordway Devil's Den Preserve*** on Pent Road (take Godfrey Road, which is off either Route 53 or 57, to Pent Road). Owned by the Nature Conservancy, Devil's Den consists of more than 1,450 acres with 5 miles of hiking trails. This is a great place to scout out examples of rare or unusual species of plants, including hog peanut and Indian cucumber root. Or you can just have a pleasant hike. If you plan to do so, be sure for your own safety that you pick up a map at the Pent Road entrance and sign in. Special programs and guided walks are held on some weekends, with attendance by reservation only. Call (203) 226–4991.

Norwalk Trivia

At one time, Norwalk was the oyster capital of Connecticut. Severe pollution changed all that for a while. Today, thanks to tough environmental legislation that cleaned up Long Island Sound, Connecticut is once again one of the country's top oyster producers. And the new home base for Connecticut's oystering industry is, once again, Norwalk.

Technically, **Norwalk's City Hall,** 125 East Street, is neither museum nor gallery, but it does contain the largest collections of Depression-era murals in the United States. During the 1930s, unemployed artists were commissioned under the Works Progress Administration (WPA) to paint murals, many portraying the art of everyday life in America, in public buildings. Most of the structures that once housed these under-appreciated masterpieces have fallen victim to the wrecker's ball, but some of Connecticut's Depression-era buildings, especially post offices, still display these modern wonders. Norwalk's WPA murals were originally painted on the walls of the old high school. When that building was torn down, the art was carefully preserved, restored, and rehung in the city hall. Free. Open Monday through Friday, 9:00 A.M. to 5:00 P.M. Call (203) 866–0202.

SoNo, shorthand for South Norwalk, was once a classic decaying inner-city neighborhood, but the area around Washington and South Main Streets has pulled itself up by its bootstraps to become a home to artists and artisans, much like Manhattan's semichic SoHo. This restored waterfront, included in the National Register of Historic Places, is now home to dozens of galleries, specialty shops, and restaurants.

One of the centers of the SoNo revival is the **Maritime Center of Norwalk** on North Water Street. Part museum, part aquarium, and part theater, what ties the center together is life on (and by) the sea. The building also contains restaurants and a nice gift shop. Open daily, 10:00 A.M. to 6:00 P.M. June 15 through Labor Day; 10:00 A.M. to 5:00 P.M. during the winter. Admission. Call (203) 852–0700.

Trivia

Watch the skies. According to Yankee Magazine, *the first recorded meteorite strike in the United States occurred in Weston in 1807. Connecticut appears to be a popular meteorite landing zone: the magazine also reported a meteorite strike on Memorial Day in 1972 in Stratford and additional strikes in 1971 and 1983 in Wethersfield.*

SoNo is known for its fine restaurants. One of the best is **Pasta Nostra.** Located at 116 Washington Street, Pasta Nostra is smack dab in the middle of SoNo. The style and the prices are high, and the attitude is as high as its prices, but the food is worth suffering for. All pasta is made fresh on site; there's also a take-away pasta store. The lunch and dinner pasta menu changes daily, featuring high-quality food such as linguine with sauce puttanesca, a zesty, quickly prepared red sauce invented

The wiffle ball was invented by David N. Mullaney of Fairfield in 1954. By the way, wiffle (the plastic ball with holes) comes from the sandlot baseball term "wiff" (strike), which is what you usually do when you try to hit that crazy ball.

by Rome's working girls. Open for dinner Wednesday through Saturday from 5:00 to 9:30 P.M. Call (203) 854–9700.

One of our favorite beaches is **Calf Pasture Park** on Calf Pasture Road. You can loll on the beach, picnic, or wander the shore looking for seashells. Open daily from 8:30 A.M. to 11:00 P.M. A food concession, bathrooms, changing areas, and eating areas are available. If you're an out-of-towner, there's a fairly stiff parking fee.

Just a short ferry ride off Norwalk, the historic **Sheffield Island Lighthouse** is a pretty cool place to spend a hot summer day. Sheffield is the outermost of the thirteen Norwalk islands and offers scenic views of both Long Island Sound and the Norwalk River. *The Island Girl,* a sixty-passenger ferry, leaves for the island from Hope Dock (corner of Water and Washington Streets in South Norwalk). Weekend and holiday service starts Memorial Day weekend; daily service runs from late June through Labor Day, with weekend trips until late September. On the round-trip cruise, the ferry's crew offers lively commentary on Norwalk's oystering past and the island's sometimes racy history and folklore. Islands clambakes are held regularly throughout the summer. Fee for ferry ride and clambake. The light, which is now on the National Register of Historic Places, was constructed in 1868 and was an active working light until 1902. For a copy of the Sheffield Island Lighthouse schedule and more information, call the Norwalk Seaport Association at (203) 838–9444. For more information about New England and Connecticut lighthouses, check out this Web address: www. zuma.lib.utk.edu/lights/newengl.html.

Norwalk's picturesque **Silvermine Tavern** was built in 1785 in the crossroads town of Silvermine. Since then, several nearby towns have swallowed up the village, but the tavern still occupies the crossroads (now Silvermine and Perry Avenues). Today, as in the past, Silvermine Tavern could very well be the platonic ideal of a picturesque New England tavern inn. The 200-year-old establishment overlooks a waterfall and a charming mill pond populated by fat ducks and swans who seem to feed quite well on the bounty cast their way by strolling guests. The ten rooms are amply furnished with antiques, including, in some cases, canopy beds.

Most people, however, come here to eat and drink. There is a cozy cocktail lounge and six dining rooms, including a main dining room decorated with more than 1,000 antiques. The food is traditional New

England cooking. Thursday night the inn serves up a locally famous buffet, and a plentiful brunch is offered on Sunday. Lunch is served from noon to 3:00 P.M.; dinner, 6:00 to 9:00 P.M. (10:00 P.M. on weekends). The inn is open all year; the restaurant closes on Tuesdays from September to May. Call (203) 847–4558.

In previous editions of this book, we called negotiating the streets of Westport's downtown shopping district on business days "pure tourist hell." We heard about that from Westport merchants, and we stand corrected—sort of. Truly, downtown Westport, with its collection of small

Dogs Off the Beaten Path in Fairfield

*S*hould Fairfield County be christened Connecticut's "Hot Dog" capital? Who knows? Who cares? We just know you can find several of the state's top dog shops in Fairfield County.

For years chef Gary Zemola and his colorful Super Duper Weenie Truck were a familiar sight around Fairfield Country. Now the SDWT is off the road (except for special occasions), and Gary cooks up his superlative dogs in a permanent home at his tiny eatery, **Super Duper Weenie** (the "Fortress of Weeni-tude"), 306 Black Rock Turnpike, Fairfield. For the uninitiated, the SDWT is a restored mobile Chevy van featured in a painting by diner artist John Baeder in his book Diners. Chef Gary, who trained at the Culinary Institute of America, creates fast food with panache. All ingredients are high-quality, but what really makes the sandwich are his homemade relishes. The fresh-cut fries also get raves. You can eat inside at the counter, but why? Head for the picnic tables outside. The quality of the food is as high as the prices are low (lunch for under a fin). Open Monday through Thursday, 11:00 A.M. to 8:00 P.M.; Friday and Sat-

urday from 11:00 A.M. to 8:00 P.M. Call (203) 334-DOGS Visit the SDW on the Web at www.superduperweenie.com.

Not far from the Birdcraft Museum and Sanctuary is **Rawley's Drive-in**, 1886 Post Road, a place where the doyen of domesticity, Martha Stewart, chows down, as do the likes of Paul Newman and David Letterman. Obviously, along with most of the people in Fairfield, Martha, Paul, and David know a good thing. This small, shingled eatery offers no-frills, fundamental drive-in eating at its best The chili dogs and plain hot dogs in butter toasted French rolls topped with the works (sauerkraut, mustard, relish, and bacon) are excellent, and the prices are rock bottom. (203) 259–9023.

Is it too Fairfield County or what that Ridgefield would have a hot dog cart named **Chez Lenard?** And, naturally, Chez Lenard's offerings are called "le hot dogs." Snobbery aside, Lenny does cook up some swell dogs. We like the "le hot dog facon Mexicaine" (chili dog) and "le hot dog Logano Suisse," an all-beef frank drenched with a cheese-fondue-like mixture. You'll find Chez Lenard open year-round on Main Street. He opens for business around 11:00 A.M.

quaint shops, has its own charm. The shops come and go, so just park and go where your fancy takes you. We'd still rather attend an accordion recital then spend time in the downtown area on peak shopping days, but don't let our grouchiness over rubbing shoulders with Yorkers stop *you* from enjoying the town.

Actually, the very best reason for visiting Westport even on the busiest days is a place called *Coffee An'*. This establishment at 343 North Main is a world-class doughnut shop. The doughnuts are made from scratch, and they keep coming fresh out of the oven all day. There are no special ingredients or secret recipes involved, but the results bear the same resemblance to franchise fare as Dom Perignon does to Ripple. Just about anything that comes out of the oven—including the plain variety—is superb, but we're particularly partial to the coconut crullers and the cinnamon twirls. Westport resident Paul Newman and Fairfield resident Jason Robards have been known to slip into Coffee An' for their Sunday morning doughnuts, but we don't know *their* preferences.

Chili-Dog Sauce Recipe

*W*hen we started collecting recipes for this book, we were naive. Of course, chefs would give us a recipe. After all, who could resist free publicity? We soon found out that most pros guard their recipes like Scrooge McDuck guards his gold, and it seems that no recipe is as highly cherished as the sauce for chili dogs. We couldn't lure a chili sauce recipe away from any famous dog house, but the following recipe has been around for as long as we've lived in Connecticut. We've seen it credited to various restaurants, but New Britain's original Metropole seems the most likely source.

1 small onion, chopped	*½ teaspoon cinnamon*
1 clove garlic, crushed	*1 teaspoon paprika*
1 tablespoon vegetable oil	*½ teaspoon nutmeg*
1 pound hamburger	*½ teaspoon allspice*
2 cups water	*salt and pepper to taste*
1 tablespoon best-quality chili powder	

Brown onions and garlic in oil. Add meat and brown. Stir with a fork to break up meat. Add water and remaining ingredients. Simmer over medium-low heat for 20 to 30 minutes until mixture is thick and water evaporates. If you prefer your chili-dog sauce with a finer texture, let it cool and then buzz it a little in a food processor. Reheat as needed. **Note:** *you can freeze leftover sauce, but spice balance will change.*

Coffee An' is open weekdays, 7:00 A.M. to 5:30 P.M.; Saturday, 7:00 A.M. to 4:00 P.M. You can eat at one of fifteen or so counter stools or, if they're empty, pull up a chair by the window. Better yet, grab a bag to go and beat it out of town with the loot. Call (203) 227–3808.

One of the oldest nature centers in Connecticut is a good place to walk off doughnuts from Coffee An'. The *Nature Center for Environmental Activities,* 10 Woodside Lane, has good trails (open dawn to dusk) and an excellent display of native plants in a courtyard. On weekends (Saturdays 2:00 to 4:00 P.M., and Sundays 2:00 to 3:30 P.M.), the hands-on marine aquarium gives kids bang-up experience with marine life. On weekends (Saturdays 11: 30 A.M. to 2:00 P.M., and Sundays 1:00 to 3:00 P.M.), the Discovery Room has many hands-on natural history activities, puzzles, artifacts to look at, and scientific equipment with which to play. The center is open Mondays through Saturdays from 9:00 A.M. to 5:00 P.M., and Sundays 1:00 to 4 P.M. There's a very modest admission fee, and family memberships are available. Call (203) 227–7253 for information on special programs.

Bridgeport

Phineas Taylor (P. T.) Barnum is probably the most famous entrepreneur in the history of entertainment. Born in 1810, in an era when entertainment was pretty much divided along class lines between the cultural and the popular, Barnum revolutionized show biz by presenting entertainments designed to appeal to people of all classes. In the process his name came to be linked in the public mind with three things: showmanship, the circus, and a legendary quote, which he never said, "There's a sucker born every minute."

Today Barnum is remembered in Bridgeport's refurbished and expanded *Barnum Museum* (820 Main Street), three stories of circus exhibits and P. T. Barnum memorabilia, housed in what has been described as a "Byzantine-Romanesque-Gothic-Barnumesque" building with a red sandstone facade and lots of domes and terra-cotta friezes. The third floor, "Showman to the World," is designed to be a sort of grand finale to any tour, and it is truly grand. Here is Barnum's famous 2,500-year-old Egyptian mummy (Pa-Ib), one of the favorite exhibits. There's also an exhibit of Barnum oddities, including the "Feejee Mermaid," a two-headed calf, and a fragment from Noah's Ark; a wonderful gallery on "clowning," and displays of memorabilia related to Jenny Lind—the so-called Swedish Nightingale—and General Tom Thumb (two of many proteges that Barnum collected during an active life as a promoter).

Bridgeport Trivia

Finally there's the most famous of the museum's holdings, William Brinley's 1,000-square-foot scale model circus, based on one that the artist saw in 1915, when he was nine years old. The model took sixty years to complete and contains more than 3,000 hand-carved miniature figures. It alone is well worth the trip.

Famous last words: On his deathbed, P. T. Barnum is reported to have said, "How were the receipts today at Madison Square Garden?"

The Barnum Museum is open Tuesday through Saturday, noon to 5:00 P.M. (mornings by appointment). Gift shop. Admission. Call (203) 331–1104.

Any town would be lucky to have a museum as good as the Barnum. Bridgeport has two. A friend once described the ***Discovery Museum*** (4450 Park Avenue) as "more fun than a basket of puppies." Puppies are pretty hard to beat in the fun category, but we agree that this is a splendid place for kids of all ages.

The Discovery was born in 1987, when the stuffy old 1950s-era Museum of Science and Industry decided on a change. Its new focus would be the relationship between the arts and physical science. This required a makeover of the museum's interior and the installation of more than fifty hands-on science exhibits. The result is a place where you can make a variety of delightful things happen by simply pulling a lever, turning a crank, or pushing a button. When your hands have had enough pulling, turning, and pushing, you can jump aboard a bicycle and pedal up the electricity to run a radio or test your reflexes by driving a bumper car or interact with the museum in what seems like a zillion and one other ways. Some museums are "don't touch" places; the Discovery is a "please touch" place. This makes it a great place to take the kids for a wild rumpus and not a bad place to be a kid yourself.

The exhibits are only part of the fun here. You can also visit the ***Henry B. duPont Planetarium*** and the ***Wonder Workshops,*** where kids can make a variety of souvenirs. As part of a special program, youngsters can even suit up and take a mission to Mars as crew members aboard a spaceship. For a small charge in addition to the museum's admission, kids ten and up can participate in one of the Challenger mini-missions that are held most weekends. You might like checking your weight on a "Martian" scale; you'll weigh about one-third less. Be sure to check out the gift shop, it's thoughtfully stocked with lots of low-priced goodies, so the kids can take home a souvenir without flattening the parental wallet. Open Tuesday through Saturday from 10:00 A.M. to 5:00 P.M.; Sunday from noon to 5:00 P.M. The planetarium shows start at 3:30 P.M. on weekdays and at 1:30 and 3:00 P.M. on weekends. Admission. Call (203) 372–3521.

Bridgeport's **Beardsley Zoological Gardens,** in Beardsley Park off Noble Avenue, is Connecticut's biggest zoo, featuring large North American mammals in addition to various exotics. There is also a children's zoo set up like a New England farm within the main zoo. The facility includes a picnic area, snack bar, and gift shop. It is open weekdays from 9:00 A.M. to 4:00 P.M. There is a modest admission charge and a fairly stiff parking fee. Call (203) 576–8082.

Bloodroot (85 Ferris Street) is one of those places that make you wonder whether you've accidentally stepped through a time warp. It's not so much the rigidly vegetarian fare. Sure they don't serve meat or fish, but lots of places are that way today. Maybe its the fact that this restaurant thinks of itself as feminist to the point of redefining what the restaurant business is all about. It's not a cafeteria, but no one waits on anyone else, either. You order your food and pay for it. Then you sit down and relax. When the food is ready, you pick it up, course by course and carry it to your table. When you're ready to leave, you clear the dishes yourself.

Bloodroot is committed to animal rights, so the only animal products that appear on the menu are eggs and milk products. You won't miss red meat, though. Soups, thick hearty ones such as curry-scented lentil, sided with a few slices of Bloodroot's homemade bread, thick with husks and shards of different grains, make a lovely meal. The pasta and salad dishes are also tasty and filling. Desserts are excellent, especially the Indian pudding.

Stargazing in Connecticut

*B*ecause it offers suburban living in close proximity to New York, a host of celebs from the world of entertainment have made their homes in Connecticut, mostly in Fairfield and Litchfield Counties. But Connecticut is also the birthplace of many well-known actors.

Bridgeport: Robert Mitchum, Peter Falk, Brian Dennehy, and John (Cheers) Ratzenberger

Hamden: Ernest Borgnine

Hartford: Sophie Tucker, Linda Evans, and Katharine Hepburn

Redding Ridge: Hope Lange

Stamford: Christopher Lloyd

Westport: Glenn Close

Bloodroot is open for lunch Tuesday, Thursday, Friday, Saturday, 11:30 A.M. to 2:30 P.M.; dinner Tuesday, Thursday, 6:00 to 9:00 P.M., Friday and Saturday, 6:00 to 10:00 P.M.; Sunday brunch, 11:30 A.M. to 2:30 P.M. No credit cards. Wheelchair accessible through a side entrance, but bathrooms may prove a problem for those in wheelchairs. Call (203) 576–9168. On the Web at: www.bloodroot.com.

Danbury

Time was, a good hat was an essential item of apparel, and you weren't really dressed without a good topper. In those days, Connecticut was hat maker to America, and Danbury was the center of the hat-making business. Today the glory days of hat making are remembered along with other Danbury history in the **Scott-Fanton Museum** at 43 Main Street. There are actually several buildings at this address, and exhibits are scattered among them. The exhibit on Danbury's hatting industry is in the 1790 John Dodd Shop. Other exhibits deal with early American life, the Revolutionary War, and the history of Danbury. Open Wednesday through Friday, 1:00 to 4:00 P.M. Gift shop. Call (203) 743–5200.

The **Military Museum of Southern New England,** 125 Park Street (just off Interstate 84, exit 3) is the product of a volunteer army of helpers who don't want the sacrifices of those who served in Word War II forgotten. What's interesting to us is that, unlike so many volunteer museums that seem to suffer from lack of a professional staff, this one thrives. In fact it's one of the best military museums we've seen anywhere.

You'll know you've arrived when you see what looks like a tank park. This is actually an outdoor display of fighting vehicles and small guns located in front of the museum building. Most of the material is American, but there are items from other countries, too (even a snappy little BA-series Soviet armored car from the early days of the Great Patriotic War). The condition of the armored fighting vehicles varies. Some have been fully restored, while others look just as you'd expect from vehicles that have been moldering away for half a century. Whatever their condition, standing directly under the guns of these steel monsters is awe-inspiring. To get a real feel for what the soldiers of that era meant by "tank fright," stand behind the 37mm antitank gun by the museum's front entrance and peer along its barrel at the tanks out in the yard. Some variant of this little pop gun was the main weapon that the grunts of most armies had for stopping enemy tanks during the first half of World War II. Really.

Wandering among the tanks in the outdoor display is fun, but the main attraction is inside.
Here, you'll find enough dioramas, maps, models, pictures, and paraphernalia of war to occupy
your attention for several hours. The most
impressive items are fully restored weapons and
vehicles exhibited against realistic back-
grounds; in some cases, accompanied by man-
nequins dressed in authentic uniforms of the
period. The experience of stepping into a recent,
but still bygone, age is enhanced by the well-
chosen World War II–era background music.
For teens and younger kids, this museum is a
wonderful way to introduce them to the feel and
flavor of a part of our history that they may
know only as memorized data from some school
assignment. There's even a modest gift shop for
small, but appropriate, souvenirs. Admission.
Open Tuesday through Saturday, 10:00 A.M. to
5:00 P.M.; Sunday, noon to 5:00 P.M. Closed Monday and holidays.
Reduced hours during the winter. Call (203) 790–9277 for information
about special events and exhibits. Web address: www.danbury. org/org/
military/index.htm.

Adults commuting into Manhattan may think of trains as something
to be endured, but most kids will always see trains as romantic and
vaguely magical. At the **Danbury Railway Museum,** 120 White Street
at Union Station, a group of dedicated volunteers is doing its bit to
keep that magic alive. They've just about finished restoring the old station and turning it into a museum of train paraphernalia and are
working hard to rehab the train yard and build a collection of restored
trains. This is a work in progress, so we're not sure what you'll see by
the time you visit. If this sort of thing appeals to you, call ahead and
ask about special events. The museum holds some neat ones, such as
shopping trips to Manhattan, Christmas and Halloween trips, and
"rare mileage" trips (their term for trips along tracks not in regular
use). Near the front of the museum is a small but interesting gift shop
specializing in "train stuff." By the way, if Union Station looks familiar,
it should. Alfred Hitchcock used it in *Strangers on a Train* as the setting
for his own cameo appearance. Open Tuesday through Saturday, 10:00
A.M. to 5:00 P.M. and Sunday noon to 5:00 P.M. Reduced hours in winter.
Call (203) 778–8337. Web address: www.danbury.org/drm.

The Danbury Fair Mall is one of the largest shopping malls in the Northeast and probably offers at least one of everything required by modern-day everyman. That might cause you to bypass Danbury center in favor of the mall experience. Don't. There are still plenty of neat shops in the downtown area. One of our favorites is the *Cow's Outside,* 286 Main Street (exit 5 off Interstate 84). We're not sure if the name comes from the fact that this is a leather store (the cow's outside) or because there really is a *cow outside* (in this case a life-size, mooing, boot-shod cow). The Cow's Outside is a leather outlet, with an emphasis on boots with prices "cheaper than in Texas." Even at outlet prices (discounts ranging from 15 to 50 percent), the boots here are on the high side, but then so's the quality. As for the selection, it's just about impossible to beat. You'll find thousands of pairs of boots, made from ostrich, alligator, lizard, and leather, in a wide range of sizes. In the summer, look for nice discounts on sandals. You'll also find leather jackets for men and women at 30- to 50-percent discounts. Open Monday through Thursday, 10:00 A.M. to 6:00 P.M.; Friday until 8:00 P.M.; Saturday, 10:00 A.M. to 6:00 P.M.; Sunday, noon to 6:00 P.M. Call (203) 797–1924.

Danbury has its share of fast-food strips and chain restaurants, not to mention the usual urban mix of "family" and "gourmet" establishments. We figure you can find the name eateries on your own. Here, we'd like to point you toward some places you might miss but shouldn't. If you're bored with over-priced chichi froufrou eateries where the chef thinks that "gourmet" and "eccentric" are synonyms, we think you should try the *Goulash Place* in a secluded residential neighborhood at 42 Highland Avenue. Even if the chow was just so-so, we'd come back just to be charmed by owner and hostess, Magda Magdolas. As it happens, the food is also first-rate, and the prices, as they say in Fargo, are indeed "reasonable."

For more than two decades, Magda and her husband John, the chef, have been feeding a host of loyal customers, most of whom found the Goulash Place by accident or referral. You won't go wrong with anything on the menu. The specialty here, though, is goulash, and there are five different varieties to sample, so choose accordingly. If you've never eaten Transylvanian goulash, take a chance. This tender stew of pork, sauerkraut, paprika, onions, and dill comes topped with a dollop of sour cream and is completely different from any other goulash you've ever tasted. All the food here is cooked to order, so the goulash arrives piping hot, with *nockerl* (pumped-up noodles) and fresh veggies. In the unlikely event that you have the self-control to save room for dessert, go for the apricot or cheese *palacsinitas* (dessert crepes). Open Tuesday through Thursday,

11:00 A.M. to 9:00 P.M.; Friday and Saturday, 11:00 A.M. to 10:00 P.M.; Sunday, 1:00 to 8:00 P.M.; closed Monday. Call (203) 744–1971. Parking is in the rear and is presided over by the owners' dog, Gypsy.

If you like motorcycles, you'll want to hit **Marcus Dairy Bar** at 5 Sugar Hollow Road (intersection of Route 7 and Interstate 84, near Danbury Fair Mall). On any given Sunday, you'll find the bikes lined up and down Sugar Hollow Road as bikers and bike-watchers bop in for morning coffee and to check out each other's rides. On a Super Sunday, it looks like every bike in New England is parked there. Super Sunday events include vendors, motorcycle crafts, shows, competitions, and club displays. By the way, the food, especially breakfast, is pretty good, plentiful, and cheap. Open daily for three meals. Call (203) 748–9427 for information about special events.

Danbury was a center of Portuguese settlement in New England, and great Portuguese cuisine is one of the city's cultural assets. If you're in the area during June, you might want to try one of several outdoor Portuguese festivals on Liberty Street: the **Feast of Saint Anthony** is the first weekend in June, **Portuguese Day** is June 10, and the **Feast of Saint John** is the third or fourth weekend in June.

East of Danbury is Newtown, where the **Second Company of the Governor's Horse Guards,** Fairfield Hills Complex, Wildlife Drive (Interstate 84, exit 11) practice, usually in full uniform. A horse guards practice is something no horse- or animal-loving kid can resist. Chartered in 1808, the Second Company of the Governor's Horse Guards was mainly used to escort the governor and distinguished visitors on ceremonial occasions. Today, the troop is a cavalry militia designated by the governor to serve the people of southwestern Connecticut. The troop's horses, all of which were donated, are mainly quarter horses and Morgans. Tours of the barns are often available. Summer practices are held in Newtown April through October on Wednesdays at 7:00 P.M. For more information call (203) 426–9046. The First Company of the Governor's Horse Guards, headquartered in Avon, also holds public drills and special events. (See page 49.)

When J. Alden Weir saw his first impressionist painting in a Paris gallery, it gave him a headache, but by 1881, the American artist was honing his own distinctively impressionistic style. Today, his home, **Weir Farm,** 735 Nod Hill Road, is a National Historic Site. Weir crafted his farm as he would a painting, mixing and matching visual elements until everything was perfect. The farm, which he called the "Land of Nod," provided inspiration for his own portraits of late nineteenth-century family life and for the works of fellow artists Childe Hassam, John Twachtman, and John Singer Sargent. The self-guided "Painting

Sites Trail" is a living landscape. It's well-marked to highlight a series of views from Weir's paintings, including Weir Pond, which he built with the prize money from his 1895 painting *The Truants*. Admission is free, but you'll want to spring for the excellent inexpensive brochure that illustrates the tour. Open April through November, 8:30 A.M. to 5:00 P.M., daily; December through March, 8:30 A.M. to 5:00 P.M., Monday through Friday. Call (203) 843–1896 for hours and information.

The ***Brookfield Craft Center*** north of Danbury on Route 25 houses a school of contemporary arts and crafts within four colonial buildings (including a 1780 gristmill) set on the banks of Still River. The associated arts-and-crafts gallery and retail shop is open Monday through Saturday, 10:00 A.M. to 5:00 P.M.; Sunday, noon to 5:00 P.M.; closed major holidays. Call (203) 775–4526. Web address: www.craftweb.com/org/brookfld/brookfld.shtml.

If your kids normally gag at being dragged off to a craft center, try bribing them with a visit to ***Mother Earth Gallery & Mining Company,*** 806 Federal Road (Route 7). It's a great way to occupy kids during school vacations. You and the kids can suit up with natty lighted miner's helmets and buckets and go digging for amethyst, quartz, mica, pyrite, tourmaline, peridot, and galena. The best part: You get to keep whatever you find. The florescent mine, glowing with green, red, orange, and blue rocks, is spooky but neat. The complex includes a gift shop that is well-stocked with products from conservation organizations such as Greenpeace. Mother Earth is one cool place for a kid's birthday party. Admission. Open Monday and Wednesday through Saturday, 10:00 A.M. to 6:00 P.M., and Sunday, noon to 5:00 P.M. Call (203) 775–6273 for information about special events.

For a walk on wine's wild side, try Brookfield's ***DiGrazia Vineyards & Winery*** (131 Tower Road). It's one of New England's smaller wineries, but it's also one of the most interesting. The grapes for its wines come from vineyards in New York as well as Sharon and Southbury, but it all comes together at the Brookfield site, which is a family-run boutique winery. While other area vintners make fruit wines or grow the French hybrids traditional to New England, Dr. Paul DiGrazia and family focus on specialties. You might find Beaujolais, port, mead (honey wine), or wines made from pears, sugar pumpkins, raspberries, or apples. If you're sensitive to sulfides, ask about the wines made with honey, which DiGrazia uses in place of sulfides. This winery has been around since 1984, and the original line has expanded greatly. They've been experimenting with these items since 1986, and they're now pretty good at it. Open daily, 11:00 A.M. to 5:00 P.M., with reduced winter hours. Free tours and tastings are run by Barbara DiGrazia on weekends and are conducted in a small, but pleasant, tasting room and retail area. Call (203) 775–1616.

When Washington's Northern Army went into winter quarters at the end of November 1778, it was disposed in an arc from New Jersey to Connecticut to ring the British garrison in New York. Three of the army's brigades had their winter encampment at Redding, where they could move east to defend the Hudson Heights or west to defend the Connecticut coast from British raiders. Their commander was Major General Israel ("Old Put") Putnam, a larger-than-life hero, who is often called "Connecticut's Paul Bunyan."

That winter was relatively mild, but the harvest had been poor, and supplies were scarce. The men, many of whom had been through the hell of Valley Forge the previous year, began to mutter about a similar privation winter in Connecticut. Then in December the state experienced one of the worst winter storms in New England history. Two days after it ended, the men of one brigade mutinied and prepared to march on the colonial assembly in Hartford to demand overdue supplies and wages. Putnam was able to break up the affair only with the greatest of difficulty. Thus began the winter encampment at Redding that came to be known as "Connecticut's Valley Forge."

The original encampment is now the site of **Putnam Memorial State Park** at the junction of Routes 58 and 107 in West Redding. These days, the twelve-man huts are just piles of stone where their chimneys stood, and the old magazine is only a stone-lined pit. The officers' barracks have been rebuilt, though, and there is a museum containing exhibits dealing with the Redding encampment. There's also a great statue by the front gate showing Old Put riding his horse down a flight of stairs to escape capture during a British raid in February 1779. Open daily, 8:00 A.M. to sunset. Call (203) 938–2285.

Nearby Ridgefield was the site of a minor 1777 skirmish known as (what else?) the **Battle of Ridgefield,** in which Benedict Arnold led the colonists against General Tryon's British. The historic 1733-vintage Keeler Tavern at 132 Main Street still carries a legacy of the battle in the form of a British cannonball embedded in the tavern wall. Now the **Keeler Tavern Museum,** the inn has been restored and furnished with authentic eighteenth-century furniture, appointments, and artifacts. Guides in colonial dress conduct half-hour tours in season. Open Wednesday, Saturday, and Sunday, 1:00 to 4:00 P.M. (last tour is at 3:30 P.M.). Gift shop. Admission. Call (203) 438–5485.

A short distance down Main Street, at number 258, is a large 1783-vintage clapboard house. It doesn't really look much different from most of the other houses on this street, historic buildings whose exteriors are kept frozen in time. This building's interior, however, is another matter. Gone now are the antique plaster and woodwork that cut up the interior space. Instead, there are broad expanses of white walls with huge, colorful canvases. Sophisticated lighting enhances the hues of the paint and brings a reflected gleam to the polished wooden floors. The quiet open spaces encourage visitors to stand before the canvas worlds and contemplate what they are seeing. This is the *Aldrich Museum of Contemporary Art,* one of America's better small art museums. This private facility is definitely contemporary, and this close to New York, it tends to get works from the best of America's young artists. Often the artists represented are relative unknowns whose first important exposure comes at the Aldrich. Their works are displayed inside, in a series of changing exhibits.

Behind the museum building is the most exciting part of the Aldrich. Sloping away from the building is a broad green lawn dotted with several dozen pieces of modern sculpture. Most are massive, towering over the strollers in their midst. All are imbued with a special strangeness that comes partly from their staid colonial surroundings. Scattered here and there about this sculpture garden are wrought iron tables and chairs where visitors can sit and chat, rest their feet, or pause for a close-up view. Overlooking this garden of unearthly delights is a terrace where you can picnic or just sit and absorb the colors and shapes.

The Aldrich is open Tuesday through Sunday, noon to 5:00 P.M. The garden is always open, even when the museum is closed. Admission. Call (203) 438–4519.

To fortify yourself before tackling art and culture at the Aldrich, you can't go wrong with breakfast at *Gail's Station House* at 378 Main Street (between Bailey Avenue and Governor Street) in Ridgefield. This is a cozy place with sort of a town clubhouse feel to it. Gail's breakfast specialty is the "skillet breakfast," cooked and served in a black cast-iron skillet. Each skillet meal includes scrambled eggs, hash-browns, and some special touch, such as chunks of lox and green onion. The pancakes here are also splendiferous, especially the apple variety. For a lighter meal, try the muffins; muffins are New England's favorite quick bread, and nobody does them much better than this place. Open for breakfast daily, 8:00 A.M. to 3:00 P.M.; lunch daily 11:30 A.M. to 3:00 P.M. Friday and Saturday, midday menu, 3:00 to 5:30 P.M. Dinner runs from 5:30 to 9:30 P.M., Friday and Saturday. Call (203) 438–9775.

Every now and then, you deserve a big splurge. To our thinking, one of the best getaways and fine dining experiences to be had in Connecticut is at the **Elms Restaurant & Tavern,** 500 Main Street. The kitchen at the historic 1799 Elms has undergone a spectacular upgrade. The menu shines with updated versions of American classics such as curried butternut squash and apple soup, succotash, sweet potato spoon bread, creamed collards, and Rhode Island johnnycakes. On the dessert menu, go for anything chocolate. Thanksgiving dinner (reservations far in advance required) at the Elms is the essence of a colonial holiday. Prices are moderate to high. The main dining room (reservations a must) is open Wednesday through Sunday from 5:00 to around 9:00 P.M. The more casual, less expensive tavern is open Tuesday through Sunday from 11:30 A.M. to 11:00 P.M. No handicapped access; no children's menu. Call (203) 438–9206.

Inn rooms, furnished with antiques and high-quality reproductions, are spacious and comfortable. The breakfast included in the room rate (high-moderate range) makes the inn a good value. Call (203) 438–2541 for more information.

If inns were film stars, Ridgefield's **Stonehenge** would be Cary Grant: nothing ostentatious, just impeccable, gracious, and charming, with a tiny touch of reserve; the perfect mix for an extended stay or an exquisite dinner. Located on Route 7 in Ridgefield, the inn features rooms of understated opulence designed for grace and comfort. The grounds, landscaped with a duck pond and gardens, are almost as inviting as the elegant interior.

The food, with a French flair, follows the same path. Fresh and well prepared, the tastefully presented cuisine is matched by professional service. If you eat dessert, the Grand Marnier dessert soufflé is the only way to go. Prices are in the high range. Dinner reservations are a must. Open for dinner Monday through Saturday from 6:00 P.M. to 9:00 P.M. Call (203) 438–6511 for reservations and details. The inn rooms are pleasant and furnished in a colonial style. Room rates are in the high-to-moderate range.

The **Bethel Cinema,** 269 Greenwood Avenue, screens art and independent films, attracting a large audience who now and again don't want to see anything with dinosaurs or space aliens. The two-screen theater is known for showing films such as *The Postman* (the Italian film; not Kevin Costner's future-age flick) long before the rest of the world hops on the bandwagon. Generally two films are shown during a run. The matinees are kind to tight budgets. The theater publishes a newsletter with information about upcoming features and film-related lectures. To get on the mailing list, call (203) 778–3100; for film information call (203) 778–2100.

After a show, we can't think of a better destination than **Dr. Mike's** at 158 Greenwood Avenue. If, as some say, (Eric) Clapton is God, then Dr. Mike must be his archangel. Our favorite Dr. Mike dip, chocolate lace ice cream, starts with rich, unflavored ice cream and then is packed to bursting with chocolate lace candy, a filigree of spun sugar dipped in bittersweet chocolate. The contrast between the crunchy candy and the puff of bland ice cream is almost indescribable, especially for a G-rated book. Dr. Mike rotates an impressive array of flavors throughout the year, but only a handful (maybe six) are on the menu at any one time because the Doc makes his product in small (five-gallon) batches. Open Sunday through Thursday, noon to 10:00 P.M.; Friday and Saturday, noon to 11:00 P.M. (Shorter hours in winter; call ahead.) Call (203) 792–4388. Note that this is a very tiny establishment, so don't plan on eating inside. There's another Dr. Mike's at 44 Main Street (junction of Routes 25 and 59), Monroe; (203) 452–0499.

One of us is actually old enough to have spent his teen years hanging out at drive-in restaurants where the uniformed carhops roller-skated out to your car and delivered the food on steel trays that clipped to the window! Of course, our MacBurger-indoctrinated nieces and nephews have no idea what he's taking about when David's cluttered mind wanders across this memory. We weep for the modern generation. In Connecticut, we know of only one place that still has carhops. The **Sycamore,** 282 Greenwood Avenue, is an old-fashioned drive-in restaurant that has been around since the 1940s. Carhop service is available spring, summer, and fall. Just pull in and flash your lights. It's not all atmosphere, either. The burgers are juicy and tasty. The brewed-there root beer (the recipe for which is a deep dark secret) can taste sweet and full or sparkly and dry, depending on its age. The malts are made with real malt powder. The egg creams are the best we've found in Connecticut, too. Prices are rock bottom. The Sycamore sponsors Cruise Nights throughout the summer, but you might see a vintage car pull in at any time (with Sundays often having a regular traffic in these items). Open Monday through Saturday, 6:30 A.M. to 8:30 P.M. (later on weekends), and Sunday 7:00 A.M. to 7:30 P.M. Call (203) 748–2716 for information.

New Haven

New Haven's **Yale University** is one of those American treasures that can be measured only in terms of first, bests, and similar benchmarks. In 1861, it granted the first doctor of philosophy degree ever awarded in the United States. In 1869 its School of Fine Arts, the first in the country, opened its doors. Yale numbers among its graduates men of the caliber of Eli Whitney and Noah Webster, and since 1789, almost 10 percent of major U.S. diplomatic appointees have been Yale grads.

Yale boasts some of the best Gothic architecture in the country. Start at Phelps Gate on College Street. Beyond the gate is the Old Campus, ringed with Gothic buildings. Dwight Hall introduced Yale to Gothic architecture in 1842. Built as the college library for the mind-boggling sum of $33,253, it was a strange marriage of spare New England Puritanism with Gothic overindulgence. It boasts thirty-two carved heads of man and beast mounted on turrets on its 90-foot tower. Over the next seventy years, other architects designed additional Gothic buildings for the Old Campus. Bingham and Vanderbilt Halls on Chapel Street and the bridge over High Street each have their own menagerie of mythological beasties.

Yale graduate James Gamble Rogers's 221-foot 1921-vintage Harkness Tower on High Street honors people and events associated with Yale history, including university founder Eli Yale and graduates Samuel F. B. Morse, Eli Whitney, Senator John C. Calhoun, James Fenimore Cooper, Noah Webster, Nathan Hale, and eighteenth-century fire-and-brimstone preacher Jonathan Edwards. Higher on the tower are figures from ancient history, such as Phidias, Homer, Aristotle, and Euclid. Rogers also designed the Sterling Memorial Library, the Sterling Law complex, and the Hall of Graduate Studies. The library's decorative sculpture has a surprisingly whimsical theme, with its bookworm perched above the Wall Street entrance. The Law School is a veritable jungle of legal symbols, including Minerva and her owl. A feisty bulldog personifies the school mascot. Free student-guided tours of Yale are available through the Yale Visitor Information Office, 149 Elm Street. Call (203) 432–2302. Tours run Monday through Friday at 10:00 A.M. and 3:00 P.M. and on weekends at 1:30 P.M.

Yale is also home to several of America's finest museums. An interesting showcase for British art and life, the **Yale Center for British Art,** at 1080 Chapel Street in New Haven, was built around the extensive collection of Paul Mellon, who spent forty years amassing works by a host of British artists. Mellon's holdings have been expanded since the center opened in

GATEWAY TO NEW ENGLAND

1977, and the building now houses the largest collection of British art outside of Great Britain. It also houses a 13,000-volume research library. The books and art in this building span five centuries of British art and life from the Elizabethan era to the present; the "golden age" of British art, from the birth of Hogarth in 1697 to Turner's death in 1851, is especially well represented. Open Tuesday through Saturday, 10:00 A.M. to 5:00 P.M.; Sunday, noon to 5:00 P.M. Call (203) 432–2800 or (203) 432–2850. Web address: www.yale.edu/ycba.

On the opposite corner of Chapel and York Streets from the Yale Center for British Art, at 1111 Chapel Street, is the *Yale University Art Gallery.* Founded in 1832, this is the oldest university art gallery in the Western Hemisphere, and its collection spans eras, cultures, and art styles. Four floors cover everything from ancient to early modern art. There's also a sculpture garden, with works by Moore, Nevelson, and others, that makes an awfully nice setting in which to dream away a spring afternoon. Open Tuesday through Saturday, 10:00 A.M. to 5:00 P.M. (until 8:00 P.M. on Thursday from September 15 to May 15); Sunday, noon to 5:00 P.M. Call (203) 432–2800.

The *Yale Peabody Museum of Natural History* (170 Whitney Avenue, at the intersection of Whitney Avenue and Sachem Street) is the largest natural history museum in New England. Big deal, you say. Ah, but all children and those adults who are truly tuned in to kid kool know that "natural history" is just an adult euphemism for what it's really all about. Dinos. The big guys. The all-time king bad butts of the natural kingdom. T-Rex, Raptor red, and their buddies.

So while the highbrows in your group wander the halls of the Center for British Art, let those with less tortured priorities saunter on over to the Yale Peabody for a sojourn among the thunder lizards. And if it's not exactly high culture, who cares? This place has the largest collection of mounted dinosaurs in the world, including a 67-foot brontosaurus. And then there's the 110-foot *Age of Reptiles* mural by Pulitzer Prize–winner Rudolph Zallinger. Sure, its been reproduced countless times in dino books from coast to coast. But it's the biggest mural of its kind in the world, and nothing beats the overwhelming experience of standing in front of the real thing. What else does a kid need?

Dinosaurs at the Yale Peabody Museum of Natural History

The Yale Peabody is open Monday through Saturday, 10:00 A.M. to 5:00 P.M.; Sunday and holidays, noon to 5:00 P.M. Admission. Call (203) 432–5050.

Famed as the birthplace of the hamburger, *Louis' Lunch* at 261–263 Crown Street in New Haven is open Tuesday and Wednesday from 11:00 A.M. to 4:00 P.M. and Thursday through Saturday from noon to 2:00 A.M. The way locals tell it, proprietor Louis Lassen invented this now ubiquitous American dish in 1895. Having some scraps of steak that he wanted to use up, the frugal Louis chopped them up fine and made patties, which he then broiled and served on toast. Among the first customers to whom he served his concoction, the story goes, were sailors from the port of Hamburg in Germany. When they asked for the name of the unknown item, Louis decided then and there to call it a "Hamburg." Of such moments are legends born.

This turn-of-the-century cafe is still serving up burgers in much the same style as Louis' original: finely chopped meat patties on white toast, not buns. Ask for a cheeseburger, they'll glop on some Cheese Whiz. Onions? Absolutely. Ketchup? No way. They get downright cranky if you ask for ketchup. Like the sign in the window says: THIS IS NOT BURGER KING. YOU GET IT MY WAY OR YOU DON'T GET THE DAMN THING AT ALL. Call (203) 562–5507.

Connecticut pizza lovers claim that *Pepe's Pizzeria Napoletana* (157 Wooster Street) in New Haven makes the best clam pizza in the Western world. There is some reason to accept that claim. Everything at Pepe's is prepared by hand on the premises. And Pepe's has never heard of a microwave. The splendiferous pies are baked in a coal-fired oven to emerge as flat crisp circles of dough with a firm chewy crust.

Pepe's special white clam pizza is topped with fresh littlenecks, olive oil, garlic, oregano, and Romano cheese. For other types of pies, if you want cheese, you have to ask for it; otherwise, you get a marvelous pie crust topped with tomato sauce. (If you can't handle the lines at Pepe's, try Sally's at 237 Wooster for very good pies.)

Pepe's is open Monday, Wednesday, and Thursday, 4:00 to 10:00 P.M.; Friday and Saturday, 11:30 A.M. to midnight; Sunday, 2:30 to 10:00 P.M. It doesn't matter when you're there; it's always crowded, and there's always a wait. Pepe's is closed during August. Call (203) 865–5762.

The *Five-Mile Point Light,* 1 Lighthouse Road in New Haven, was built in 1847. The 65-foot-high stone lighthouse was a functional light until it was taken out of service in 1877. Now it dominates Lighthouse Point Park. The park includes lots of nature trails and a bird sanctuary, but the main reason to visit is the 1916-vintage carousel. It's one of the biggest we've seen (52 feet in diameter), and holds seventy-two figures: sixty-nine horses, one camel, and two dragons (in our opinion, the only place to ride). It's believed that well-known artists Charles Carmel and Charles I. D. Looff worked on this ride. The park is free; there's a small admission for the carousel. Carousel rides available Tuesday through Sunday, 11:00 A.M. to 6:00 P.M. from Memorial Day through Labor Day. Call (203) 946–8005.

The *Shore Line Trolley Museum* at 17 River Street in East Havencan show off more than a hundred classic trolleys, including the world's oldest rapid transit car, the world's first electric freight locomotive, and a rare parlor car. There are also some interpretive displays, including hands-on exhibits and audio-video displays. We suspect, though, that most people will be drawn by the trolley rides. The museum offers 3-mile round-trip rides in vintage trolley cars on the nation's oldest operating suburban transportation line. Hard-core trolley freaks are also welcome to hang around the carbarn watching the restoration process. You can picnic on the grounds, and there's also a gift shop.

This attraction charges a fairly hefty admission, but group rates for parties of fifteen or more are available; parking is free. Trolleys run every thirty minutes, and the round-trip takes an hour. For most of the year, the museum opens at 11:00 A.M.; the last trolley leaves at 5:00 P.M. Charters are available in winter. This facility is open seasonally according to a rather arcane schedule, so call (203) 467–6927 to make sure that it's operating when you want to visit.

A Big Brew-Ha-Ha

Recent years have seen a real leap in the number of Connecticut microbreweries. Hammer and Nail Brewers is one of the best.

Hammer and Nail Brewers, *900 Main Street (Route 73), Oakville section of Watertown; (888)* NAIL– HAM *and (860) 274–5911. An authentic microbrewery, the beers are available only in Connecticut. Try the Brown Ale, Vienna Style Lager, or one of the seasonal beers. Tours and tastings are held on Saturdays at 11:00 A.M. and 3:00 P.M. Call ahead to make sure tours are being held. Souvenirs and company merchandise are sold at the company store.*

Fair Haven Woodworks at 72 Blatchley Avenue advertises itself as "where SoHo meets Vermont." Put another way, this woodworking shop and gallery offers sophisticated furniture and accessories characterized by fine workmanship. Fair Haven has been hand-building its own models of quality furniture for fifteen years. While most of the pieces, especially the settees, side chairs, and Morris chairs, obviously owe their inspiration to the Arts and Crafts movement, these are not slavish reproductions of old Gustav Stickley designs, but lighter, modern designs that are rooted in a shared tradition. Commissions are welcome, and you choose the type of wood, finishes, and fabrics from a selection that includes just about the largest collection of authentic William Morris patterns we've ever seen.

In addition to its own unique brand of furniture, the two-story gallery at Fair Haven Woodworks also showcases the work of other furniture designers in the same tradition. And if you had in mind something smaller than a sideboard server, the gallery also has a variety of Arts and Crafts–style decorative items, including copperwork, kilim rugs and pillows, mica lamps and stained glass. Open: Monday, Thursday, Friday, 10:00 A.M. to 8:00 P.M.; Saturday, 10:00 A.M. to 6:00 P.M.; Sunday, noon to 4:00 P.M. Call (800) 404–4754 for more information.

When in New Haven, be sure to make a side trip north of the city to suburban Hamden. The town's ***Eli Whitney Museum*** (Whitney Avenue at Armory Street) is New England's oldest continuously operating industrial site. It includes displays tracing two centuries of industrial growth on the site plus various technology-oriented interactive hands-on exhibits. The museum is mainly devoted, however, to the achievements of Eli Whitney, one of the towering figures of the industrial revolution. Whitney was a local firearms manufacturer who pioneered the use of interchangeable parts. He also changed the course of American history by inventing the cotton gin, a device that became the foundation of the Southern plantation economy, spurred the spread of slavery, and contributed mightily to the political crisis that ended in America's Civil War. The museum is open Wednesday, Thursday, Friday, and Sunday from noon to 5:00 P.M. and Saturday from 10:00 A.M. to 3:00 P.M., with shortened hours during the summer. Call (203) 777–1833 or (203) 777–0299.

Hamden also contains some great picnic spots, most of them located within the confines of ***Sleeping Giant State Park*** on Route 10. According to a legend that predates European settlement, the basalt mountain where the park is sited is actually an evil giant by the name of Hobbomock, who was put to sleep to prevent him from doing harm to local residents. When you approach it from the north, the chain of high, wooded hills that make up the park really does resemble a sleeping giant, hence the park's fanciful name. Many of Sleeping Giant's eleven color-coded trails lead to gentle or moderate hikes, so even if you're out of shape you can still get in a good walk. All told, the park's 13,000-plus acres include more than 28 miles of trails to explore, some with spectacular views.

For information, write the Sleeping Giant Park Association, P. O. Box 14, Quinnipiac College, Hamden 06518. As with any hike, it's a good idea to check in with the ranger station. The telephone number of the ranger station on the mountain is (203) 789–7498.

Our vote for best ice-cream parlor in Connecticut goes to **Wentworth's** (3697 Whitney Avenue, Route 10) in Hamden. Located just down the road from Sleeping Giant State Park, Wentworth's occupies a clapboard house on your right as you're leaving Hamden. Wentworth's makes all of its own ice cream on site. Incredibly dense and not too sweet, Wentworth's products seem to capture the essence of each of the dozens of flavors in its ever-changing repertoire. Almond Amaretto (one of many "adult" flavors that use real liquor) will win you over even if you don't care for sweet liqueurs. The best flavor of all, though, is the peach, a gift of ambrosia lovingly crafted from fresh tree-ripened fruit. For kids, there are silly flavors such as Cookie Monster, neon blue vanilla with cookie bits.

Wentworth's is open daily, noon to 9:00 P.M. (until 11:00 P.M. in the summer). It usually closes for a few months during the winter. Call (203) 281–7429 for current hours and to find out when peach ice-cream season starts.

Its extensive collection of rare books, maps, and prints aside, what we *really* like about **Whitlock Farm Booksellers** in Bethany is that it's so quiet, isolated, and hard to find. That makes it our little secret; a secret we share with only a few hundred other regulars. The address is 20 Sperry Road, and it's a straight shot down that back road from Route 69 (the old Litchfield Turnpike), but, even knowing all that, it's easy to miss this place. If you're traveling south on Sperry, look to your left for two big red barns. If you find yourself on Dillon Road or back on the Litchfield Turnpike, you've gone too far. Don't worry about it. Just turn around and try the road from the other direction; once you've seen the lovely, pastoral countryside around Bethany, you won't mind seeing it some more.

Most of Whitlock's inventory of 50,000-plus books is packed into two rustic barns. The turkey barn serves as the main office and showroom for the more expensive items and is a bonanza for collectors of military

Only in Connecticut

history, philosophy, and Connecticut history. Less expensive books and more recent books (including popular fiction, science fiction, magazines, and paperbacks) are housed in the sheep barn. A separate building contains a loft full of old maps and prints. Open Tuesday through Sunday, 9:00 A.M. to 5:00 P.M. Call (203) 393–1240.

If you've never seen cider being made, stop in at **McConney's Farm** on Roosevelt Drive in Derby any time from mid-August to Christmas or during late March. After watching the pressing, you can sample the result. The farm also sells local apples, candy apples, and fresh home-baked apple crisp and apple pies; and the greenhouse is open during spring and summer. Open 9:00 A.M. to 6:00 P.M. daily. Call (203) 735–1133.

There's something about a sunflower that just makes us feel happy. If you're of the same mind, then don't miss taking a summer or fall drive to Ernie and Sabrina Santoro's **Sunflower Farms,** 767 Derby-Milford Road, (off Route 34 or Route 121 or exit 56 from the Merritt Parkway) in Orange. The Santoros are the largest growers of ornamental sunflowers in Connecticut. Throughout the late summer and into the fall, their two-acre farm blazes with brilliant sunflowers in a surprising range of colors from the traditional golden yellow to cream and wine. It's not unusual to find painters and photographers mingling with garden lovers as everyone tries to take in the essence of summer in a flower. You can buy flowers potted or in bouquets. In May and early June, they'll sell you seedlings for your own sunflower garden. In the fall, Sabrina paints pumpkins with great flair and creativity in traditional harvest and Halloween motifs and in some not-so-traditional motifs such as customer's pets and kids, crows, and Elvis and other famous personalities. Open during summer and fall, Monday through Friday from noon to 6:00 P.M. and weekends from 10:00 A.M. until 6:00 P.M. Call (203) 795–6829.

When intrepid OPBers, Pat and Erasmus "Ray" J. Struglia recommended we visit **Rich Farm Ice Cream Shop,** 691 Oxford Road (Route 67) in Oxford, we hopped to it. We admire Dave Rich's philosophy of farming his land rather than selling it off for condos, and he churns up some really good ice cream, made from milk from his own herd of Holsteins. In summer, the place is packed and you might wait on line a good 15 to 20 minutes. You won't be bored because this is a real farm with real farm looks and real farm smells. At haying time during the summer, just a whiff of the new-mown hay distills summer in a sniff. As for the ice cream, you can choose from among twenty-five flavors with seasonal favorites such pumpkin and stuff for the kiddies like Cookie Monster. We prefer to keep things simple and stick with a good old-fashioned chocolate cone. The ice cream shop also makes ice-cream cakes and seasonal treats such as ice-cream Yule logs. Operating hours seem to vary with the season, so please call ahead. From early spring through Columbus Day, open Tuesday through Sunday. From Columbus Day through about mid-December, open Tuesday through Sunday from 2:00 P.M. to 5:00 P.M. Closed during winter. Call (203) 881–1040 to hear a message listing current operating hours.

Ed and Lorraine Warren of Monroe have been Connecticut's, maybe the country's, premier investigators of other-worldly occurrences for a very long time now. Their **Warren Occult Museum** is one spooky place, definitely not for the faint of heart or the easily suggestible. The Warrens have investigated ghosts, spirits, and apparitions for years at such places as the United States Military Academy at West Point and Amityville. Your tour of their establishment starts only after Mr. Warren has provided each member of the tour with an aura of protection. The stories behind many of the displays are both truly terrifying and truly sad. Visitors are cautioned not to touch any of the artifacts as they still hold incredible evil. One display of local interest are photos of Monroe's famed White Lady ghost; other displays include evil dolls and cursed chairs. Tours of the museum are by appointment only. The Warrens also host a Supernatural Halloween Program, which includes a dinner, guest speakers, and a special screening of a horror film. Their Halloween celebration starts in the late afternoon and continues on through, what

Connecticut Haunts

*W*est of the Shelton-Derby area is Monroe, which is home to what might be Connecticut's most famous ghost, the **White Lady,** who is said to haunt the Stepney Cemetery near Monroe and nearby Pepper Street. Visitors to the cemetery report that the apparition wears a white nightgown with a bonnet. Others say they've seen not only the White Lady but also shadowy specters who try to grab her. Ed Warren of Monroe, Connecticut's top ghostbuster, believes she is a Mrs. Knot, whose husband was murdered near Easton in the 1940s. It is believed Mrs. Knot met the same fate as her husband shortly after his unfortunate demise. The White Lady—or perhaps another lady in white—is also said to haunt the **Union Cemetery,** near the Easton Baptist Church on Route 59 in Easton. As with any cemetery, visit with respect and only during the cemetery's operating hours.

else, the witching hour. Call (203) 268–8235 for information about tours and special programs.

South-central Connecticut

ay before there were golden arches on every street corner, the central Connecticut towns of Meriden and Middletown had developed a local specialty called the "steamed cheeseburger." Steaming the burgers makes them incredibly juicy and reduces the sharp Wisconsin cheddar to just the right degree of molten wonderfulness. Locals know to order theirs in the form of a "trilby" (a regional term for anything served up with mustard and onions). You do the same. Your best bet for a quality burger is probably *Ted's Restaurant* (1046 Broad Street in Meriden). We recommend having your trilby with one of Ted's special chocolate shakes. The decor here can be downright scary, but

It's A-maze-ing

orn and hay mazes, which are very popular in the Midwest, are just now starting to show up in New England. It's a fun fall activity for the whole family. Since the mazes are located at farms or nurseries, you can combine your family's pumpkin-gathering expedition with a trip through a maze.

Steck's Nursery at 100 Putnam Park Road, Bethel, (203) 748–1385 creates a wonderful hay maze every fall. It's open from October 1 through mid-November, daily 9:00 A.M. to 5:00 P.M. The maze is made completely of hay bales and kids can crawl through hay tunnels, climb on top of hay pyramids, and work their way through the intricate maze. Free.

Jones Family Farm at 266 Israel Hill Road and Route 110 in Shelton, (203) 929–8425 is a fun-filled family farm throughout the year, but for us, the highlight is October's corn maze. After

you're through tunneling through the maze, you can take a hayride, gather pumpkins from the pumpkin patch, or take home some corn stalks to make your own corn maze. (Wouldn't your UPS driver just adore negotiating your corn maze to deliver packages!) In the summer you can PYO strawberries and blueberries (starts in mid-June); winter brings a chance to cut your own Christmas tree, wind your way through the Christmas tree maze, and visit with Santa. You'll find berry picking and Christmas tree cutting at *Valley Farm;* the corn maze, pumpkin patch, and Christmas tree maze are located at Pumpkin Seed Farm. Both locations are just off Route 110, a hop, skip, and a jump apart. Open 8:00 A.M. to 8:00 P.M. Monday through Saturday, Sunday from 8:00 A.M. to noon. Hours change in the winter, so call ahead for information and directions.

the food is worth the trip. Open Monday through Saturday, 11:30 A.M. to 10:00 P.M. or so. Call ahead to check hours. Call (203) 237–6660.

Early in the nineteenth century, Connecticut entrepreneurs tried to change the patterns of commerce in the state by digging a canal paralleling the path of modern-day Route 10. The Farmington Canal (1828–1847) never really caught on, and the venture was eventually abandoned. Not much remains of the old canal except in the town of Cheshire, west of Meriden. There, at 487 North Brookvale Road (Route 42), you'll find a restored section of the canal at *Lock 12 Historical Park.* In addition to the canal, the grounds contain a museum, a lockkeeper's house, a helicoidal bridge, and a picnic area. The park is open daily from March through November between 10:00 A.M. and dusk. The museum is open by appointment only except for limited Sunday hours in the fall. Call (203) 272–2743.

At *Roaring Brook Falls,* just off Roaring Brook Road (just west of the junction of Route 70 and I–84), you'll find a wonderful hiking trail and overlook—the perfect place for a spring or fall picnic—and the foundation of an old mill to explore. But the draw here is Connecticut's second highest waterfalls, Roaring Brook Falls, an 80-foot main waterfall with smaller cascades above and below. Open from dawn to dusk. Call (203) 272–2743 for information.

Your kids might think that animation starts with the Simpsons and ends with Beavis and what's-his-name, but a visit to the *Barker Character, Comic, and Cartoon Museum,* 1188 Highland Avenue (Route 10) in Cheshire will set 'em straight. Herb Barker, the museum's guiding light, is a longtime collector of 'toon memorabilia, and he's packed a lot of history into his jewel-box museum. Naturally you'll find a lot of cartoon cells on view, but our favorite parts of the collection are the lunch boxes and pull toys featuring cartoon characters from our youth and the collection of McDonald's Happy Meals toys, once giveaways, now pricey collectibles. Animators and illustrators such as George Wildman of Popeye fame often visit the museum for talks and special events. The museum is open 11:00 A.M. to 5:00 P.M., Tuesday through Saturday. Call (203) 272–2357 for information about special events.

Brix Restaurant, 1721 Highland Avenue, Cheshire. In case you're wondering brix isn't a cute spelling for bricks; brix is a measurement of the sugar content of grapes, must, or wine that indicates how ripe the grapes were when harvested. Got that? Cool, pop quiz later. Jokes aside, Brix is a very unlikely restaurant for Connecticut; it feels like places we've visited in California's Napa Valley, but we're very glad it's located just a short hop down Route 10 from us.

Menu offerings are rotated seasonally, so what we enjoyed from the fall menu may not be around when you visit. Here's just a sampling of dishes we enjoyed. We know goat cheese is something of a yuppie cliché, but we love Brix's warm goat cheese over baby greens with a sweet beet vinaigrette. The pizza Popeye is a fusion of New Haven thin crispy crust and a California-designer pizza, strewn with fresh spinach, caramelized onions, black olives, and ricotta. On the dinner menu, the perennial dining-out fave, rack of lamb, appears roasted perfectly with a wonderful side sauce of garlic and rosemary. The dessert list features some tried and true goodies like a creamy tiramisu. Prices are moderate for the quality of food and service. FYI: Connecticut foodies who love Farmington's delightful Gristmill Restaurant should be aware cooking genes run in the family—the Gristmill's owner's daughter is the eminence behind Brix. Open for lunch, Monday through Friday, 11:30 A.M. to 2:00 P.M.; dinner, Monday through Friday, 5:30 to 9:30 P.M.; Saturday, 5:30 to 10:00 P.M. Brix is a Cheshire hot spot, so reservations, especially on weekends, are advised. Call (203) 272–3584 for information and reservations.

For years we buzzed right past **Sweet Claude's** on Route 10 on our way to Wentworth's for ice cream. What a mistake! Sweet Claude's dishes some of the best ice cream in the state in a rainbow of more than forty-five flavors. People on restricted diets can still spend quality time with their favorite treats because Fred Clason (the Claude behind the name) stocks tofutti, sugar-free, or lactose-free ice cream and several other variations on fat-free, low-fat, and no-fat. We like their more adult (and higher butterfat concoctions) like the sublime bananas foster, a creamy banana ice cream with a praline taste. We're clueless about this, but kids tend to glom onto the special flavors like smurf (vibrantly red raspberry ice cream filled with marshmallows and stripes of equally vibrant blue). Open Tuesday through Sunday; shorter hours in winter. Call (203) 272–4237 for more information.

Ten miles or so northwest of Cheshire is the city of Waterbury. The brass industry moved into the city in the mid-1800s, and the "Brass Capital of the World," as it was then known, was largely built on wealth derived from brass manufacturing. In the years since, the industry has moved elsewhere, but its architectural legacy remains. During the heyday of brass, Waterbury residents erected hundreds of rambling Victorian mansions and imposing public buildings. Entire neighborhoods of these buildings are preserved almost intact, and as part of an ongoing renaissance program, other neighborhoods have been restored to their former glory. As a result much of modern-day Waterbury is a living museum of nineteenth- and early twentieth-century architecture.

Watches, time, and timekeeping pretty much put the Waterbury area on the map. In the 1850s, Waterbury Clock and Waterbury Watch made clocks and watches inexpensively, which made giving the gift of a timepiece (once prized and expensive) possible for everyone. Around 1900, watchmaker Robert Ingersoll partnered with Waterbury Watch to make the popular $1.00 "Yankee" watch. In just two short decades, almost 40 million Yankees were sold. You can see the history of timekeeping and watch the industrial progress of this part of the Nutmeg State at the *Timexpo Museum,* 175 Union Street, Brass Mill Commons (exit 22 off I–84). The museum traces the history of timekeeping with an emphasis on the Waterbury-based Timex Corporation. You'll see about 150 years worth of clocks and watches as well as those famous John Cameron Swayze commercial of our youth ("takes a licking and keeps on ticking"). Interactive displays and games keep kids interested and occupied. Per-haps the strangest part of the museum is a 40-foot replica of an Easter Island statue and a interactive display that challenges visitors to guess where the inhabitants of Easter Island came from. We're not sure what it has to do with watchmaking, but it's way cool. Admission; reduced admission for kids and seniors. Open Tuesday through Saturday from 10:00 A.M. to 5:00 P.M. and Sunday from noon until 5:00 P.M. Visit the museum on the Web at www.timexpo.com.

Preserving food in tin cans was a good invention, but getting the food out of tins and into the mouth was, perhaps, a better one. So when in 1858, Ezra J. Warner of Waterbury found a way to quickly open tins, tummies all across American thanked him. Unfortunately, his invention looked more like something from a slasher movie than the latest housewife's helper. You stuck a rather intimidatingly big, curved blade into the tin and rammed it around. Since the opener tended to open the user as well as the tin, about ten years later, someone else invented the less dangerous cutting-wheel can opener.

In 1790, the Grilley brother of Waterbury made Connecticut's first buttons.

If you're interested in architecture, you'll want to visit the *Hillside Historic District,* once home to Waterbury's captains of industry. Now carried on the National Register of Historic Places, the district includes 310 structures dating from the nineteenth and early twentieth centuries. The center of Waterbury's restoration program, however, is the tree-lined city green, one of the most beautiful greens in any northeastern city. Within a few blocks of the green you'll find scores of lovingly restored structures. Among the more interesting are

The Holy Land in Miniature

*O*ne of the most frequently asked questions at our book signings and talks is: Do you know anything about the cross you can see from Interstate 84 in Waterbury? We don't know everything, but we do know that the cross is what remains of Waterbury's Holy Land, an early version of a religious theme park. As you travel west on the interstate (exit 22) toward Waterbury, the cross is the most visible part of Holy Land, a model in miniature of Jerusalem and Bethlehem. Once upon a time, Holy Land was such a flourish-ing attraction that busloads of the faithful trekked to Waterbury from all over the East to see the Biblical scenes rendered in miniature and other attractions. Holy Land's been closed for many years now, and time, the weather, and vandalism have pretty much reduced the park to rubble. There don't seem to be any objections to visitors, at their own risk, wandering through the once-flourishing attraction. If you're of a mind to learn more, the Waterbury Public Library keeps an extensive file on Holy Land.

a marvelously misplaced railroad station modeled on the Palazzo Pubblico in Siena, Italy. There are also five municipal buildings designed by prominent American architect Cass Gilbert.

The modernized and expanded Masonic Hall, at 144 West Main Street on the northwest corner of the green, houses Waterbury's **Mattatuck Museum.** This establishment is an oddly satisfying combination of industrial museum and art gallery. The gallery portion includes items spanning three centuries and is devoted to the works of American masters who have an association with Connecticut. The museum portion contains displays of household items and furnishings dating from 1713 to 1940 as well as exhibits dealing with local history, especially the history of the region's industrial development. Its holdings include collections of nineteenth-century furniture, novelty clocks and watches, early cameras, and art deco tableware. The most curious item is Charles Goodyear's rubber desk. The museum is open Tuesday through Saturday from 10:00 A.M. to 5:00 P.M. Except during July and August, it is also open Sunday from noon to 5:00 P.M. There is a gift shop and cafe on site. Call (203) 753–0381.

Wandering the halls of the Mattatuck or pounding the pavements on an architectural tour can burn a lot of calories, and Waterbury has some great eateries where you can replenish them. A large Italian population means that some of the best of these serve Italian cuisine. Two area restaurants that are particularly well thought of are **Bacco's** at

1230 Thomaston Avenue (203–755–1173) and *Faces* at 702 Highland Avenue (203–753–1181).

When you drive past the Waterbury green, slow down long enough to take a gander at the massive statue of a lively prancing horse. Knight, the name of the horse depicted by the statue, was owned by Waterbury heiress Caroline Welton, who lived in Rose Hill, one of Waterbury's most lavish mansions. Caroline Welton died tragically in 1885 in a mountain climbing accident, but before her death, she was active in the social movement to prevent cruelty to animals. When originally installed in 1888, the statue included a horse trough at its front and two troughs at its back for dogs and cats. It's such a popular landmark in Waterbury that residents frequently make dates to "meet at the horse."

If you have a mind to pick up a souvenir of your visit, do stop in at **Howland-Hughes Department Store** (120 Bank Street). This is the oldest free-standing department store in Connecticut. It's been serving Waterbury since 1890 and is one of those old-fashioned stores that emphasize personal service and civility. At Howland-Hughes, you'll find a selection of best-in-class Connecticut crafts and manufactured goods. You could, for example, choose a gift from an array of handsome pewter from Woodbury Pewterers. Or, if you are one of those unmodern souls who still mends and sews, you might want to paw over the selection of metal buttons from the Waterbury Company, which at 180 years, is America's oldest button maker; this company made buttons for both sides in the Civil War and today makes them for both houses of Congress. Open Tuesday through Saturday from 9:30 A.M. to 5:00 P.M. Call (203) 753–4121.

Uncle Willie's, 1101 Huntington Avenue, Waterbury. Who'd a thunk it that too-chic-for-its-own-good Fairfield County would harbor Connecticut's best BBQ joints? When it come to rib joints, Uncle Willie's might just be the prince of pork. At this no-frills place, they serve up huge slabs of pig meat, smoky, meltingly tender, and savory with a variety of barbecue sauces, including Wichita Falls hot and Memphis classic sweet. If you aren't in the mood for ribs, try any of the other stellar barbecue offerings: pulled pork and beef brisket. Besides barbecue, you'll find other down-home cooking—fried okra (probably an acquired taste for most Yankees) and collards. Barbecue side dishes includes good, creamy cole slaw; cornbread; and smashed potatoes, both plain and sparked up with a dash of jalapeno peppers. For dessert, go traditional—try the sweet potato pie or the peach cobbler. Open Monday through Saturday, 11:00 A.M. to 8:00 P.M. Call (203) 596–7677 for more information.

DON'T MISS

Here are some short takes on other attractions, dining, shopping, and lodging in the Gateway to New England.

ATTRACTIONS

Meeker's Hardware, White Street, Danbury. It's the only hardware store on the National Register of Historic Places and still the home of the nickel Coke. Open Monday through Saturday, 7:00 A.M. to 3:00 P.M. Call (203) 748–8017.

St. James Church, 25 West Street, Danbury, features Gothic Revival architecture and Tiffany glass. It houses the Bulkley Memorial Carillon, the first made in the United States. Open daily.

St. Peter Church, built in 1870, at Main and Center Streets features glorious stained-glass windows.

Birdcraft Museum and Sanctuary, 314 Unquowa Road (near exit 21, Interstate 95), Fairfield; (203) 259–0416. This is the first privately owned bird sanctuary. Situated on six acres of woods and ponds, this site is now owned by the Connecticut Audubon Society. A small but nice museum.

Tarrywile Mansion and Park, 70 Southern Boulevard, Danbury; (203) 744–3130. Victorian mansion and gardens with hiking.

Railroad Museum of New England, 176 Chase River Road, Waterbury; (203) 575–1931. Ride the "Naugy" through 17 miles of Connecticut's most picturesque scenery. Train runs May through October. Call for schedule and information about special events.

Bishop Farm and Winery, 500 South Meriden Road, Cheshire; (203) 272–8243. Would they call it a winery in France? Perhaps *non,* but this a is a pleasant place to visit at harvest. The grape wines are made from grapes grown in Stonington, and the fruit wines come from the products of the Bishop Farm in Cheshire. Wines include Cheshire red, white, and blush, and tangy apple wine. Open seasonally from July 1 through December 26. Open weekdays, 10:00 A.M. to 5:00 P.M.; weekends, 9:00 A.M. to 5:00 P.M.

SHOPPING

United Crafts, 127 West Putnam Avenue, Greenwich; (203) 869–4898. A gallery of beautiful Arts and Crafts stoneware, bronzes, and textiles. Be sure to check out the dark green pine-cone-motif stoneware, a prime example of the marriage of beauty and utility exemplified by the Arts and Crafts movement. Web address: www.ucrafts.com.

Images, 32 North Colony Road (Route 5), Wallingford; (203) 265–7065. This quaint shop full of heirloom linens looks like it's out of the pages of *Victoria* magazine. In fact, the store and its owner, Debra Bonito, have been featured in the magazine. The linens are gorgeous and top quality. It's the perfect place to find a wonderful shower or anniversary gift or to indulge in a little "I'm worth it" shopping. Open Monday through Friday, 10:00 A.M. to 4:00 P.M.; Saturday, 11:00 A.M. to 4:00 P.M.

Bovano Enamelware, Route 10, Cheshire; (203) 272–3200. For more than forty years, artisans at Bovano Enamelware have been enameling beautiful birds and flowers on copper. You've probably seen their work in upscale gift and department stores. There are no tours of the workshop, but you can visit Bovano's beautiful gift shop to buy their metalwork, as well as Crabtree & Evelyn potpourri, greeting cards, gorgeous dried flower arrangements, and lots of cutie-patootie country gifts. Open Tuesday through Sunday. Shorter hours in winter; call ahead.

RESTAURANTS

Leo's, Route 25 (South Main Street), Newtown; (203) 426–6881. We were tipped to Leo's by an online buddy who recommends the place for a no-frills breakfast or brunch of gigantic proportions at very low prices. Our pal recommends any of the waffles, including the ones topped with homemade rice pudding. On weekends, it's busy, so plan on a short wait. Kids are well treated. You can dine on the patio in nice weather.

Long Ridge Tavern,

2653 Long Ridge Road, Stamford; (203) 329–7818. Very good new American cuisine, excellent desserts, and a comfortable atmosphere. Kids welcome. Moderate to high. Lunch served Tuesday through Saturday, noon to 3:00 P.M.; dinner served Tuesday through Sunday, from 5:30 to around 10:00 P.M. Sunday brunch served 11:30 A.M. to 3:00 P.M. Reservations on the weekends are a good idea.

Blackrock Castle,

2895 Fairfield Avenue, Bridgeport; (203) 336–3990. The place to go in Connecticut to celebrate St. Patrick's Day, inspired cooking with an Irish flair (and twenty-three different beers and ales on tap). Entertainment. Reservations suggested, especially weekends.

Whistle Stop Muffin Co.,

20 Portland Avenue, Ridgefield; (203) 544–8139. This tiny place, housed in a railroad station, serves muffins to busy commuters. On any given day, they offer a dozen different types. Sticky buns, scones, and warm gooey cinnamon rolls are also on the menu. Open from Memorial Day to Labor Day, Monday through Friday, 6:00 A.M. to 9:00 P.M.; Saturday and Sunday, 8:00 A.M. to 9:00 P.M. and until 6:00 P.M. the rest of the year.

Claire's Cornucopia,

1000 Chapel Street, New Haven; (203) 562–3888. Around for a very long time and greatly loved, this vegetarian restaurant is known for its veggie breakfasts and vegetarian Mexican food. Open daily from 8:00 A.M. to 9:00 P.M. (10:00 P.M. on Friday and Saturday); closed major holidays.

Marjolaine, 961 State

Street, New Haven; (203) 789–8589. A bakery and coffee house famous for its fine pastries. This is a decent place to rest your feet after the Yale museum trek. Open Tuesday through Friday, 8:00 A.M. to 6:00 P.M.; Saturday, 8:00 A.M. to 5:00 P.M.; Sunday, 8:00 A.M. to 1:00 P.M.

LODGING

The Homestead Inn,

420 Field Point Road, Greenwich; (203)869–7500. Want to know how the other 2 percent live? Try dinner or a getaway weekend at the Homestead. Very expensive, but worth it. Six suites, fourteen doubles, a hundred rooms, all with private bath and every possible luxury. Don't skip breakfast on the enclosed front dining porch. Open all year; restaurant closed Labor Day.

House on the Hill B&B,

92 Woodlawn Terrace, Waterbury; (203) 757–9901. Owner Marianne Vandenburgh's twenty-room, 1888 Victorian really does sit on a hill. Its Victorian atmosphere and period ornamentation is very popular with the Victoria magazine set. Moderate to high.

Coast and Country

Connecticut has 253 miles of shoreline, all of it bordering Long Island Sound. This shore was settled shortly after the first towns were built in the Connecticut River Valley. Today the southwestern portion of the state's coastal plain has been largely urbanized, while most of the eastern portion has been given over to tourism. It is the less densely portion of this coastline (between New Haven and Rhode Island) that most people envision as the Connecticut shore. Home to fried-clam shacks and posh inns, popular sandy beaches and lonely ruined lighthouses, modern submarines and ancient whalers, riverboats and coastal mail packets, the Connecticut shore reflects the romance of the sea like few other places on earth.

Even if you're not a big fan of the sea, this part of Connecticut has much to offer. The inland portion of the coastal plain and the lower reaches of the Thames and Connecticut Rivers, in fact all of New London and Middlesex Counties and the easternmost part of New Haven County, are all part of what we call the "Shore." Here you'll find attractions as disparate as the historic Bee and Thistle Inn and a classic diner in Middletown, the glorious wedding cake architecture of the Goodspeed Opera House and the Gothic extravagance of Gillette Castle, or the famous hunt breakfasts at the Gris and the renowned chili dogs and shakes at Higgies in Higganum.

The Western Shore

According to legend, Captain William Kidd was a black-hearted pirate and bloody-handed murderer who savagely preyed upon America's coasts. Well, not exactly. As a matter of public record, the real Captain Kidd was a Scottish-born merchant transplanted to America, who was commissioned in 1695 to hunt down the pirate Thomas Tew (of Newport) in the Indian Ocean. While pursuing Tew, Kidd stretched the limits of his commission, which embarrassed his prominent British backers (including the Crown). When he returned home, Kidd was

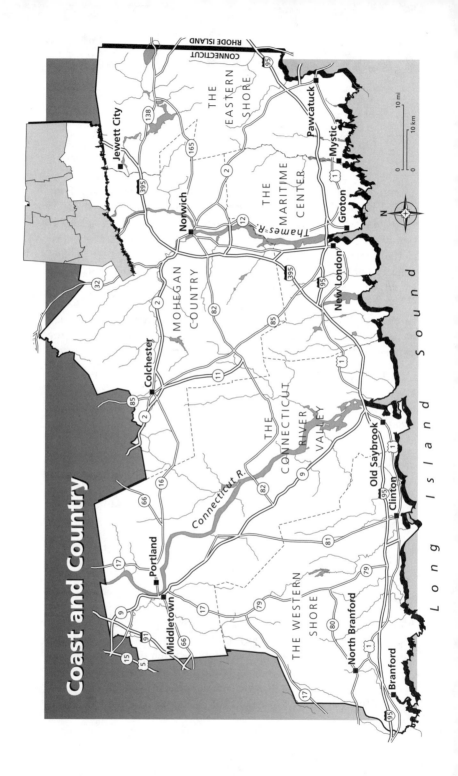

Coast and Country

COAST AND COUNTRY

seized and, after a rigged trial in which evidence of his innocence was suppressed, convicted of murder and piracy and hanged in 1701.

Whether your view of Captain Kidd leans toward the mythical or the historical, it's hard to resist the tantalizing legends of pirate gold and buried treasure. Many of these tales are linked to the state's Thimble Islands, just off the coast from Branford's Stony Creek, and local residents nurture the Kidd mythology. The residents of High Island, for example, refer to their home as Kidd's Island and enhance its piratical flavor by flying the skull and crossbones and painting their cottages black. And on Money Island, where Kidd is widely supposed to have buried some of his treasure in a cave, shovels and spades get a good workout every summer as people try to locate the buried booty.

From early May through October, your can tour the **Thimble Islands** on the *Volsunga IV* with Captain Bob (dock phone 203–488–9978; reservations and schedules 203–481–3345); the *Sea Mist II* with Captain Mike (203–488–8905); or the *Islander* (203–397–3921). The boats leave from the Stony Creek Dock, 34 Sachem Road in Stony Creek, and cruise the Thimble Islands, delivering mail and supplies to island residents and offering nonresidents an interesting tour, replete with lively commentary dealing with tales of dark doings and pirate gold. The captains like to brag they know the waters so well, that in pea-soup-thick fog, they can find their way around with falling back on "potato navigation." Potato navigation is tossing a potato, preferably from Maine, over the bow. If you hear a splash, it's safe to keep on going. Cruises start mid-May and run through Columbus Day. No Monday cruises in May, June, and September through Columbus Day. No Monday afternoon cruises in July. Visit Captain Bob or the Web at www. thimbleislands.com; e-mail: captbob@thimbleislands.com. Note: No reservations for children under 12.

One note: All the islands are privately held. Unless you're an invited guest, don't plan on getting off the boat to explore; uninvited guests are understandably not welcome.

If you're hungry for seafood after your cruise, try **Lenny's Indian Head Inn** on Route 146 in the Indian Neck section of Branford; (203) 488–1500. Lenny's offers lobsters fresh off the boat and fish and seafood so fresh it practically swims into the kitchen. It's a comfortable place with wooden booths and customers from all walks of life, from Crickers to tourists looking for a real New England seafood place. Open for lunch and dinner, Tuesday through Saturday.

The Stony Creek Market, 178 Thimble Island Road, is another local hangout. It's good for lunch or for picking up sandwiches and salads for an impromptu picnic. Open Tuesday through Saturday for lunch and dinner. Call (203) 488–0145.

Branford Craft Gallery at Bittersweet Herb Farm is a melange of two dozen shops and studios occupying the barns and chicken coops of a 150-year-old farm at 779 East Main Street (Route 1). Among the craftspeople plying their trade at the center are leatherworkers, glassblowers, potters, and woodcarvers. There's also a frame gallery and gift shop. A restaurant on the property serves lunch and Sunday brunch. Open Tuesday through Saturday, 11:00 A.M. to 5:00 P.M.; Sunday, noon to 5:00 P.M. Call (203) 488–4689.

The site's rambling old farmhouse is occupied by **Bittersweet Herb Farm,** a locally famous merchandiser of herbs and herbal products. The interior of the house is awash in herbs and spices. They line the walls and mantels and hang from the beams, occupying every possible space. There are scads of dried cooking herbs and spices, potpourri blends, bouquets of dried flowers, herbal teas, and herbed vinegars and honeys. All of these things you would expect to find. Bittersweet, however, also makes and sells its own seasonings, salad dressings, and herbal butters and dips, many of which are unique to this establishment. Open Monday through Saturday, 10:00 A.M. to 5:00 P.M.; Sunday, 11:00 A.M. to 5:00 P.M. Call (203) 488–4689.

Back down along the coast and closer to East Haven, **Judie's European Baked Goods** (126 Shore Drive) bakes some of the best bread in Connecticut. Judie's has been around for twenty years, and most folks still think it's the top boutique bakery in the state. Certainly more than one shoreline restaurant has based its reputation on the fact that they serve Judie's breads. Owner Judie Saleeby, who does the baking, claims she got her start making mud pies as a child. You'll find more than seventy varieties of bread here, including Tempestuous Harvest Yam Yam Bread. Don't get too hung up on names and exotic ingredients, though. You will not, for example, find a better baguette, even in Paris. One of these crusty

FAVORITE PLACES IN COAST AND COUNTRY

1. *Thimble Islands*
2. *Valley Railroad Company*
3. *O'Rourke's Diner*
4. *Gillette Castle*
5. *Mashantucket-Pequot Museum and Research Center*

numbers with a bit of cheese and a little wine makes for a nice shoreline picnic. The bakery is open Tuesday through Thursday, 6:30 A.M. to 4:00 P.M.; Friday and Saturday from 6:30 A.M. to 5:00 P.M.; Sunday, 6:30 A.M. to 2:00 P.M. Cash only. Call (203) 488–2257.

Are Connecticut residents hungrier than residents of other states, or are they just more food conscious? We don't know, but anecdotal experience tells us people in Connecticut like to talk food a lot, and whenever they do, the talk quickly turns to pizza. Who makes the best crust? Best sauce? Most generous topping? A few years back we had a client in Branford, so we made the trip to the shoreline several times a month. We wanted to talk technology, but the client wanted to talk pizza. And the pizza he called the best in Connecticut was none other than Branford's own **Born in America Pizza,** Bushy Hill Plaza. After trying their pizza, we agree that it's something special (nearly as good as our personal favorite—Harry's in West Hartford and Simsbury). Born in America is a tiny, unassuming pizza place, tucked away into a pretty ordinary strip mall. The eatery is divided into two parts: one-half serves take-out, and the other half is a small sit-down restaurant decorated in bright colors and posters. The tables and chairs are roomy and comfortable. On our first visit we learned that chef Darrell Janis went for and won the gold in the 1997 "pizza Olympics" in Las Vegas. His Full House pizza (white sauce, duck, Portobello mushrooms, and spicy chorizo sausage topped with smoked gouda, mozzarella, roasted garlic, tomatoes, and scallions) sure sounds like luxury on a pizza crust, but we have to confess we've never tried it. We always go for a simpler pizza, a few veggies, sweet and flavorful red sauce, and just a tad of mozzarella on the chewy and tender crust. Chef Darrell must like to experiment; we arrived on an early winter afternoon just before New Year's Eve to find the day's special pizza consisted of traditional New Year's good-luck ingredients—knockwurst and sauerkraut. Nope, didn't try that one either. Born in America also offers appetizers, salads, grinders, and such daily specials as a sublime-sounding roasted lamb shank. All those wonderful pizzas to choose from—part of the wonder of being born in America. Open Sunday, Tuesday, and Wednesday from 4:30 P.M. to 10:00 P.M.; Thursday from 11:30 A.M. to 10:00 P.M. and Friday and Saturday from 11:30 A.M. to 11:00 P.M. Closed for most major holidays. Operating hours seem to be somewhat idiosyncratic, so call ahead before you visit.

Guilford Trivia

Guilford has the largest town green in New England.

While looking for something lost, have you ever muttered, "Now where in the Sam Hill is it?" And did you ever wonder who Sam Hill was? Well, he was a real guy, who lived in Guilford (1678–1752). Old Sam was the town clerk for thirty-five years, judge of the probate court for twelve years, and deputy to the general court for at least twenty-two sessions. He ran for so many offices that people used to say "running like Sam Hill" when they meant someone was persistent. Poor Sam's name—which had become known throughout the country and which sounds so much like the common name for the nether regions—eventually lost that connotation and became a polite euphemism for "hell."

Although the recent addition of upscale frozen yogurt shops and trendy clothing stores has somewhat lessened the appeal of Guilford to us, it's still a charming place to spend a lazy afternoon. The side streets off the town green are studded with any number of interesting places well worth a leisurely poke.

Over at 411 Church Street is the **Guilford Handicrafts Center,** a small school of arts and crafts with a gallery that does about ten shows per year, and a shop that is open year-round. Open Monday through Saturday, 10:00 A.M. to 5:00 P.M.; Thursday evenings until 7:00 P.M.; Sunday, noon to 5:00 P.M. Call (203) 453–5947. On the Web at www.handicraftcenter.org.

To take home a perfect souvenir of your visit to Guilford, stop by **Whitfield Jewelry** for crafts made from pink granite cut in nearby Beatties's Quarry.

On Whitfield Street, you'll find the **Whitfield House Museum.** Built back in 1639 as a combination minister's home, stronghold, and meeting hall, the Henry Whitfield House is reputedly the oldest stone house in New England. Today it's a showcase for seventeenth- and eighteenth-century antique furnishings. There's also a pretty fair herb garden on the grounds. Open Wednesday through Sunday, 10:00 A.M. to 4:30 P.M. December 15 through January 31 by appointment only. Admission. Call (203) 453–2457.

If you like old houses or antique furnishings, there are also two other houses worth looking at in Guilford. Both are on Boston Street. The 1660-vintage **Hyland House** (number 84) is a classic colonial saltbox noted for its unusual woodwork and for no less than three walk-in fireplaces. The 1774-vintage **Thomas Griswold House** (number 171) is another saltbox that has been turned into a museum of local history. In addition to the usual collection of furnishings, this house has some period costumes and a restored blacksmith shop. Both of these houses keep seasonal hours mid-June to October 1, Tuesday through Sunday, 11:00 A.M. to 4:00 P.M.; October, weekends only, 11:00 A.M. to 4:00 P.M.; also open by appointment, and both charge a small admission. Call (203) 453–9477 for information on the Hyland House and (203) 453–3176 or (203) 453–5452 for information on the Thomas Griswold House.

Almost twenty years ago—in our first years as Nutmeggers—one of our favorite haunts was the Stone House Restaurant, 506 Whitfield Street in Guilford. We loved the lobsters, literally minutes off the boat and onto your plate; we loved the waitresses at lunch; we loved the view; and we even loved the somewhat threatening feral cats who roamed the parking lot, making us very happy that cats do not grow to the size of Dobermans. Much to our dismay the cozy Stone House folded many years ago. Since then, several restaurants with trendy decor, catchy names, and various cuisines have come and gone in that location. Now a new **Stone House** has opened at 506 Whitfield Street. Do we love it as much as the Stone House of our memories? No, but memories are like that—hard to replace. The new eatery follows a sort-of updated old Stone House menu. We like the generous calamari appetizer. It's not leaden or greasy, but seems, at least to us, pan seared rather than deep fried. We've not tried but have heard good things about the diver scallops and many of the desserts. Still we miss the Stone House's carrot cake. The wine list offers some nice wines from California and other parts of the world. Open for lunch from 11:30 A.M. to 3:00 P.M., Tuesday through Saturday; for dinner Tuesday through Thursday from 5:00 P.M. to 9:00 P.M., Friday and Saturday from 5:00 P.M. to 10:00 P.M., and Sunday from 5:00 P.M. to 8:00 P.M. We've heard there's a Sunday brunch from noon until 3:00 P.M. but haven't tried it, so take your chances. Call (203) 458–3700 for more information.

Henry Whitfield House

For a beautiful water view, follow Whitfield Street south from the green to Guilford Harbor. You'll find some thoughtfully placed comfortable benches, just right for sitting a spell. If you're of a mind to see some more beautiful scenery, follow Mulberry Point Road (off Route 146) to its end. You can't park at the point, but you can see Faulkner Point Lighthouse off in the distance.

The Place (891 Boston Post Road; Route 1) in Guilford has been serving excellent grilled food in the rough to legions of satisfied customers for the past twenty summers. If you've not been there, do stop by for the grilled seafood (or whatever). Steaks, chicken, clams, corn on the cob, lobster, they all get grilled over the same 18-foot firepit. Seating is outdoors at tables made from discarded telephone wire spools, and the sound system is a boom box. For foul weather days, there's a tent. This definitely ain't the Ritz, but the elegant simplicity of the food compensates for the lack of amenities. You'll never look at clams the same way once you've tasted them hot off the grill, their natural sweetness enhanced by a touch of wood smoke and sparked by a splash of hot sauce. The grilled lobster is also wonderful, but don't wear white, because your hands (indeed, most of you from the waist up) can easily end up speckled with char from tearing apart the blackened shells to search out every last morsel of sweet meat. Better yet, forget the "don't wear white" rule and just bring a change of clothes. The owners invite you to "make your own dining statement" by augmenting all that good grilled stuff with your own alcoholic beverages, tablecloths, flowers, candles, or other embellishments; there are a couple of package stores close by. Open seasonally from May until about Columbus Day weekend. Open Monday through Thursday, 5:00 to 11:00 P.M.; Friday, 5:00 to midnight; Saturday, noon to midnight; Sunday, noon to 10:00 P.M. Call (860) 453–9276.

Cider fanciers, don't leave the Guilford area without stopping at *Bishop's Orchards Farm Market* at 1355 Boston Post Road (Route 1). Started in 1910 as a produce stand, Bishop's has grown to a sizable cider mill and pick-your-own/cut-your-own farm with sidelines in Vermont cheeses, local honey and eggs, and fresh herbs. The cider mill makes splendid apple cider, but try the pear cider, too. It's a little thicker than apple cider and maybe a little sweeter, but the fresh pear taste is quite unusual and invigorating. Open Monday through Saturday, 8:00 A.M. to 6:00 P.M. and Sunday, 9:00 A.M. to 6:00 P.M. Call (203) 453–2338. Web address: www.bishopsorchards.com.

The 1785 *Allis-Bushnell House & Museum* at 853 Boston Post Road in neighboring Madison is noted for the unusual corner fireplaces and original paneling that graces its period rooms. It's now home to the Madison Historical Society, which maintains collections of toys, dolls, costumes, kitchenware, and china. Modest admission. Open May through October on Wednesday, Friday, and Saturday from 1:00 P.M. to 4:00 P.M. Open other times by appointment. Wednesday, Friday, and Saturday, 1:00 to 4:00 P.M. Call (203) 245–4567.

Another historic home in Madison comes complete with a family ghost. The 1685 ***Deacon John Graves House at Tunxis Farm,*** 581 Boston Post Road, was owned and occupied for 300 years by the descendants of Deacon John Graves. Open mid-June through Labor Day, Wednesday through

Sweet Treats

*I*f you're looking for an interesting souvenir for the folks back home that won't break your budget—or if you just want a taste of Connecticut history—check out gourmet, candy, and souvenir shops throughout the state for these two regional sweet treats: Chocolate Lace candy and Rock Candy Mountain.

Chocolate Lace *got its start in czarist Russia at the turn of the century, when a woman named Eugenia Tay made a magical candy that required a snowstorm. Her technique was to boil sugar and drizzle the hot syrup on the fresh snow, thus making delicate lacy patterns of caramelized sugar. When the substance hardened (almost immediately), the pieces of "lace" were brought indoors and dipped in chocolate. Hence the name of Chocolate Lace.*

When the Tay family fled Russia in 1917, they settled in New York, where Eugenia Tay went into the candy business. At first she used cold marble as a drizzling surface to allow regular production; it's difficult to run a business whose inventory depends on frequent

snowstorms. Eventually, though, a machine, affectionately dubbed "Veronica Lace," was developed to automate the process of creating the lacy patterns. For around $9.00 for a seven-ounce box, you can present your nearest and dearest with a treat worthy of a Russian czar. Alas, the Chocolate Lace factory is not open for tours.

Rock Candy. *Everything old is new again.* ***Dryden & Palmer,*** *located in Branford, makes old-fashioned rock candy. This treat is a revelation to many modern kids, but Dryden & Palmer have been turning it out since 1880. In addition to crystal-clear nuggets of rock candy, they also manufacture rock candy swizzle sticks in bright jewel-tones and a variety of flavors. Great in fancy cocktails, the rock candy swizzle sticks never fail to charm young or old as stirrers for hot or iced tea or hot chocolate. A swizzle stick costs about 40 cents. Available in candy shops around Connecticut. The Dryden & Palmer factory is not open for public tours.*

Saturday from 1:00 P.M. to 4:00 P.M.; Labor Day through Columbus Day on Saturday and Sunday from 10:00 A.M. to 4:00 P.M. For more information call (203) 245–4798.

Madison is also home to the **Meigs Point Nature Center,** located in **Hammonasset Beach State Park,** the largest of Connecticut's shoreline parks. The beach is overrun with visitors in summer, making for heavy traffic and other hassles, so we advise a trip to the nature center during the off-season, roughly October to Memorial Day. There's an especially pleasant sense of desolation about Hammonasset in winter. The Meigs Point Nature Center is open daily throughout the year from 8:00 A.M. to 5:00 P.M. Call (203) 245–2785.

A good place to stop to rest weary feet and catch up on the latest doings of the Royals is **Front Parlour at The British Shoppe,** 45 Wall Street, an English outpost in a 1690s colonial home, not far from the late twentieth-century sprawl that's the Boston Post Road. John and Barbara Jago-Ford from Devon, England, sell British teas and other comestibles at the British Shoppe. The tearoom, located in the front of the house, is called the Front Parlor. The decor of the tea shop blends a certain rough-hewn colonial character with English Victorian charm. Tables are layered with dainty embroidered cloths, and your tea is served on flower-sprigged china, accompanied by whimsical butter spreaders and a host of spoons. Photographs of the royal family adorn the walls as does a letter acknowledging the Jago-Ford's sympathy letter on the death of Princes Diana. By the way, the Jago-Fords are happy to share their opinions on the Royals—just don't ask about Fergie unless you want a real earful! For your tea, you can have scones and cream, crumpets, or tea sandwiches, wispy little wafers with savory fillings, and desserts, including a lovely lemony cake. The tea is, as they say, strong enough to trot a mouse on. Robust lunches with offerings such as Cornish pasties or steak and kidney pie are also served. Open for tea, Monday through Saturday, 2:00 to 4:00 P.M.; lunch, Monday through Saturday, 11:30 A.M. to 4:00 P.M. No reservations. Web address: www. thebritishshoppe.com. E-mail: gourmet@the britishhoppe.com. Call (203) 245–4521 or (800) 842–6674 for more information.

East of Madison is Clinton, home to one of Connecticut's better known shopping venues, the **Clinton Crossing Premium Outlet Mall,** 20 Killingworth Turnpike (exit 63 off Interstate 95); (860) 664–0700. This collection of top-shelf stores offers brands such as Coach and Donna Karan at pretty good discounts. You can sign up for online notification of sales and other special events at the mall's Web site: www. chcelseagca.com/location/clinton/clin.html.

Not far from Clinton Crossing is a hidden jewel called ***Chamard Vineyards,*** 115 Cow Hill Road. This operation certainly looks like a famous French winery, complete with elegant tasting room and vine-wreathed entrance. But how good can the wine really be? As it turns out, really quite good. This is an artistic operation that focuses on a small but excellent line. The specialty is chardonnay, and in 1991, Chamard's chardonnay came in second to a much pricier French wine in a taste test conducted by *Cooks Illustrated.* The winery also produces good reds, including a merlot. Open for tours and tastings, year-round from Wednesday through Saturday, 11:00 A.M. to 4:00 P.M. Call (860) 664–0299.

The Connecticut River Valley

W hen the six men who formed the Company of Military Historians got together to do so in 1949, it is doubtful that any of them realized that one day it would be the largest international organization of military historians in the world. The organization has its offices in the ***Military Historians Headquarters & Museum*** in the old post office building on North Main Street in Westbrook. Here the organization has assembled the largest collection of American military uniforms and insignia in the country. Also on display is a collection of restored twentieth-century military vehicles, all in operating condition, ranging from the World War II–era M-29 Weasel to a Jeep from the Vietnam era. There's also a research library and a music room containing a display of bandsmen's uniforms and a collection of thousands of recordings of military music, which can be borrowed or copied. Open Tuesday through Friday, 8:30 A.M. to 3:30 P.M. or by appointment. Call (860) 399–9460.

Chamard Vineyards

Essex Trivia

Can't make it to Punxsutawney, Pennsylvania, for Groundhog Day (February 2)? Head on down to Essex for their Groundhog Day festival, which features Essex Ed, their homegrown version of Punxsutawney Phil. There's the usual does-he-doesn't-he-see his shadow silliness, a grand parade, and lots of family activities. Be sure to get a photo of the larger-than-life Essex Ed papier-mâché sculpture that's popped atop the Essex Rotary for the festivities. Call the Southeastern Connecticut Tourism District at 1–800 TO–ENJOY for more information on Essex's groundhog fest.

Crowded and touristy, **Lenny and Joe's Fish Tale Restaurant** (86 Boston Post Road) still has the best fried clams around, and the servings are huge. If you've never eaten whole-belly clams, this is a good place to start; but, be forewarned, you'll never again be satisfied with those sad little strips with which the rest of America gets stuck. Lenny and Joe's also has good lobster rolls, fresh coleslaw, and grand onion rings and fried zucchini. In the spring you can get a Connecticut River shad dinner. Be prepared to wait, though. Most days, there's a line. Open daily, 11:00 A.M. to 9:00 P.M. (until 10:00 P.M. on Friday and Saturday). Call (860) 669–0767. There's a second restaurant at 1301 Post Road in Madison. Call (203) 245–7289.

With one of the best anchorages on the Connecticut River, Essex has always had intimate ties with the river. The main street of Essex is called Main Street, and it still looks very much like its eighteenth-century counterpart. Clapboard houses, fan-shaped windows, and fences abound, and in the shops that line the street, pricey purveyors of antiques, clothing, and gifts ply their trade on tourists from around the world.

There used to be two shipyards in the town, and from 1754 there was a West Indies warehouse next to the town dock, where goods from Africa and the Indies were unloaded for redistribution across the state. It was next to that warehouse at the Hayden Shipyards that America built its first warship, *Oliver Cromwell*, in 1776.

It is therefore fitting that the Connecticut River Foundation's **Connecticut River Museum** at Steamboat Dock in Essex now occupies the 1813-vintage Hayden Chandlery and General Store at the end of Main Street. The museum traces the history of Connecticut by tracing the history of the Connecticut River and of steam power. Among the exhibits is a gorgeous scale model of the Victorian pleasure ship, *City of Hartford,* which sank in the Connecticut River on March 29, 1876, after striking and carrying away the Middletown railroad bridge. Another model shows David Bushnell's 1775-vintage *American Turtle,* the first submarine ever constructed. One of the most interesting (and appropriate) exhibits is a model of the *Oliver Cromwell.* The museum also contains nautical paintings, shipbuilding tools, and memorabilia.

COAST AND COUNTRY

Be sure to ring the brass bell from a turn-of-the-century steamship (next to a sign requesting visitors to ring it just once). Open April 1 through December 31, Tuesday through Sunday, 10:00 A.M. to 5:00 P.M. Gift shop. Admission. Research library and reading room usable for a separate fee. Call (860) 767–8269. Web address: www.ctriver museum.org. E-mail: crm@ctrivermuseum.org.

Before looking at the exhibits in the Connecticut River Museum, you might want to actually spend some time on the water, maybe even see some of the eagles that inhabit the river's banks. If so, you are within a few yards of your embarkation point. Eagle-spotting and feeding cruises along the Connecticut regularly depart from **Steamboat Dock** next to the Connecticut River Museum. Feeding times are 8:00 to 11:00 A.M., February and March. Call (860) 443–7259.

If you've never visited the 1776-vintage **Griswold Inn,** don't leave Essex without doing so. People who know and love this place often call it the "Gris" (pronounced "Griz"). Located at 36 Main Street, about 100 yards from the river, the inn has fourteen rooms, three petite suites, and eight suites, all with private bath and telephones. The Garden Suite has two double beds and a full bath upstairs and a living room with a wood fireplace downstairs.

The Gris serves lunch and dinner daily Monday through Saturday, plus a Sunday brunch in the form of the justly famous Hunt Breakfast. This tradition goes back to the War of 1812, when officers of the British Army, which was then occupying Essex, forcefully suggested that the establishment start serving a regular Sunday Hunt Breakfast. Today the Hunt Breakfast table groans with an array of food that includes fried chicken, lamb kidneys and mushrooms, and creamed ham and eggs over English muffins. It's almost, but not quite, enough to make you forgive the British for burning New London during the same war.

A number of the inn's downstairs rooms have been turned into dining rooms. You can, for example, eat in the book-lined library or in the Steamboat Room with its lifelike mural of steamboating on the river. No matter where you land, you'll have an interesting experience. Open throughout the year except for Christmas Eve and Christmas Day. Call (860) 767–1776.

If the river formed Essex's early history, the railroad had much to do with its later development. The **Valley Railroad Company** on Route 154 was chartered in 1868. It still runs a steam train, with an optional riverboat ride, along the Connecticut River. Four or more trains per day make the 12-mile round-trip from Essex to Deep River, and all but the last train connect with the riverboat. Boats make a round-trip from Deep River to Gillette Castle and East Haddam. Before or after the excursion, guests can tour a variety of vintage train cars, visit the gift and snack shops (both in old railroad cars), or check out at the carbarn. The railroad runs a varying schedule from May through October and from Thanksgiving through Christmas. Generally, tickets are available at the station in Essex, but specials such as a *Murder Mystery Train* and a *Ghost Train* may require reservations. Modest children's fares; somewhat steeper adult fares. Call (860) 767–0103 or (800) 277–3987. Web address: www.valleyrr.com. E-mail: valley.railroad@snet.net.

The Griswold Inn

Essex used to be famous for manufacturing piano keys, and Ivoryton was the center of the ivory trade that supported that industry. In fact the town's name derives from the fact that it used to import "ivory by the ton." Both the legal ivory trade of olden days and the local piano works have ceased to be. Now the main source of music in Essex is the *Museum of Fife & Drum* (62 North Main Street in Ivoryton), where the Company of Fifes and Drummers is headquartered. Exhibits trace the development of military parades in America from the Revolutionary War to the present day and include many uniforms and musical instruments, including drums dating back to 1793. There's a special display of Civil War–era musical instruments. This is the only museum in the world devoted to fife and drum, so don't miss it if you're in the area. Open weekends, 1:00 to 5:00 P.M., June 30 through September 30 or by appointment. Note the museum is closed the third weekend of July and fourth weekend of August. Admission. Call (860) 399–6519 or (860) 526–5940. Visit them on the Web at www.companyoffifeanddrum.org/museum.html. E-mail at companyhq@companyoffifeanddrum.org.

Ivoryton is also home to one of the state's better inns. Named for a spectacular 200-year-old tree that graces its front yard, the *Copper Beech Inn* at 46 Main Street (Route 9, exit 3), offers two styles of accommodation. For the traditional-minded, the elegant 1890-vintage main building boasts four guestrooms with antique and country furnishings. The refurbished carriage house in the rear has nine rooms with a mix of more modern amenities and traditional furnishings. The inn's award-winning country-French restaurant opens to the public for dinner, with seatings on Wednesday and Thursday, from 5:30 to 7:30 P.M.; Friday, 5:30 to 8:30 P.M.; Saturday, 5:30 to 9:00 P.M.; Sunday, 3:00 to 7:00–8:00 P.M.; and Sunday prix fixe lunch, 1:00 to 3:00 P.M. Call (860) 767–0330 for reservations.

Settled in 1635 as part of Old Saybrook, the sleepy village of Deep River is known throughout the state as the site of the *Ancient Muster,* held the third Saturday of each July. At that time the tiny village on the Connecticut welcomes thousands of visitors who come to witness an historical pageant staged by a hundred fife and drum corps. Call the Connecticut River Valley & Shoreline Visitors Council at (800) 486–3346 for more information.

The rest of the year, not much happens in Deep River. History lives mainly in the *1840 Stone House* on South Main Street, where the local historical society maintains a small museum filled with such items

The XYZ Bank Robber

*T*his romantic Connecticut folktale reads more like a story from the Old West than old New England. On a mid-December day in 1899, four men tried to rob the Deep River Savings Bank. Unfortunately for them, but fortunately for the citizens of Deep River, the bank had been tipped that a robbery was likely. When the four robbers arrived at the bank, one of them tried to pry open a window. Captain Harry Tyler, a bank guard, felled the would-be robber with one shot. His companions in crime turned tail and ran. The robber's body was carried to the local undertaker, where it was examined and photographed. No identification was found on the body and no one turned up to claim it. After the news of the aborted robbery became known, Mr. Tyler received an anonymous letter asking that the young robber be buried under a headstone marked XYZ. And so he was interred in Fountain Hill Cemetery. Every year for almost forty years, a woman, her identity shielded by a flowing black veil, arrived in Deep River to lay flowers on the grave. The citizens of Deep River, true to their mind-your-own-business Yankee heritage, never questioned her and let her carry out her sad duty without interference. The Deep River Savings Bank is now Citizens Bank.

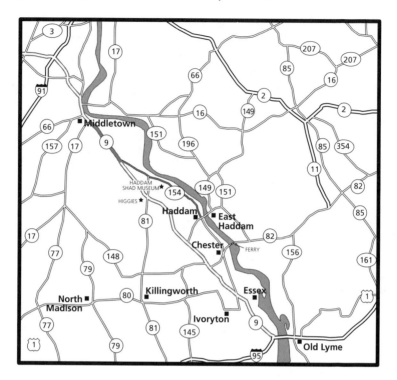

A Road Trip through the Connecticut River Valley's Past:

Route 154 between Middletown and Deep River

*T*he sky-blue, Connecticut-shaped road sign reads SCENIC ROAD NEXT 9.2 MILES. For most of those miles, Route 154 winds through some of Connecticut's prettiest country. It's part of what gives the Coast and Country region its Country tag. In its day the road has served as both a dirt path and a commercial turnpike, but today it lives its life as a quiet country road.

Heading south from Middletown toward Haddam, taking Route 9 to Route 154, you'll come upon a large rock set well back from the road. This is **Bible Rock** and its cleft marks the

line between Middletown and Haddam. Look carefully because the rock is well back from the road and easy to miss when leaves cover the trees.

Located about .3 mile from the junction of Routes 81 and 154 on Route 154 north of Higganum Center is a Connecticut institution called **Higgies** (also known as Higgies Roadside Eatery). This restaurant has been around since 1945 and has a reputation for the "best dogs and shakes" in the area. The owner prides herself on using only top-quality products, and "real hard ice cream, none of that soft serve stuff." The shakes must be pretty good because customers show up as regular as clockwork. A shake, flanked by a couple of chili dogs topped with a homemade meat sauce made from a recipe that's more than forty years old makes a perfect nostalgic lunch. The restaurant has a small dining room, but the best way to enjoy a Higgies lunch is outside at a picnic table under the trees. Open daily from about the first of May through Halloween. Monday to Saturday 11:00 A.M. to 8:00 P.M., Sunday, noon to 8:00 P.M. Call (860) 345–4403.

Continue south on Route 154 and you'll pass some beautiful Victorian, Beaux Arts, and Gothic Revival houses. About 2 miles out of Higganum Center, there's a former Catholic church, now a private residence, perched overlooking the Connecticut River, the perfect brooding realization of Gothic architecture.

Another famous spot on Route 154 is the **Pilot House,** another local institution. Its claim to fame is a secret relish served with sandwiches. This is one of those ramshackle drive-in restaurants that families make annual pilgrimages to. Open Tuesday through Sunday, 11:00 A.M. to 9:00 P.M. from May through late October. At the end of the drive, you'll end up at the East Haddam Swing Bridge and the Goodspeed Opera House. It always leaves us scratching our heads and marveling at someone's inventiveness as the bridge slowly swings parallel to the river to allow boats to pass and then just as slowly swings back to allow cars to pass.

as nineteenth-century furnishings, maritime memorabilia, locally made cut glass, and Indian artifacts. Open July and August on Tuesday, Thursday, and Sunday from 2:00 to 4:00 P.M. Donation requested. Call (860) 526–5685.

Our grannies called armoires clothespresses or wardrobes and used them in place of closets. Today, armoires are hot properties for storing televisions, VCRs, DVDs, and computers, and we've never seen a better stock than at **Irish Country Furniture,** at the intersection of Union Street and Route 154, in Deep River. The shop also stocks wooden hutches, farm tables, and kitchen chairs, in short, everything you need to furnish your house in country style. All pieces are imported; in fact a huge container arrives from Ireland several times a year loaded with goodies. Prices are excellent, much better than most antiques stores. Open Wednesday through Sunday, 10:00 A.M. to 5:00 P.M. and by appointment. Call (860) 526–9757.

Deep River has another really neat store that's worth a separate side trip to see. *The Great American Trading Company Factory Outlet Store* (39 Main Street) occupies a historic building once used by the Underground Railroad; the story is on a plaque on the building's exterior. The company

Old Saybrook Trivia

The Ingram House in Old Saybrook is—at least as far as we know—the only octagonal house still standing in Connecticut. It was purchased, prefab, from the Sears-Roebuck catalog and constructed on site in about 1890. The Old Saybrook Chamber of Commerce offers a walking-tour booklet of many interesting sites in Old Saybrook, including the Ingram House. Stop by the chamber's office on Main Street (Route 154) to pick up a copy or call the chamber at (860) 388–3266 for more information. The Chamber of Commerce is open Monday through Friday from 9:00 A.M. to 5:00 P.M. On the Web at www.oldsaybrookct.com.

itself manufactures for various merchandisers those spiffy and expensive wooden games, toys, boxes, and marbles you see in the avalanche of yupoid catalogs that hit your home a couple of months before Christmas. The outlet store sells seconds—which could mean nothing more than a small mar on the finish or some smudged paint —at very reasonable prices. For a fraction of the dollars you might send that catalog company, you can put together an inlaid and beautifully painted Chinese Checkers board, or a set of marbles (sold by the pound), or a box of just about any size or shape. The gorgeous wooden boxes are beautifully mitered with the kind of solid dovetailed joints you don't often see these days. On a recent visit, they were selling nicely balanced seconds of wooden yo-yos for half a buck. This is a nice, old-fashioned place to introduce youngsters to toys that run without batteries and chips. Open Monday through Sunday, 10:00 A.M. to 5:00 P.M. Call (860) 526–4335.

Being contrarians by nature, we visit the Shore in the winter when the crowds are gone. Unfortunately, most of the clam shacks and ice cream stands where we like to eat close up in the off-season. That's why we're glad **Johnny Ad's,** 910 Boston Post Road, in Old Saybrook, stays open year-around. Johnny Ad's is something of a shoreline landmark. In the summer, it's a popular destination for tourists, in the winter the locals have it all to themselves. Depending on the season, you can eat inside in the restaurant or take your food outdoors to the picnic tables and fight the seagulls for it. The lobster roll is the genuine, butter-drenched Shore favorite and the fried whole-belly clams are crunchy and briny. Open 11:00 A.M. to 3:00 P.M. on Monday and Tuesday; 11:00 A.M. to 4:30 P.M. Wednesday and Thursday; 11:00 A.M. to 7:30 P.M. Saturday; 11:00 A.M. to 6:00 P.M. Sunday. Call (860) 388–4032 for information.

In Old Saybrook itself, there's an old building worth checking out. The **James Pharmacy** at 2 Pennyworth Lane played host to General Lafayette in 1824, as the sign outside states. Beside its gorgeous marble counters, vintage tables and chairs, and lucious ice-cream creations, it is also notable for being a pharmacy and soda fountain once owned by Ada

Portland Trivia

Portland supplied so much brownstone for Manhattan town houses that it was called the "city that changed the face of New York City."

James, who, in 1917, became the state's first black female pharmacist. Open Wednesday through Sunday from noon to 10:00 P.M. Call (860) 395–1229 for more information.

Appropriately, Chester is also home to a four-star establishment widely respected as one of the best French restaurants in the state. Specializing in French country cooking, **Restaurant du Village** (59 Main Street, P.O. Box 377) has long been noted for quaint charm and quality cuisine. Its already outstanding reputation has been enhanced under owners Michel and Cynthia Keller. Michel does most of the cooking, while Cynthia manages the house, but both are noted chefs. The menu changes seasonally, with crusty fresh-baked breads, tasty soups, and to-die-for desserts as a constant. Michel has been adding to the menu unique variations on dishes from his native Alsace. There is also an excellent and surprisingly affordable wine list. Open for dinner Tuesday through Sunday, 5:30 to 9:00 P.M.; Sunday from 5:00 to 8:00 P.M. Call (860) 526–5301. There are two seatings an evening; reservations strongly suggested.

If driving through the Connecticut Valley has whetted your appetite for shad roe, then head for **Me & McGee Restaurant,** 40 Saybrook Road (in the Higganum section of Haddam). It's one of the few places we know that still takes time to prepare this Connecticut springtime food. You can have your shad roe cooked in the traditional method with bacon or served with a piece of shad, cooked with lemon, garlic, and white wine. When shad isn't in season or if you aren't a shad fancier (we aren't), Me and McGee offers plenty of country-cooking delights. Breakfasts are approximately the size of Ohio. Try Emilie's Casserole, a toss of cheese, eggs, sausage, and home fries—all the bad breakfast stuff people adore. Lunch dishes are equally generous and interesting. Open daily for breakfast and lunch from 6:00 A.M. to 2:30 P.M. Call (860) 345–3777.

The **Sundial Herb Garden** on Hidden Lake Road in Higganum is actually a collection of formal gardens, including a seventeenth-century knot garden, an eighteenth-century-style garden, and a topiary garden with a fountain. There's also an herb shop and tearoom on site, and on Sundays the management offers "tea talks" that include a tour of the gardens followed by tea and dessert. Open for tea and garden tours by reservation. The shop is open January though mid-October on Friday and Saturday from 10:00 A.M. to 5:00 P.M. Call for Christmas shop hours. The gardens are open for browsing from mid-May to mid-October on Friday and Saturday from 10:00 A.M. to 5:00 P.M. Visit on the Web at www.sundial gardens.com. E-mail at sundialgardens@snet.net. Call (860) 345–4290.

O'Rourke's Diner at the end of Main Street by the bridge in Middletown is a slice of contemporary life in a classic setting. This place is popular with students and faculty from Wesleyan University, and it's not unusual for the college president to occupy a counter stool between an out-of-state tourist and a street person from one of Main Street's residential hotels. The building at 728 Main has been a diner since the early 1920s. In fact it's listed on the National Register of Historic Places. It's been altered some over the years, but the original establishment started life as a Mountain View dining car, the two hundred and twenty-third made, in an era when Mountain View was building some of America's most stylish diners. O'Rourke's recently celebrated half a century of ownership by the same family.

The current owner, Brian O'Rourke, started working in the diner, helping his uncle, when he was ten years old. Brian is a self-taught cook, which may be an advantage. The food here is plentiful and cheap as you would expect, but it's also quite imaginative. One newspaper has listed O'Rourke's Diner as one of the top ten places in the United States to get a good meal for under $10.

The lunch menu usually features half a dozen homemade soups. There may be, for example, a choice of gazpacho, Creole sausage and seafood chowder, clam chowder, and black bean. Entrees include such diner standbys as meat loaf; if you know and like diner food, you'll probably have a pretty good idea of what to order. Weekends, Brian does special breakfasts. Each month there's a special omelette; in July, for example, it's smoked salmon and asparagus topped with Hollandaise. There's also a different pancake special each week, like double blueberry (blueberry pancakes with blueberry syrup). O'Rourke's also does its own jams, breads, and muffins, including magnificent Irish soda bread and a terrific banana chocolate chip muffin. Open Tuesday through Friday, 4:30 A.M. to 3:00 P.M., and weekends, 4:30 A.M. to 1:00 P.M. Call (860) 346–6101.

Groton may get the lion's share of attention when it comes to subs, but Middletown has its own small gem of a submarine museum that grew out of one man's passion. Bernard Basatura, a retired machinist, has owned and operated his *Submarine Library Museum,* 440 Washington Street, for more than forty-three years. Today his museum contains dozens of submarine and naval artifacts donated from all over the world. Like many Nutmeggers, a visit to Groton whetted his appetite for subs and submarine paraphernalia. His collection spans everything from the periscope two-man, Japanese submarine, something of a rarity, to flooring from the *Nautilus,* the first nuclear-powered submarine.

Open April 1 to December 1 on weekends from 10:00 A.M. to 5:00 P.M. or by appointment. Call (860) 346–0388.

Don't leave Middletown without stopping at the **Middlesex Fruitery,** 191 Main Street. This is an old-fashioned, family-run greengrocer with primo produce. Not only do the owners personally select your produce for you, but they carry it out to your car. Open Tuesday through Saturday, 8:30 A.M. to 5:30 P.M. Call (860) 346–4372.

Mazotta's Restaurant & Bakery, 650 South Main Street, Middletown. For as long as we can remember, Mazotta's has been a place to go for hefty portions of good Italian food, friendly service, and reasonable prices. It's such a mainstay of our life that we often forget how good it truly is. We were reminded when we took some visiting relatives out for a casual family dinner and had to pry a family member off the dessert case. (You walk past the dessert case to get to the dining room.) Hard to believe but some areas of this country are cannoli-deprived. Any of the traditional Italian menu offerings are good choices. We like the Sicilian orange and onions salad composed of thinly sliced sweet orange, purple onion, and black olive tossed with a light vinegar and oil dressing. The pastas are marvelous, especially the veggie lasagna. Lighter appetites can opt for a small pizza or a hot oven grinder. And then there's dessert. We always go for the cannoli, but we certainly wouldn't pass up the Italian cookies or rum cake if someone happened to drop some on our plate. All of the desserts go well with the house cappuccino or espresso. Open Tuesday to Sunday. The bakery opens at 8:30 A.M., and the restaurant serves lunch and dinner starting at 11:00 A.M. Closed Monday. Call (860) 346–4146 for information.

South and east of Middletown at the junction of Routes 66 and 147 in the village of Middlefield is another of our favorite stops for road food. With its rural surroundings, **Guida's Drive-in** (pronounced *Guy-das,* not *G-we-das*) is just about a perfect place for a springtime hot-dog lunch. The claim to fame here is the "10-inch pedigreed hot dogs," which come sizzling from the grill, nestled in a toasted bun. The accompanying chili sauce is hot, spicy, and vinegary and just right with mustard and onions. The shakes are honest, luxuriously thick, and made from hard ice cream the way God intended. Open Monday through Saturday, 6:00 A.M. to 8:00 P.M. and Sunday, 8:00 A.M. to 7:00 P.M. Call (860) 349–9039.

East Haddam is the heart of the lower Connecticut River Valley's resort country and was once a mecca for New Yorkers seeking to avoid the crowding closer to the shore. It isn't as popular as it once was, but the area is still liberally sprinkled with holiday camps, lodges, gift shops, antiques stores, and similar establishments.

East Haddam is the only town in the state to occupy both sides of the Connecticut, and as you approach the eastern part of the township from across the river, you pass over the longest swinging bridge in New England. This uncommon bridge actually pivots sideways to open a path for passing boats. The first thing you see on the other side is a glorious three-story American Gothic palace that looks like a wedding cake and dominates the East Haddam skyline. This symphony in gingerbread is the **Goodspeed Opera House.** Founded by William Goodspeed over a century ago, the Goodspeed is widely known as "the birthplace of the American musical," thanks to the number of Broadway hits that received their first tryouts there. An extended summer season —from April through December—of professional theater is still offered in this recently renovated structure. Call (860) 873–8668 for details. Visit on the Web at www.goodspeed.org.

While you're in East Haddam, stop by **St. Stephen's Church** in the center of town. The church bell up in the belfry was cast for a Spanish monastery in A.D. 815 and is probably the oldest bell in the New World. Behind the church is the **Nathan Hale Schoolhouse,** a one-room establishment where Hale taught in 1773–74. Originally called Union School, it was renamed for Hale after he became an acknowledged American hero. Today the schoolhouse is a museum containing Hale possessions and displays of artifacts relating to local history. The church and school are open between Memorial Day and Labor Day, weekends and holidays, 2:00 to 4:00 P.M. Admission. Call (860) 873–3399.

The real name of the **Merchant House,** 1583 Saybrook Road, in Haddam is Ye Olde Tyler Merchant House, but we call it Arts and Crafts heaven. We're slowly transitioning our home furniture from Victorian to Art and Crafts and Mission, so when we drove past the Merchant House and saw the huge banner advertising Stickley reproductions, we pulled over so fast we almost caused an accident. (Apologies to the nice lady in the Blazer who was behind us!) Pick a furniture maker's name from the Art and Crafts and Mission movements and you'll find high-quality reproductions at the Merchant House. We love the oak Harvey Ellis writing desk and covet the prairie settles. There's way too much on display to do justice to the selection, so just drop by to browse and drool. Besides the glorious furniture, the Merchant House carries lots of gift items like potpourri and fragrant lotions, creams, and potions. The Christmas shop carries some of the most interesting and unusual ornaments and decorations around; we cherish the teensy Arts and Crafts mice we picked up two years ago. Stuff from the Christmas shop starts flying off the shelves in early October, so shop early. Take a minute to peruse the watercolors of historic and well-known Connecticut attractions; they make wonderful souvenirs or presents to commemorate a special occasion. One of our friends gave his wife a watercolor of Simsbury Chart House, the place where he proposed marriage. You'll see drawings of lots of the places described in this book. Monday through Sunday, 10:00 A.M. to 7:00 P.M.; Friday until 9:00 P.M. Hours can vary depending on the season; call ahead: (860) 345–4195 or (800) 613–0105.

Historians don't agree on how the **Devil's Hopyard** in East Haddam got its name, but they do agree that there are a lot of fascinating legends surrounding the 860-acre state park outside of the town of East Haddam. The most lurid one has Satan himself playing in the house band while the locally renowned Black Witches of Haddam held sabbat in the area. According to this legend, Mister Scratch would sit on a rock near the 60-foot cascade of Chapman's Falls in the center of the park and play while his minions cavorted.

Nutmeggers' Yankee forebearers were kind of obsessed with Satan, and the sabbat origin certainly *seems* reasonable. Sadly, the origin of the park's strange name is probably more commonplace than legend admits. There are those who maintain that a local farmer and noted bootlegger named Dibble once cultivated a hopyard along Eight Mile River and brewed his harvest into a particularly potent moonshine. According to this version, the park's name began as "Dibble's Hopyard," which later evolved into "Devil's Hopyard."

Whatever the true origin of its name, there is no denying that this isolated, heavily forested, and reputedly haunted park is a truly spooky place at night. During daylight, though, the Devil's Hopyard is one of the most popular picnic spots in this part of Connecticut, and the big rocks around Chapman Falls are especially nice for spreading a blanket and whiling away a summer's afternoon. For a daytime visit, take Route 156

(Hopyard Road) and follow the signs. There are some picnic shelters scattered around the park, but most people just lay out a spread near the falls. The park is open from 8:00 A.M. until sunset. Call (860) 566–2304.

The granite pile that is Hadlyme's *Gillette Castle* (67 River Road, off Route 82) was built over a five-year period from 1914 to 1919 as the retirement home of the famous actor William Gillette, who designed the structure, including its unique, hand-carved interior furnishings and appointments. Built on 122 acres of wooded land, the twenty-four-room mansion is now a museum, kept almost as it was when Gillette lived there. Among the actor's possessions on display are his collection of over one hundred scrapbooks filled with pictures of felines; like all sane men Gillette was an ardent cat lover. Gillette's best-known stage role was as British detective Sherlock Holmes, and Gillette Castle also houses the largest collection of Holmessiana in the world, including a complete recreation of Holmes's sitting room at 221B Baker Street.

Gillette specified in his will that the property not "fall into the hands of some blithering saphead who has no conception of where he is or with what he is surrounded." Today, Gillette Castle is owned by the state, and those who manage the property seem to have a very fine idea indeed of where they are and with what they are surrounded. While there is ample parking, the facilities are generally modest, and the beauty of this spot has been well preserved. Whatever you do, don't forget to bring a camera when you visit. The view down the Connecticut River from the castle's broad terraces is one of the best in the state. In late winter and early spring, before the facility opens for the season, you can sometimes stand on the main terrace in splendid isolation and watch eagles soar above the river. If you visit during the tourist season, be sure to spring for a tour of the castle's interior, which is, if anything, even more eccentric than the exterior.

Gillette Castle and the associated gift shop and snack shop are open daily, 11:00 A.M. to 5:00 P.M., Memorial Day to Columbus Day; weekends from 10:00 A.M. to 4:00 P.M. between Columbus Day and the last weekend before Christmas. There is a modest admission for house tours, but none to walk the grounds or picnic in any of the delightful glens and groves that have been set aside for this purpose. When this edition went to press, Gillette Castle was closed for renovations until Memorial Day 2002, so call ahead to avoid disappointment. Visitors can still walk around on the grounds, but cannot tour the castle. Call (860) 526–2336. To read the press release about renovations and monitor opening day announcement, go to www.dep.state.ct.us/whatshape/press/2001/ps0326.htm.

Castle enthusiasts recommend approaching the castle for the first time from across the Connecticut river in Chester. Just follow Route 148 to the river and take the **Chester-Hadlyme Ferry** across. This is the second oldest continuously operating ferry in the United States (after the Glastonbury–Rocky Hill Ferry). It runs Monday through Friday from 7:00 A.M. to 6:45 P.M. and weekends from 10:30 A.M. to 5:00 P.M. between mid-April and mid-November and can accommodate up to eight cars at a time. There's a minimal charge. By taking the ferry, you'll see the site of the castle much as William Gillette first saw it.

Gillette Castle

Allegra Farm on Town Street (Route 82) in East Haddam calls itself a "living history museum." We call it a chance to see what transportation was like in the nineteenth century. In fact, horses and carriages from Allegra Farm were featured in the movie *Amistad*. The museum, located in a post-and-beam carriage house and livery stables, is chockful of carriages, sleighs, coaches, and any other horse-drawn vehicle you can imagine. One you've taken in all the vehicles, you can go outdoors and check out the creatures that draw them as well as some chickens, sheep, and a llama. We love the English Shires and Percherons, gentle giant plow horses, and the sweet miniature horses. Horse-drawn carriage, sleigh, or hayrides are available on reservation. All the horse-drawn rides provide refreshments that vary with the seasons, from iced mint tea to hot chocolate served by a campfire. In the spring and summer, carriages from Allegra Farm are a familiar sight carrying wedding parties throughout the Connecticut River valley. The museum is open by appointment. Horse-drawn rides are available by reservation. You'll find Allegra Farm on Route 82, about 2 miles from Gillette Castle and just past Ye Old Christmas Shop. Call (860) 873–9658 for information and reservations.

Moodus, near Mount Tom, is the site of another curious phenomenon steeped in legend. At more or less regular intervals, loud noises like the voices of the damned can be heard throughout the town. These are the famous "*Moodus Noises.*"

The Native Americans said these noises were the voice of an evil spirit who lived on Mount Tom. Other stories blame giant peels growing in caverns beneath Moodus for the sounds. Early colonists attributed the noises to an ongoing battle between the Good Witches of East Haddam and the feared Black Witches of Haddam. According to this myth, when the battle between good and evil goes on too long, a benevolent spirit, Old Machemoodus (for whom the town of Moodus is named), awakes and waves his sapphire wand, clearing away the evil witches and ending the battle. The Black Witches of Haddam then gather their powers once again, and the battle is rejoined, causing more Moodus noises.

According to geologists, the true cause of the noises is the rubbing of tectonic plates against each other along a fault line, a phenomenon known to generate earthquakes. In fact, in 1791, Moodus was shaken by two quakes, which were felt as far away as New York and Boston. A future quake is expected sometime during the next few centuries, and there have been predictions that some day Moodus will be swallowed up by the fault and disappear into the earth forever.

The *Florence Griswold Museum,* 96 Lyme Street in Old Lyme, isn't a particularly large museum, but it's one of the nicer ones in Connecticut. Back in the nineteenth century, Florence Griswold turned her ship-

Baa-d to the Bone

*O*K, visiting **Sankow's Beaver Brook Farm,** *139 Beaver Brook Road in Old Lyme, is one of those times when we carnivores hang our heads in shame. It's hard to reconcile the sight of sweet, gamboling spring lambs with the succulent rack of lamb we order in restaurants. The farm does sell its lamb meat (and very good lamb meat it is), but we never have the heart to buy it. Instead, we major in their incredibly fluffy and luxurious sheepskins (wonderful baby gifts) and their all-natural woolen clothing, such as vests, hats,*

and very cute sweaters finished with pewter farm-animal buttons—all made from the farm's own sheep. Farm owner Susan Sankow is happy to show you her flock, and farm tours are available by reservation. Occasionally Susan teaches classes on spinning. At Christmas, things turn festive with visits by Santa and hayrides through the fields. Farm store is open daily from 9:00 A.M. to 4:00 P.M. Call (860) 434–2843 or (800) 501–WOOL for information about farm tours, wool products, special events, and classes.

captain father's 1841 house into a sort of boardinghouse and salon for painters. The light is supposed to be particularly good in this part of the state, something to do with large bodies of reflective water; the shore is very near, and the Lieutenant River runs behind the house. Anyway, a whole community of artists ended up boarding at the Griswold home, where they worked, played, and inspired each other to greater efforts.

As a result Old Lyme came to be a major center of American impressionism, and the doors and woodwork throughout Florence Griswold's home came to be decorated with original paintings by the likes of Willard Metcalf, Henry Ward Ranger, and Childe Hassam. The vast Griswold collection, including the works of some 110 local artists, is displayed for the public inside the Griswold home. The museum is open from April through December from 10:00 A.M. to 5:00 P.M. Open Sunday from 1:00 to 5:00 P.M. Open January through March on Wednesday to Sunday from 1:00 to 5:00 P.M. Call (860) 434–5542. Visit on the Web at: www.flogris.org.

Near the museum (at number 100) is the *Bee and Thistle Inn.* Built in 1756, this place has enough charm for several country inns. The Bee and Thistle occupies five acres along the Lieutenant River. Half of the dozen or so guest rooms have fireplaces. All are beautifully decorated, with big comfortable beds smothered in quilts or toasty afghans, just right for burrowing. Once in your bed, if you don't want to leave it, relax. The inn offers breakfast in bed, the ultimate treat in a stressful world. Alas, lunch and dinner are served only in the dining room. The lunch menu tends toward hearty homemade soups and light dewy-fresh salads. The dinner menu is mostly American cuisine, with French and Asian touches, topped off with the inn's famous dessert extravaganzas. A wonderful clam chowder is served here, with sweet fresh clams, rugged salt pork, potatoes, rich cream, and just a whisper of thyme. The menu changes four times a year to take advantage of New England's seasonal bounties, but the bread basket always comes with hot scones and honey. Open year-round except for Christmas Eve, Christmas Day, and the two weeks after New Year's. Breakfast, lunch, and dinner are served daily except Tuesday. Breakfast is from 8:00 to 10:00 A.M., lunch is from 11:30 A.M. to 2:00 P.M., and dinner is from 6:00 to 9:00 P.M. There's also a Sunday brunch from 11:00 A.M. to 2:00 P.M. From November through early May, tea is served Monday, Wednesday, and Thursday from 3:30 to 5:00 P.M. Prix fixe; reservations required. Call (860) 434–1667.

Old Lyme's *Nut Museum* out on number 303 Ferry Road is hard to classify. Truth is, there isn't universal agreement that this is a proper museum, despite the fact that the state lists it as such. Call it rather an inspired madness. Founder Elizabeth Tashjian clearly loves nuts, and she is dedicated to elevating their status in the world. Her museum reflects her passion. As an aside, whatever you do, don't call her the "nut lady." She doesn't take it well. Two rooms in her Victorian Gothic home are given over to nut jewelry, nut carvings, nut paintings, nut toys, and nut sculpture. The "museum" is home to the world's largest nut, a 35-pound coco-de-mer grown on an island in the Indian Ocean. Open by appointment only. Admission is $3.00 and one nut. Call (860) 434-7636. Visit the Nut Museum on the Web to hear Ms. Tashjian's stirring rendition of "The Nut Anthem": www.roadsideamerica.com/nut/index.html.

We are dedicated to sleuthing out the places that "only the locals know," so we were happy to follow up on a tip from a friend and find *Flanders Fish Market and Restaurant*, 22 Chesterfield Road (Route 161) in East Lyme. It is a place you probably wouldn't find on your own, but once found, it becomes a regular on your "always-eat-here-when-at-the-Shore" list. It's an unpretentious place, where good food and friendly service are more important than tricky vertical presentations or whatever other food nonsense is in vogue these days. On the menu you'll find not only Shore-perennials like lobster bisque and oyster stew, but also the increasingly rare clear, broth-based clam chowder. We like their clam fritters, the hot lobster roll, and the blackened swordfish. The side dishes, sometimes forgotten in fish places, are especially good, including the Flanders fries and the sweet potatoes, either fried or baked. For dessert, try the crisp of the day. The restaurant knows how to treat kids well, so fish-detesting kids can opt for the peanut butter and jelly sandwich and a milkshake and come way happy and well fed. On nice days, it's fun to take your food outside and eat in the picnic area. If you liked your lobster so much you want to share it with the folks back home, they ship lobsters anywhere in the United States. Lobster line: (800) 242-6055 (in Connecticut); (800) 638-8189 (nationwide). Open Sunday through Friday from 8:00 A.M. to 9:00 P.M., Friday and Saturday from 8:00 A.M. to 10:00 P.M. We found the restaurant a bit tricky to find, so try these directions: exit 74 from I-95, take a left at the end of the exit, go through the traffic light and watch for restaurant on the left. On the Web at www.flandersfish.com.

One of the nicest off-the-beaten-path places we've found lately has the additional, always welcome, advantage of being free. The *Connecticut Department of Environmental Protection Marine Headquarters,* Ferry Road, Old Lyme, offers a way-cool boardwalk with the added allure of that universal kid favorite, trains. This is a wonderful, out-of-the-way destination for parents and kids. (Don't be put off by the DEAD END sign on Ferry Road. Just go all the way to the end, and turn into DEP marine headquarters; the parking lot is beyond the main building.)

The boardwalk meanders along the river and ends at a marsh. At the marsh you'll find an elevated platform, ideal for bird-watching or just watching the river flow. Markers along the walk identify the different animals you might see. The fisherfolk who congregate along the river are more than willing to tell tales of the big one that got away to willing little ears.

The boardwalk also rambles under a railway bridge that gives you a very unusual view of speeding trains: Underneath! Free. The best time of year to visit is spring through fall. Trains cross the bridge mornings (about 9:30 A.M. to 1:00 P.M.) and afternoons (around 4:00 to around 6:30 P.M.). The site offers free parking, is handicapped accessible, and had well-maintained picnic tables and bathroom facilities. The park closes at sunset.

Mohegan Country

The *Sands World Wide Games Factory Outlet* on Mill Street in Colchester has a stupendous selection of puzzles, games, and related items. Items range in sophistication from kiddie games (ages five and up) to heavy-duty adult strategy games, from Lego blocks to *Dungeons & Dragons*. For those who refuse to let their kid-side show, there are even some beautifully crafted chess sets, chess being an acceptably "adult" form of play. There is also a selection of new and discontinued arts-and-crafts items. Most of the inventory is of American invention, but there are also some interesting foreign products on display.

Most products are discounted 30 to 40 percent, with seconds discounted up to 60 percent. The store also sells some first-quality current games at retail prices. Open Tuesday through Friday, 9:00 A.M. to 4:30 P.M. and Thursday, until 6:00 P.M.; Saturday, 10:00 A.M. to 4:00 P.M. Call (860) 537–2325.

Located off Route 16, the 1872-vintage *Comstock Bridge* (now honorably retired) is one of Connecticut's three remaining covered bridges. It is now used mainly by salmon fishermen and folks just watching the river flow. The handicapped area was designed by Peter Reneson, a polio victim, who grew up in Colchester. Call (860) 267–2519.

Lebanon and the Jonathan Trumbull family are practically synonymous. Trumbull was the only colonial governor (1769–1784) to support the American War of Independence. He organized George Washington's supply line almost single-handedly, and it was largely thanks to Trumbull that Connecticut came to be called "the Supply State." Today there are at least three buildings in Lebanon associated with the Trumbulls and the governor's historic efforts to support the Revolution. All three are located very near each other on West Town Street (Route 87) on the green.

The 1735 *Jonathan Trumbull House* was once the governor's home. Today it is furnished with period furniture and administered by the Daughters of the American Revolution. Also on this site is *Wadsworth Stable.* George Washington didn't sleep there, but his horse did. Finally, the property also contains the home of Dr. William Beaumont, the "father of physiology." The *Beaumont home* houses a display of surgical instruments. Open Tuesday through Saturday, 2:00 to 5:00 P.M. Adult admission. Call (860) 642–7558.

The 1769-vintage *Jonathan Trumbull, Jr., House* is a center-chimney farmhouse with eight intricately carved corner fireplaces and a gorgeous original cherry staircase with a molded rail. Today it is furnished with both reproductions and period antiques. Open on Saturday from May 30 to the last Saturday in September from 1:30 P.M. to 4:30 P.M.; on Sunday from May 30 to August 31 from 1:30 P.M. to 4:30 P.M. Adult admission. Call (860) 642–6100.

Built in 1727 as the *Trumbull Family Store,* the *Revolutionary War Office* on West Town Street was where the Council of Safety met to plan the logistical effort that kept Washington's army in the field during the Revolutionary War. Open Saturday, 1:30 to 5:00 P.M., May 30 through the last Saturday in September. Adult admission. Call (860) 642–7558.

Located at the confluence of the Yantic and Shetucket Rivers, Norwich was founded in the second half of the seventeenth century. By 1776 it was the second largest city in Connecticut, and it was a major Patriot stronghold during the Revolutionary War. Among Norwich's sons who fought in that war was Benedict Arnold, the talented American general who tried to turn West Point over to the British and who later burned New London. *Benedict Arnold's birthplace* at 299 Washington Street can still be seen today.

A block from Arnold's birthplace is the *Christopher Leffingwell House* (348 Washington Street), a unique restoration of two small saltbox houses joined together to form a single home. The oldest portion dates from 1675. In 1701, Ensign Thomas Leffingwell opened a tavern on the premises, and there his son entertained George Washington in 1776 when the general was on his way to Lebanon. Open April 1 to December

1 on Tuesday through Sunday from 1:00 P.M. to 4:00 P.M. or by appointment. Admission. Call (860) 889–9440.

There must be a dozen other historic buildings scattered along Washington and Town Streets, most within easy walking distance of each other. One with an interesting history is the *Samuel Huntington House* at 34 East Town Street. Samuel Huntington was Norwich's most prominent citizen after Benedict Arnold; he signed the Declaration of Independence and presided over the signing of the Articles of Confederation. There's also the *Joseph Carpenter House,* which dates from the 1770s, when it was home to one of New England's most successful silversmiths. The homes are private and can be viewed only from the street.

Norwich also contains several sites of interest to fanciers of Native American lore. Over on Yantic Street by Yantic Falls is *Indian Leap.* After the Battle of East Great Plains in 1643, the Mohegans pursued a band of fleeing Narragansetts into this gorge, forcing them to jump to their deaths. And on Sachem Street you'll find the *Royal Indian Burial Ground,* the last resting place of Uncas, the Mohegan chief who gave Europeans the land on which the settlement of Norwich was constructed. President Andrew Jackson laid the cornerstone of Uncas's monument in 1833.

The *Slater Memorial Museum and Converse Art Gallery,* on the campus of the Norwich Free Academy, doesn't have the romantic lure of some of Norwich's historical attractions, but it's well worth a visit, especially if you've never been able to get to the Louvre or any of the other great European sculpture galleries. This imposing three-story Romanesque structure was built in 1888 to house a truly impressive collection of plaster casts of famous Greek, Roman, and Renaissance sculpture. The casts are still the main attraction; but in addition to that collection (one of the three finest in the United States), the museum also has displays of antique American and European furniture, Native Americans artifacts, textiles, and various fine art, including one of the best collections of Hudson River art in America. Open September through June from Tuesday to Friday, 9:00 A.M. to 4:00 P.M.; weekends, 1:00 to 4:00 P.M. Open July and August, from Tuesday through Sunday, 1:00 to 4:00 P.M. Modest admission. Call (860) 887–2506.

Early in the seventeenth century, a Pequot subchief named Uncas formed a new tribe, the Mohegans. During the Pequot Wars of 1638, Uncas and his people sided with the British, beginning a century of intimate involvement in the affairs of European settlers. The Mohegans and Pequots eventually united under Uncas's leadership, and they became a powerful force in southwestern Connecticut. The first major American novelist, James Fenimore Cooper, recounted part of their story in his 1826 sensation *The Last of the Mohicans,* one of his famous *Leatherstocking Tales.*

Actually, the Mohicans (Mohegans) didn't quite die out in the manner that Cooper suggests. There are about six hundred of them left, including thirty-five in Connecticut. In 1931, John Tantaquidgeon, a direct descendant of Chief Uncas, founded the **Tantaquidgeon Indian Museum** on the Norwich–New London Road (Route 32) in Uncasville. Here the culture and history of the Mohegans and other New England Indians are presented in a series of displays featuring artifacts of stone, wood, and bone made by Indian craftsmen, living and dead. Artifacts from other tribes of the Southeast, Southwest, and Plains are housed in their own sections. Open May through September, Tuesday through Sunday, 10:00 A.M. to 3:00 P.M. Donation requested. Call (860) 848–9145.

There are several other points of interest related to the Mohegans in Montville. Just 200 yards from the Tantaquidgeon Indian Museum is the **Mohegan Congregational Church,** an 1831 meetinghouse that is still in use. West of Mohegan Hill, off Raymond Hill Road, is **Cochegan Rock,** the site of secret meetings between Uncas and his councilors (and said to be the largest boulder in Connecticut). Farther north, near the village of Mohegan, is **Fort Shantok State Park,** which contains an old Indian fort and a Mohegan burial ground, among other points of interest.

Nestled in Niantic is an absolutely awesome children's museum, the **Children's Museum of Southeastern Connecticut,** 409 Main Street. Frequently children's museums overflow with activities for kids over five, but fall short for those under five, so this interactive educational center is a real discovery. The exhibits and activities are designed to appeal, but never talk down to, kids and are engaging enough to capture the attention of adults, too.

Nursery Rhyme Land is a wonderful place for toddlers to explore as is Kidsville, a kids-size town. The Discovery Room, best for kids six and up, brings the wonders of science to life. We liked the activity that lets kids "play doctor" and bandage and splint up each other or mom and dad. Throughout the year, the museum features a number of exhibits, field trips, seminars, and musical performances of interest to kids, including a respected summer camp program that focuses on the environment, science, and the arts. Admission. Open Tuesday through Saturday, 9:30 A.M. to 4:30 P.M.; Friday until 8:00 P.M.; Sunday from noon to 5:00 P.M. Open Memorial Day to Labor Day and school vacations from 9:30 A.M. to 4:30 P.M. Open Mondays during the summer and school holidays. A picnic area is available, with snacks sold from April through November. Admission; kids under 2, free. Call (860) 691–1255. Web address: www.Hcat.conncoll. edu/childrensmuseumsect.

Mystic derives its name from the Pequot Native American word Mistuket.

The Eastern Shore

I f you're planning a trip to Connecticut, you probably know as much as we do about Mystic, Mystic Seaport, and other Mystic attractions. After all, this is just about the most popular tourist destination in the state, and the folks at Mystic do a wonderful job of getting the word out about this attraction. All we'll say here is that Mystic Seaport is a grouping of some sixty buildings and four vessels from all over the New England coast that re-create life in an old Yankee seaport. There's lots to see and the admission is steep, so plan to arrive early to avoid crowds and to make the most of your time. Open April 6 to October 15, daily 9:00 A.M. to 5:00 P.M.; mid-June through August, 9:00 A.M. to 8:00 P.M. Call (860) 572–5315. Web address: www. mystic.org.

A neat place to stay in Mystic is the **Red Brook Inn,** 2750 Gold Star Highway, Mystic. Its description sounds lovely but pretty typical for a high-end B&B in a tourist spot. Guest rooms are in two historic colonial (1756) buildings on a beautifully landscaped, seven-acre property. Some of the ten antique-filled rooms have fireplaces and whirlpools. Unlike other inns, though, the Red Brook Inn has a ghost or several of them. Over the years, guests and staff report cold spots that move throughout the inn and the sounds of voices where no voice should be heard. Moderate to expensive. Call (860) 572–0349.

If you've come to Mystic, there's a good chance you arrived with children. That being the case, your best bet for lodging is probably the **Mystic Hilton,** 20 Coogan Boulevard; (800) HILTONS. It's close to the aquarium, the seaport, and Old Mystick Village. Best of all, they know what kids like, and the staff seem to genuinely like children. There are a plethora of child-oriented activities, such as face painting, magic shows, and kids' barbecues. Lots of amenities for big people, too. The restaurant, The Mooring, offers excellent seafood and desserts. Open year-round; moderate to high.

An nice alternative to the hustle and bustle of Mystic is Stonington. There's a lot to enjoy in this small town, and all of it at a quieter pace than Mystic.

The town of Stonington is perched on a mile-long peninsula so narrow that you can stand on some cross streets and see the ocean on either side. Were it not for the town's protected harbor, it is unlikely that anyone would ever have chosen to build in such a confined space. That harbor, however, made Stonington a center of New England's whaling and sealing industries in the first half of the nineteenth century. It also helped make Stonington an important railroad terminus. In the early days of railroading, before rail bridges crossed the state's major rivers, Stonington was on the most direct route between Boston and New

Eating in Mystic

*M*ystic has its share of formal dining, but we like its more relaxed family places. Number one on most lists for travelers to Mystic is **Mystic Pizza,** 56 West Main Street, Mystic. Until the movie Mystic Pizza came out, this was just another small town pizza parlor. Now it's a movie-trivia-buff pilgrimage. Everyone wants to see where a young Julia Roberts served up pies. Movie buffs will have a good time with all the movie memorabilia on the walls (and for sale) in the restaurant. The pizza's pretty good, but let's face it, the charm comes from eating in the same place the movie was filmed. Serves lunch and dinner. Call (860) 536–3700; Web address: dhinet.com/dtmystic/pizza/.

Next the to drawbridge at 2 Main Street you'll find **Mystic Drawbridge Ice Cream Shoppe,** a cute ice-cream parlor that locals claim has the best ice cream around. The Kona-coffee flavor, made from Hawaiian coffee ground on the premises, and the Barbados buttered rum come highly recommended. It's open daily. Call (860) 572–7978. By the way, that cute drawbridge is called a bascule (French for seesaw), and you'll have plenty of opportunity to contemplate its rare

beauty, because car traffic along Main Street goes into gridlock when it's raised to allow boats to pass.

Kitchen Little at 81½ Greenmanville Avenue, near Mystic Seaport, has been lauded in more travel guides and articles than you can shake a stick at. As you'd guess from the name, this is a small restaurant. In fact the breakfasts are almost bigger than the restaurant itself. Size and fame conspire to draw crowds, so be prepared for a short wait. Eggs, any way, shape, or form are big here, but we like the French toast or ham-and-cheese-stuffed pancake sandwich. Lunch offerings are equally good and generous; prices are beyond reasonable. Call (860) 536–2122 for hours and information.

You'll find the **Sea Swirl** at the junction of Route 1 and Route 27. When food pundits compile their "Best of" lists, the Sea Swirl is a perennial on the Best Fried Clam list. Without a doubt, this tiny drive-in is the best place in Connecticut for fried whole-belly clams. The other fried seafood offerings are similarly stellar. Open daily seasonally (roughly May through Columbus Day). Call (860) 536–3452.

York, and seventeen separate tracks once converged on the town. In those times, passengers arriving by rail from Boston had to board steamboats in Stonington harbor for the trip to New York.

At the height of Stonington's fortunes, the town's two main streets were packed cheek by jowl with commercial buildings and the fancy homes of wealthy merchants. Then whaling and sealing fell off, the railroad moved on, and Stonington, which lacked the real estate to expand into a bedroom community, was left frozen in the mid-nineteenth century. Most of the beautiful federal and Greek Rrevival homes are still there, only now they're B&Bs, restaurants, antiques stores, and crafts shops.

The town dock on Pearl Street (1 block west of Water Street and 1 block north of Grand Street) is an exception of sorts to Stonington's Brigadoonish aura; it's still a working fishing dock. In fact, Stonington has the only active fishing fleet left in Connecticut. Stonington's annual June *Blessing of the Fleet* is a festive event. You can get information and a free calendar of events by calling (800) TO-ENJOY. And by the way, it was from this harbor that Captain Nathaniel Palmer embarked on the 1820 sailing trip that resulted in the discovery of Antarctica.

Cannon Square, toward the south end of Market Street, marks the site where the Stonington militia successfully fought off the British in August 1814. It and the surrounding streets are the center of Stonington's historic district. Stroll up Main Street from the square (away from the Point) and admire the architecture of the 1827-vintage *Old Customs House* and the elegant 1780-vintage *Colonel Amos Palmer House,* both worth more than a passing glance.

Down at the end of Water Street (at number 7) is our favorite haunt in Stonington, the *Old Lighthouse Museum.* Originally constructed in 1823, this first government-operated lighthouse in Connecticut was moved to its present location in 1840. It is now a museum housing an eclectic collection of nineteenth-century portraits, whaling and fishing gear and related nautical paraphernalia, small exhibits on lighthouses and ice-harvesting, memorabilia from the Revolutionary War–era Battle of Stonington, antique riches from the town's China trade, and a children's room with an antique dollhouse. If you care to climb the narrow winding stairway to the top of the lighthouse, you'll be rewarded by a stunning view of Long Island Sound, including Fisher's Island. Open May through June and September through October from Tuesday through Sunday, 10:00 A.M. to 5:00 P.M. Open July and August daily from 10:00 A.M. to 5:00 P.M. Admission. Call (860) 535–1440.

Old Lighthouse Museum

If you're at the museum around day's end, linger a while to see a spectacular sunset over Stonington Point. Pull into the small parking area at the foot of Water Street, just past a private beach and the museum.

The Mashantucket Pequot Museum and Research Center, 111 Pequot Trail on the Mashantucket Pequot Reservation in Mashantucket, is, without a doubt, the most beautiful, stunning, and moving museum we've ever visited. Mashantucket Pequots invested $135 million of the monies earned from the nearby Foxwoods Casino in building this state-of-the-art museum and research center. The museum brings to life the story and history of the Mashantucket Pequot people, a history spanning 20,000 years from the last Ice Age to today, and that of other Native American tribal nations.

The life of woodland Native Americans is portrayed in stunning detail with dazzling multisensory dioramas and exhibits. Based on years of scholarly research and the works of Native American artisans, you'll see re-creations of life in a sixteenth-century Pequot village, a seventeenth-century Pequot fort, and an eighteenth-century farmstead. You can hunt caribou along simulated glacial crevasses—complete with chill, howling winds and the sounds of creaking ice. When you visit the village, you'll hear the sounds of children playing and women working and smell the smokes from many campfires. The detail of each diorama is magnificent, especially the life-size, hand-painted Indian figures, cast from living Native Americans. In a specially designed theater you can watch a thirty-minute film called *The Witness,* which recounts the 1637 massacre of 600 Pequot people at the Mystic fort.

Don't miss the 185-foot stone and glass observation tower, which gives you a sweeping view of the area. In fall, this is one of the best places in the state to take in the brilliant reds and golds of a New England autumn. We like visiting the tower before going through the museum. Somehow seeing the sweep of the Pequots' homeland makes the exhibits and dioramas much more meaningful.

The museum is located close to the Foxwoods Resort Casino. Continue past the main entrance to Foxwoods and take a right at the next traffic light onto Route 214. Drive ⅓ mile and turn right onto the Pequot Trail. The Public Safety Building will be on the left. Continue until you reach the museum parking lot.

All areas of the museum are fully wheelchair accessible. Open Memorial Day through Labor Day daily from 10:00 A.M. to 7:00 P.M., last admission at 6:00 P.M. Winter hours are Wednesday through Monday, 10:00 A.M. to 6:00 P.M., last admission at 5:00 P.M. Closed major holidays. Because of the time it takes to appreciate the museum, last admissions are one hour before closing times. Fairly stiff admission charge, but worth it. Call (860) 572–6800 for information about tours and special events. On the Web at: www.mashantucket.com.

Stepping into ***Randall's Ordinary*** on Route 2 (P.O. Box 243) in North Stonington is like returning to an earlier century. The wide floorboards, the flickering firelight, and the rich tang of wood smoke mingled with

The Mashantucket Pequot Museum and Research Center

cooking odors emanating from the fireplaces all conjure images of the distant past. The Randall family's original clapboard inn dates to 1685, with additions made in 1720 and 1790. There's a lot of history in this structure, which is now a landmark on the National Register of Historic Places. Be sure to check out the heavy shutters that were hung for protection from Indian attacks during the colonial period. Also ask to see the trapdoor used to conceal escaped slaves when the inn was a station on the Underground Railroad in the 1830s.

Secluded on twenty-seven acres of rolling woodlands, the inn is a calm retreat from the hustle and bustle of twenty-first century life. Be sure you arrive early enough to take a stroll through the grounds and visit with the oxen and pigs on the property.

Food here is cooked the way the Randalls did: over an open hearth. Cooks and servers also dress much the way the first owners did, in authentic colonial garb. Dinner features one 7:00 P.M. seating and is prix fixe with three entree choices, usually fish or seafood, poultry, and red meat. The pan-roasted Nantucket scallops are the boffo dish, along with the bread basket that includes spider bread (corn bread baked in a "spider," a.k.a. cast-iron skillet). Dessert is usually a sampling of traditional New England desserts such as Indian pudding, long baked, molasses-spiked, and served with a dab of ice cream, and strawberry fool, strawberries blended with softly whipped cream.

Open for breakfast, lunch, and dinner year-round. A continental breakfast is included in the price of a room. Breakfast is served daily from 7:00 to 11:00 A.M.; lunch is from noon to 3:00 P.M. If you plan to take dinner at the Ordinary, be certain to make reservations well in advance. Call (860) 599–4540.

If B&Bs are more your style—or if you just like old things—then you might try North Stonington's *Antiques and Accommodations* (32 Main Street). The four guestrooms and all the public rooms in this restored 1861-vintage Victorian home are lovingly furnished with formal antique furniture and odd accessories. What makes this place truly one-of-a-kind, though, is that these gorgeous furnishings are for sale to the guests. Do you like that Victorian bureau in your room or the four-poster bed you slept in last night? For a modest price, you can have them shipped home. Did your significant other fall in love with that silver brush set on the dressing table? You can make them a gift that will always have special meaning. Even if you don't see anything that tickles your fancy, you'll enjoy your stay at this elegant little B&B. Everything done here is carried off with taste and style. From the fresh-cut flowers and decanter of sherry that greets new arrivals to the breakfasts served by candlelight, every element has that small touch of class that makes for a memorable experience. Call (860) 535–1736 or (800) 554–7829 for information and reservations.

The first diesel-powered submarine was built in Groton in 1912.

The Maritime Center

roton is the birthplace of the atomic submarine and the site of the nation's largest submarine base. This history is commemorated at the **USS Nautilus Memorial** on the U.S. submarine base off Route 12. In addition to touring the world's first nuclear sub, you can spend hours in the 12,000-square-foot **Historic Ship Nautilus and Submarine Force Museum,** which includes extensive exhibits tracing the history of America's submarine fleet. The museum also offers a pair of top-notch multimedia shows in two different theaters: one tracing the history of the Submarine Force and one dealing specifically with *Nautilus.* Open May 15 through October 31 Wednesday through Monday from 9:00 A.M. to 5:00 P.M.; Tuesday, from 1:00 P.M. to 5:00 P.M. Open November 1 through May 14 Wednesday through Monday from 9:00 A.M. to 4:00 P.M. Closed major holidays, the last full week of October, and the first full week of May. Call (860) 694–3174 or (800) 343–0079.

Groton's **Fort Griswold Battlefield State Park** commemorates the warfare of a different era. Located at Monument Street and Park Avenue, the park is the site of a 1781 massacre of American troops conducted by a force of 800 British soldiers under the command of the traitor Benedict Arnold. At that time Yankee privateers based in New London were a thorn in the side of the British in New York, and Arnold came to burn the town, which he did, destroying 150 buildings. The part of his force that advanced up the east bank of the Thames suffered heavy casualties assaulting Fort Griswold, which was held by a force of 150 militia under the command of Colonel William Ledyard. When Ledyard finally surrendered, he was murdered with his own sword, and eighty of his men were slaughtered.

Many of Fort Griswold's old emplacements remain, and there are some interesting historical displays. In addition the 134-foot monument tower provides a nice view of the coast. The park is open year around. The museum and monument are open from Memorial Day through Labor Day daily from 10:00 A.M. to 5:00 P.M. Open Labor Day through Columbus Day, weekends from 10:00 A.M. to 5:00 P.M. Call (860) 445–1729.

This is just our observation, but kids are generally bloodthirsty little monsters. Tell them you're taking an environmental cruise, chances are you'll get yawns; hum the theme song from *Jaws* and mention sharks and they're in the car in a New-York minute. For budding Cousteaus and their parents, **Project Oceanology,** Avery Point, makes an interesting and educational day trip (don't forget to hint at the possibility of shark attacks). You'll cruise the waters off Groton to learn about the environment and marine life in ways you never could at an aquarium. The boats, *Enviro-Lab II* and *III,* are oceanographic research vessels, staffed by marine research scientists and teachers. They really communicate their love for the sea and give kids a chance to participate in lots of hands-on adventures such as catching lobsters and taking and analyzing samples from the ocean using oceanographic sampling instruments. It's so engaging you can probably drop the shark patter about five minutes after boarding. Meanwhile, *you* can kick back and enjoy some beautiful ocean views, including a slice of the southeastern Connecticut coastline

Norm's Texas Beef Stew

1 to 1½ pounds cubed stewing beef
2 tablespoons oil or butter
1 onion, chopped fine
2 stalks celery, chopped fine
2 carrots, chopped fine
1 16-ounce can pinto beans, drained and rinsed (You can substitute an equal amount of diced raw potato, but the pinto beans bring out the "Texas" in the stew.)
1 28-ounce can tomatoes, diced with liquid (or an equal amount of diced raw tomatoes)
2 to 3 cups beef stock (either home-made or canned, low salt)
1 cup fresh or frozen corn
1 cup fresh or frozen green peas
1 cup fresh or frozen green beans
(You can omit any of the vegetables or double up on the ones you like and leave out the ones you don't.)
1 cup barbecue sauce (Norm's recommends Bullseye brand.)

Serves 6–8

Heat oil in large pan (Dutch oven or something with a lid) over medium heat.

Dry beef well and sauté in oil until very brown.

Add the beef stock and the tomatoes and simmer covered for about one hour until about half done. Stir frequently.

Add the chopped onion, carrots, celery, and pinto beans to beef mixture.

Continue to simmer over low heat, stirring often, for about 45 minutes or until beef is very tender.

Add corn, peas, beans, and barbecue sauce. Continue to simmer until vegetables are tender, maybe about 15 minutes.

Cook stew and then refrigerate overnight. Reheat and serve.

and some postcard-pretty lighthouses. Admission. Call (203) 445–9007 or (800) 364–8472 for cruise schedules.

A lobster tidbit: It takes between five and seven years for a lobster to reach salable weight. Want to pick the very freshest live lobster? Easy, just pick the friskiest one with its tail curled tightly under its body.

Some places *belong* in the movies. **Norm's Diner,** at 171 Bridge Street, is one of them. It's down near the shoreline with its smokes and mists and is the sort of venue where, on foggy nights, you expect hard-boiled detective Philip Marlowe to burst through the door and pistol whip some bad actor to his knees under the steely gaze of a approving clientele. Despite this film noir quality, so far all we've encountered at Norm's are nice, quiet guys who look like retired machinists from Electric Boat.

The slightly battered exterior of this 1954-vintage metal-sided Silk City features a handsome barreled roof, adorned with the requisite neon sign proclaiming its name to the world. The interior is done up in shades of green and pink. The counter is a pale green. The Formica tables are salmon pink. Green vinyl adorns the booths and stool seats. The rims of the stools are shiny metal with alternating stripes of bright candy pink. This is definitely 1950s decor.

Norm's is a good place for late-night breakfast. Norm's cheesecake is locally famous and made on-site from a top secret recipe. Open Monday through Friday, twenty-four hours a day; Saturday, 10:00 A.M. to 2:00 P.M.; Sunday, the diner closes at 2:00 P.M. and doesn't reopen until Monday at 5:00 A.M. Saturday and Sunday, breakfast and lunch menu only. Call (860) 445–5026.

One of the best places in the world to eat lobster is **Abbott's Lobster in the Rough** (117 Pearl Street), down by the shipyards in Noank. You have your choice of eating indoors in the dining room or outdoors at picnic tables scattered around the lawn and pier. Take outdoors; on good days, you can see three states. The view of the sea and the passing trawlers and sailboats is worth the small loss of comfort.

During the summer, Abbott's serves thousands of pounds of lobster a day, so just assume they wrote the book on cooking crustaceans. Your lobsters come steamed fresh from the pot, the way nature intended, with butter, coleslaw, and chips on the side. Nothing fancy, but you came to Abbott's for lobster, and lobster is what you get. Try it the way we do: Order a large lobster (2½ pounds or more, depending on your lobster obsession) to split and fixings for two dinners. That way, you'll get more lobster and less shell for your money. The lobster rolls at Abbott's are a lazy person's way to get around the cracking, picking, sucking, and lip-smacking that go with demolishing a whole lobster. Each lobster roll consists of a quarter pound of premium butter-soaked lobster on a toasted bun. Abbott's also serves a classic shore dinner with steamers, cooked shrimp, and clam chowder in addition to the lobster.

However you take your lobster, be prepared to wait. This is a very popular place. Open noon to 9:00 P.M. daily May through Labor Day; noon to 9:00 P.M. weekends between Labor Day to Columbus Day. Call (860) 536–7719.

Hammonasset gets most of the press, but for our money, **Rocky Neck State Park** (exit 72 off Interstate 95 in Niantic) is the better location, especially for off-season picnics. If you like things historical, be sure to check out the pavilion, constructed as a Works Progress Administration project. For picnics, though, we recommend walking out to the end of the rocky point, where you have the waters of Long Island Sound on three sides. This is a beautiful and peaceful place to pitch a blanket and share a meal. Be sure to bring some stale bread or a couple of anchovy pizzas for the gulls; they seem to expect it. The park has a picnic area and a place to cook. Open daily from 8:00 A.M. to sunset. Parking rates Memorial Day through Labor Day, $5.00 for Connecticut vehicles and $8.00 for out-of-state vehicles on weekdays; weekends and holidays, $7.00 for Connecticut vehicles and $12.00 for out-of-state vehicles. Mid-April through Memorial Day and Labor Day through the end of September parking is free weekdays and $5.00 for Connecticut vehicles and $8.00 for out-of- state vehicles on weekends. Call (860) 739–5471.

Ledyard Township, north of Groton, is the site of the eleven-acre **Ledyard Powered-Up—Powered-Down Sawmill** (Iron Street; Route 214), an unusual restored 1860-vintage water-powered vertical sawmill. The park also has a working blacksmith shop, a restored gristmill with a two-acre mill pond, an 1878 "Lane" Shingle Mill, ice-harvesting equipment, and a picnic area. The park staff includes a working blacksmith and a working tinsmith. The saw operates Saturdays from 1:00 to 4:00 P.M. during April and May and from mid-October to November. Call (860) 464–8888 or (860) 433–4050.

At its founding in 1876, the original name of the **U.S. Coast Guard Academy,** 15 Mohegan Avenue, New London, was Revenue Cutter School of Instruction. Today visitors are welcome year-round to tour the academy. Tours are free and self-guided. When it's in port, the three-masted training barque *Eagle* is open to the public on Friday, Saturday, and Sunday from noon to 5:00 P.M. Full-dress reviews, held at Washington parade field, happen most Fridays at 4:00 P.M. in the spring and fall. USCG sweatshirts and other souvenirs are for sale at the gift shop. The campus is open daily from 9:00 A.M. to 5:00 P.M.; the visitor's center is open May to October daily from 10:00 A.M. to 5:00 P.M. The museum is open Monday through Friday from 9:00 A.M. to 4:30 P.M., Saturday, 10:00 A.M. to 5:00 P.M.; Sunday, noon to 5:00 P.M. In the summer the academy offers some wonderful band concerts of patriotic and popular music; call for concert schedule. When in port, *Tall Ship Eagle* is open to visitors Friday through Sunday, 1:00 P.M. to 5:00 P.M. Pets must be on a leash and cameras are permitted. There are no picnic facilities at the academy, but you can spread a blanket at Riverside Park, next to the academy. Much of the parking is restricted or reserved; park at the visitor's center or next to the museum. Call (860) 444–8270.

The grinder sandwich was supposedly invented by Benny Capablo in New London in 1926. Despite our proximity to the sub base at Groton, Nutmeggers stick with the handle grinder. Submarine sandwich is really a Pennsylvaniaism. Other names for the same over-stuffed sandwich: hoagies, poor boys, wedgies, and bombers.

Huddled beneath the eight-lane Gold Star Bridge is **Ye Olde Towne Mill** *(860–447–5250), the nation's oldest industrial power plant (1650).*

New London's Shaw Mansion is considered the cradle of the American Navy. It was Connecticut's naval office during the Revolutionary War.

Though often crowded to the point of distraction, downtown New London has so much going for it that it would be a shame to miss the experience if you are anywhere in the vicinity. We recommend a fall or spring walking tour, including the *Captain's Walk* and *Whale Oil Row.* Points of interest include *Ye Ancient Burial Ground* and the *New London County Courthouse,* built in 1784 and still in use. In late July, New London hosts America's longest-running polka festival. Come prepared to eat and dance the day and night away. Admission. The festival is held at Ocean Beach Park, from noon to midnight.

Energetic walkers may want to head all the way down to Bank Street to see the granite-walled 1833-vintage *New London Maritime Society, U.S. Custom House, & Museum of American Maritime History.* This is the oldest operating custom house in America, and the only one in Connecticut. The front doors were assembled from planks taken from the frigate USS *Constitution* ("Old Ironsides"). Open Tuesday and Thursday from 2:00 P.M. to 4:00 P.M. Admission. Call (860) 447–2501.

British soldiers led by Benedict Arnold burned New London in 1781, and just about every structure in the city today postdates that episode. The exception is the 1678-vintage *Joshua Hempsted House* (11 Hempsted Street), the home of a famous Connecticut diarist and now the oldest surviving house in New London. One of the interesting features of this home is that it is insulated with seaweed. Open Thursday through Sunday from noon to 4:00 P.M. from May 15 to October 15 and by appointment. Admission varies. Call (860) 443–7949.

Our favorite walk is down Whale Oil Row, with its flanking of 1832-vintage Greek Revival houses built by the leading figures in the whaling industry. New London was the center of the whaling industry in Connecticut. During the years 1784–1907, it was home port to 196 whaling vessels, over twice as many as ventured from all other Connecticut ports put together. The men who ran this business were the OPEC of their age, and New London was their Riyadh. The industry peaked in 1846 and died off rapidly thereafter, but Whale Oil Row still carries some of the aura of those days when Connecticut whale oil helped light the lamps of America.

New London has another—literary—side that's every bit as fascinating as its seagoing heritage. Eugene O'Neill, arguably America's greatest playwright, spent part of his childhood in **Monte Cristo Cottage** (325 Pequot Avenue) in New London. Named for O'Neill's actor father's best-known stage role, Monte Cristo Cottage is a pretty little gingerbread structure that looks like it should be filled with light and laughter. Alas, the years that O'Neill and his brother Jamie spent there were more like one of the Grimms' darker fairy tales. Both father James and brother Jamie were heavy drinkers. O'Neill's mother, Ella, addicted to morphine from O'Neill's birth, battled her own demons throughout his childhood. Ella is said to haunt the tiny cottage. The Tyrone family in *Long Day's Journey into Night* is a reflection and expression of the misery of O'Neill's summers at the cottage. The comedy *Ah! Wilderness*, also set in Monte Cristo, portrays a life that O'Neill never knew except as an outsider; he based his happy and slightly zany characters on the McGinleys, the family of a childhood friend.

The cottage where O'Neill's dark dreams were born is a conglomeration of small buildings, all wrapped up in the Victorian pseudogentility of gingerbread, wraparound verandas, and turrets. Inside, especially on the second floor, the rooms are grim, claustrophobic cells. The first floor of the cottage is fully restored and furnished. In a room adjacent to the living room, a short multimedia show narrated by the late actress Geraldine Fitzgerald describes O'Neill's life in New London in the early 1900s. Open Memorial Day through Labor Day, Tuesday through Saturday from 10:00 A.M. to 5:00 P.M., Sunday from 1:00 to 5:00 P.M. Moderate admission. Call (860) 443–0051.

The *Lyman Allyn Art Museum* at 625 Williams Avenue in New London is one of Connecticut's lesser known gems and a delight for kids. There's a wonderful room chockful of Indian artifacts and a collection of antique dollhouses and toys. In addition the museum has collections of Egyptian, Roman, medieval, and Greek artifacts as well as various changing exhibits. The small museum shop is a real find, offering both antiques and reproductions. Also located on the museum grounds is the historic Deshon-Allyn House, a nineteenth-century mansion that was home to whaling captain Lyman Allyn; the first floor is furnished and open to visitors. The museum has a noncirculating reference library of art and art history books available for use during museum hours. Open July through Labor Day, Tuesday through Saturday from 10:00 A.M. to 5:00 P.M., and Sunday from 1:00 to 5:00 P.M.; closed major holidays. Admission; kids under twelve, free. Handicapped accessible. Wheelchairs and ASL interpreter available by previous reservation. Call (860) 443–2545. On the Web at lymanallyn.conncoll.edu.

Ledge Lighthouse in New London Harbor has a ghost named Ernie. Some believe the haunt is a former lighthouse keeper who cut his own throat and then jumped off the structure, depressed by marital problems. Some reports say the ghost is a tall bearded man dressed in a slicker and rain hat. The prankster ghost has been known to untie

New London Ledge Lighthouse

boats, hide coffee cups and radios, and slam doors. The Ledge Lighthouse is atop a 65-foot, 3-story square building in the water at the meeting of the Thames River, Fisher's Island Sound, and Long Island Sound in New London Harbor.

As far as we know, there are no ghosts at New London's **Lighthouse Inn.** Originally a 1902-vintage mansion called Meadow Court, the building at 6 Guthrie Place in New London became the Lighthouse Inn in 1928. The exterior suggests Spanish Moorish influences, but the interior is elegant Victorian and best described as opulent and unique. Many of the furnishings are antiques, rescued from flea markets; most of the rest are quality reproductions. The three formal dining rooms offer a good view of the green lawns that roll down to Long Island Sound. Service is excellent, and the food is well prepared. The seafood, especially the famous clam bisque, gets high marks for both preparation and freshness. Open for lunch Monday through Saturday, 11:45 A.M. to 2:30 P.M. Open for dinner daily 5:00 to 9:00 P.M. Sunday brunch, 11:30 A.M. to 2:30 P.M. Call (860) 443–8411.

DON'T MISS

Here are some brief looks at other Coast and Country attractions:

ATTRACTIONS

Thankful Arnold House, Hayden Hill and Walkley Hill Roads, Route 154, Higganum; (860) 345–2400. A three-story gambrel-roof house with some unusual architectural features and design. The gardens and heritage herb garden are notable. Open Monday through Wednesday from 10:00 A.M. to 4:00 P.M. Guided tours by "resident ghost." Call ahead to confirm schedule.

The **Sunbeam Express** leaves from Captain John's Sport Fishing Center, Waterford; (860) 443–7259. The *Sunbeam Express* cruises the waters of Long Island Sound on whale-watching expeditions. Besides whales, you can see other sea critters like dolphins, sharks, and turtles. An on-board naturalist makes sure you spot all the sea life there is to see and answers questions. If you prefer, you can just tip back your head and doze in the sun and enjoy being on the water. Whale-watching cruise on Thursdays and Sundays; reservations a must. There's a fairly stiff (but worth it) per person charge for the cruise. On the Web at www.sunbeamfleet.com; e-mail at sunbeamfleet@snet.com.

SHOPPING

Old Bank Antiques, 66 East Main Street, East Hampton; (860) 267–0790. A multidealer shop housed in a turn-of-the-century bank. Antiques tucked everywhere, including the old vault. A cute place, especially good for china, silver, and collectibles. Open Wednesday through Sunday, 10:00 A.M. to 5:00 P.M.; Thursday evening until 9:00 P.M. Longer hours around the holidays.

Madison Trust Antiques —Consignments, 891 Boston Post Road, Madison; (203) 245–3976. Beautiful furniture, rugs, silver, and china at very good prices. Call ahead for hours.

Richard D. Scofield Historic Lighting,

One West Main Street, Chester; (860) 526–1800. Handmade reproductions of everything from seventeenth-century candle holders to hanging lanterns and odd, but beautiful, lamps. Call ahead for hours.

Essex Saybrook Antiques Village,

345 Middle Turnpike, Old Saybrook; (860) 388–0689; fax: (860) 388–1179. We love this group shop, which is always crammed to the rafters with good things. It's a good place to browse and pick up decorating ideas because the dealers go all out to display their wares in cute and cunning ways. We love their old toys, Maxfield Parrish prints, and art pottery. When you stop by, make sure you visit our friends, Pat and Marcia, of Firemark Antiques and check out their vintage kitchen treasures. Open seven days a week, 11:00 A.M. to 5:00 P.M.; from Memorial Day through January 2; from January 2 to Memorial Day, closed Monday. Visit them on the Web at: www.esavantiqs.com.

RESTAURANTS

Hallmark Ice Cream,

Route 156, Old Lyme; (203) 434–1998. We like their thirty different flavors of made-there ice cream. The "fur children" like the "kibbles & cream" frozen

dessert for pets. Open daily, April through November, 11:00 A.M. to 11:00 P.M.

It's Only Natural,

686 Main Street, Middletown; (860) 346–9210. Award-winning vegan food (no eggs or dairy products). Macrobiotic food, also. Wonderful, healthy, fresh-tasting food; inexpensive.

Pat's Kountry Kitchen and Pat's Kountry Kollectibles,

70 Mill Rock Road East, (junction of Routes 1 and 154), Old Saybrook; (860) 388–4784 (restaurant) or (860) 395–3349 (shop). Comforting food such as clam hash. This eatery takes care of people on special diets by cooking up tasty low-fat or sugar-free dishes. A nice touch for kids: Pat's big stuffed bears can join you for breakfast if there's room at your table. Open daily from 7:00 A.M. If you can't leave without taking a bear with you, you can buy one in Pat's gift shop, which carries a good stock of teddy bears and bear paraphernalia.

Cafe Routier, 1080 Boston

Post Road, Old Saybrook; (860) 388–6270. Our fathers held firm to the maxim that you should "always eat where the truckers eat for a four-square meal." Well, Cafe Routier might cause our dads to raise their eyebrows. From the outside, Cafe Routier does look like

a truck stop, but inside is a different story. Inside you'll find eclectic furnishings and one of the best French bistros in the state; in fact so good that noted French chef and author Jacques Pepin dines there regularly. The menu changes frequently. We've enjoyed such tried-and-true bistro favorites as calves liver with bacon and a pan sauce of reduced balsamic vinegar or lamb stew with crisply tender baby veggies. For dessert, what else but tart tartin, a caramelized, upside-down apple pie. Open 5:00 to 9:00 P.M. Sunday and Tuesday through Thursday; Friday and Saturday from 5:00 to 10:00 P.M. Reservations are advised.

Paul's Pasta Shop,

223 Thames Street, Groton; (860) 445–5276. Paul's is another place the locals will never tell you about, but it's a great lunch spot. We like the made-there lobster ravioli or one of their top-notch grinders like the turkey and cheddar topped with apples and cranberry jelly, sort of Thanksgiving dinner on a roll. You can also take away any of the prepared food or buy your own pasta and sauce. Open seven days, 11:00 A.M. to 9:00 P.M.

Al Forno, 1654 Boston Post

Road, Old Saybrook; (860) 399–2346. Al Forno is another place where local chefs gather on their day off to eat and talk food. We could make a meal out of chef Bob Zemmel's Tuscan bread alone, but Al Forno's pizzas are so divine, we always pace ourselves with the bread. We love the crispy, thin-crusted fresh tomato pizza in the summer. In the winter, the hearty pastas will warm the cockles of your heart. We like the pillowy, potato gnocchi with marinara sauce or plain with a simple sprinkle of Parmesan cheese and butter. The wine list includes some excellent Tuscan wines, which are marvels with the pizza and pastas. Reservations recommended, especially in summer. Open Sunday through Thursday, noon to 9:00 P.M.; Friday and Saturday, from noon to 10:00 P.M.

LODGING

Roseledge Farm B&B, 418 Route 164, Preston; (860) 892–4739. A 1720 B&B with canopy-topped high featherbeds, fireplaces, and private baths. There's a maze of tunnels under the house and barn, escape ways from Indian attacks. A hearty New England breakfast is cooked

over an open fireplace, with plenty of baked goods for snacking and nibbling. There are animals on the property and beautiful gardens. One of our online buddies reports sighting several ghosts, including a wolf and some kitties. All seem peaceful. The room journal in the Blue Room keeps mysteriously disappearing. Moderate.

Madison Beach Hotel, 94 West Wharf Road, Madison; (203) 245–1404. Beautiful gray-shingled beach resort/hotel, complete with a lovely, Victorian-style wrap-around porch with lots of rocking chairs. No-frills, family meals served in the Wharf Restaurant (open for lunch and dinner). Moderate (includes breakfast).

Tidewater Inn, 949 Boston Post Road, Madison; (203) 245–8457. A former stagecoach stop, offering nine guest rooms, all with private baths, two with fireplaces. Antiques, reproductions, estate furniture, full breakfast, fruit and home-baked goodies, and coconut French toast. Moderate to high; off-season rates are more reasonable.

House of 1833 B&B, 72 North Stonington Road, Mystic; (860) 536–6325 or (800) FOR–1833. An elegant and romantic Greek Revival mansion with beautiful grounds and a swimming pool. Five guest rooms all with private baths have antique and reproduction furnishings. Some have canopy beds or private porches, fireplaces or whirlpool tubs. The country gourmet breakfast and afternoon tea and snacks are special. Moderate to expensive. Children welcome midweek only. No smoking; no pets.

Old Lyme Inn, 85 Lyme Street, Old Lyme; (860) 434–2600 or (800) 434–5352. Open year-round, this pleasant inn welcomes not only children but also your pets (make arrangements ahead of time). Thirteen rooms, all with private baths. Handicapped accessible. Continental breakfast with room. Lunch and dinner served. Visit on the Web at www.oldlymeinn. com; e-mail at innkeeper@ oldlymeinn.com.

The Quiet Corner

ast of Hartford is an area that the state's tourism board calls the "Quiet Corner." Bounded on the north by Massachusetts and on the east by Rhode Island, the Quiet Corner encompasses the lightly populated, slightly bucolic uplands of Tolland and Windham Counties. It is an area of peace and tranquillity that has escaped both the dozer blades of the state's developers and the attention of the chic set. In truth the Quiet Corner has such an air of serenity that in many places you can easily imagine that this is the way all of Connecticut looked 350 years ago. Fertile

With Pup

In recent years walking your dog off-leash in a public park has become something of a political statement in some parts of Connecticut. Witness all the madness when dog lovers and dog avoiders went toe-to-toe (or paw-to-paw) in our hometown of Avon. Dog lovers (the authors included) relished walking their dogs off-leash in certain areas of Fisher Meadow Conservation Area, but after months of testy town council meetings, lots of silly publicity about Avon's Dog Wars, and a referendum, the town council put dog lovers and their furry companions on a short leash. Dog lovers might enjoy a frolic with Fido in Bolton's watershed area. The watershed area is actually a collection of wilderness areas in the Bolton Notch and Valley Falls area, including Bolton Notch Park, Valley Falls Park, Freja Park, and the Shenipisit Trail.

You'll find several marked trails through the woods, perfect for hiking and streams, just right for a little canine sync swim. Be careful on the trails, however, as the marking isn't quite ready for prime time. Autumn seems to be the prime time to see the area in all its glory, but we like late spring walks. Remember whatever you carry into Connecticut state parks, you must carry out, including trash and garbage. It goes without saying that cleaning up after your dog is also expected. Visitors are expected to keep their dogs on a leash. The Bolton watershed area is located off exit 5 off I-384. Take a left at the exit to the commuter parking lot at the junction of Routes 6 and 44. Park in the commuter lot. Enter the watershed area just south of the parking lot. The area is open during daylight hours.

The Quiet Corner

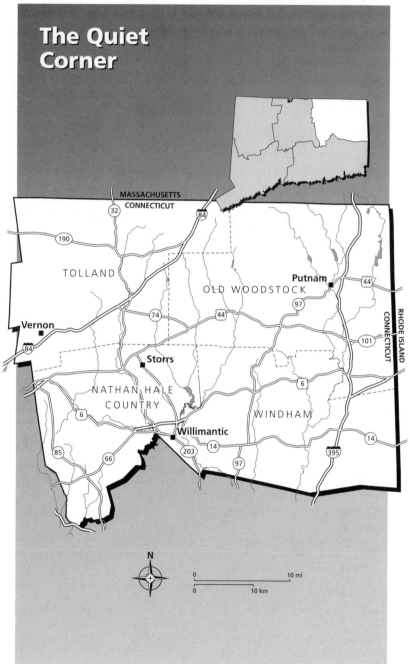

MASSACHUSETTS
CONNECTICUT

32

84

190

TOLLAND

OLD WOODSTOCK

Putnam

44

Vernon

74

44

97

101

84

RHODE ISLAND
CONNECTICUT

Storrs

6

NATHAN HALE
COUNTRY

WINDHAM

6

Willimantic

85

66

203

14

14

97

395

N

0   10 mi

0   10 km

farmland abounds. There are country inns that wouldn't be out of place in France. Herb and flower gardens are among the region's most popular attractions. With some exceptions, the antiques here are neither quite as antique nor nearly as pricey as those sold in the trendier stores across the state in Litchfield County. And if other regions have more to offer the casual traveler, for the patient, the Quiet Corner has its own rewards.

Nathan Hale Country

You can easily miss the turn onto Silver Road from Route 44 in Coventry. But, hard as it is to find, *Caprilands* is, for many people, the crossroads of the world. Visitors flock to the fifty-acre herb farm at 534 Silver Road from the far corners of the earth, and the guest book is as likely to contain the names of visitors from distant New Zealand as from nearby Hartford.

Part of the lure of Caprilands was its famous mistress. Adelma Grenier Simmons, the farm's owner and the grande dame of American herbalists, was famous for her lectures on herbs and for her herb-spangled lunches, which varied with the season. The eccentric Ms. Simmons, who died in 1997, often dressed in swirling cloaks, odd hats, and exotic jewelry and liked to describe herself as "the Agatha Christie of the herb world." Adelma Simmons's husband and family are determined that Caprilands will continue exactly as its famous mistress wished.

Caprilands' main attractions are its thirty-one theme gardens filled with more than 300 varieties of herbs, spices, and wild grasses. Visitors are free to wander among these little worlds at their own pace, and each is a unique delight. We like the identification and eighteenth-century gardens, because their sundials set us thinking of ages past, when people looked at time in terms of the rhythms of nature rather than as a driving force in its own right.

You might think that spring and summer would be the best times to visit Caprilands, but every season is special, and each offers something new and different to see, smell, and taste. Christmas is celebrated with style at Caprilands, but so are even older festivals, such as Lammas in August.

The herb farm is open daily from 9:00 A.M. to 5:00 P.M. year-round, and herbal luncheons (including a tour of the gardens, a lecture, and a five-course meal) are offered at noon, Monday through Saturday, April through December. High tea is served throughout the year on Sundays at 2:00 P.M. Reservations for teas and luncheons are absolutely essential. Call (860) 742–7244.

Near Caprilands, at 224 Boston Turnpike (the junction of Routes 44 and 31 north), is *Memory Lane Countryside Antique Center.* Gail and Gene Dickson's multidealer shop consists of a house, a large barn, and several sheds full of antiques. Two dozen different dealers have items on display here, so a wide variety of styles and tastes are represented. The large airy barn is mostly furniture, organized into a dozen or so separate displays, including some of the better nineteenth-century oak furniture in the area; there's almost always something that we've never seen anywhere else before. The house also contains some quality furniture and a raft of smaller items: jewelry, glassware, tools, and the like. There's one whole room given over to some of the best estate, antique, and plain old costume jewelry in the state, most of it very reasonably priced. Don't leave without saying "hey" to the kitties who preside over the premises. Open Wednesday through Sunday, 10:00 A.M. to 5:00 P.M. Call (860) 742–0346.

One of the joys of writing an off-the-beaten-path book is meeting people who do something they love and do it well. So it is with Anthony Maulucci and his *Nutmeg Vineyard* on Bunker Hill Road in Coventry (watch for the Connecticut Wine Trail sign). A garrulous Connecticut Transit bus driver we used to ride with first told us about Nutmeg. Go for the red he said; we're glad we took his advice. What makes Nutmeg special, beyond Anthony's dedication, is that it's Connecticut's only organic vineyard. It's a small operation, with only forty or so acres of vines. You won't find much in the way of amenities, but there is a tasting room where you can try a sample. Nutmeg makes about a dozen grape wines, some sweet and some dry; it also brews fruit wines. Open weekends, 11:00 A.M. to 5:00 P.M.; other times by chance or appointment. Call (860) 742–8402.

The small village of picturesque shops you see clustered around a pond on North Main Street in Marlborough is the *Marlborough Country Barn.* Actually, it's several barns and outbuildings, including a country restaurant called Sadler's Ordinary. We come here to shop for country furniture, including beautiful country kitchen tables made in Pennsylvania's Lancaster County, and gifts, or to shamelessly steal decorating tips. The people who work at the complex are patient, helpful, and always willing to help solve decorating problems. You'll find everything from wood stoves to Christmas ornaments to penny candy for sale. We love browsing through the beautifully decorated room settings; there's always something new and different to pique our interest. The Christmas shop is open all year and carries lovely ornaments and decorative accessories. We suggest hitting the Christmas shop early—around Labor Day—because after Veteran's Day things get awfully crowded and

THE QUIET CORNER

FAVORITE PLACES IN
THE QUIET CORNER

1. *Antiquing in Putnam*
2. *Caprilands*
3. *Memory Lane Country-side Antique Center*
4. *Prudence Crandall House Museum*
5. *The Golden Lamb Buttery*

boisterous. Take a break from shopping with breakfast, lunch, or dinner at *Sadler's Ordinary,* a low-ceilinged, old tavern decorated with lots of cutie-pie stuff. If you visit in winter, ask to sit near the fireplace; it's a cheerful place to eat. We love the food at Sadler's, especially the old-fashioned New England dishes like chicken pot pie and salmon cakes. And we love the bread baskets, full of sweet quick breads and just-out-of-the-oven sunflower bread, crunchy with sunflower seeds. For dessert, try the old-fashioned, creamy tapioca pudding covered with a cloud of freshly whipped cream or our favorite, cream cheese–pecan pie. If you prefer, you can grab a snack at the bakery in the front of the restaurant and settle down at one of the picnic tables to rest your feet and relax. Throughout the year, the Country Barn holds several special events, such as antique shows in early June and Winnie the Pooh's birthday party in early October. Unless you have an incredible fondness for small children and just can't get enough of their shrill, piping voices, avoid the Pooh party like the plague. The Christmas open house, usually held in mid-November, is a fun, if somewhat hectic and bustling, event. A word or two of advice: go early and wear comfortable shoes. Open from Tuesday through Saturday, 10:00 A.M. to 5:30 P.M.; Fridays until 8:00; Sunday, noon to 5:00 P.M. Call (860) 295–8231 or 800-853-8893. On the Web at www.marlboroughbarn.com.

Our favorite dessert at Sadler's Ordinary is their cream cheese–pecan pie, a treat we've found on no other menu, so we wanted to share the recipe with our readers. We begged, we groveled, we pleaded, and we batted our eyelashes (actually, Deborah batted her eyelashes; David just tried to pretend he didn't know her), but the good folks at Sadler's Ordinary stood resolute—nope, no recipe. So we did a little research on the Web and then cobbled together a recipe that produces a pie almost as good as Sadler's. (See next page.)

Nathan Hale is Connecticut's official state hero, and there are Nutmeggers who feel about him kinda the way Tennesseans feel about Elvis. Hale (Yale class of 1773) was a fervent patriot who left his position as a local schoolmaster to join the rebellion against the British as soon as word arrived of the doings up at Lexington and Concord. He fought with the Continental Army through most of 1776. In September of that year, he slipped into New York to gather information on British strength and deployments. After being caught (possibly as a result of being betrayed by a cousin), Hale was hanged by the British for spying. He was just

Almost as Good as Sadler's Ordinary Cream Cheese—Pecan Pie

Ingredients

1 9½-inch deep dish pie shell, unbaked (Your own recipe or a premade crust like Pillsbury's All Ready Ready Piecrust)

1 8-oz. package cream cheese, at room temperature (Light cream cheese works just fine.)

1 egg

1 tsp. vanilla

⅓ cup sugar

¼ tsp. salt

3 eggs

¼ cup sugar

1 cup light corn syrup (Karo)

1 tsp. vanilla

1¼ cup whole pecans (or chopped pecans)

How to

1. Preheat oven to 375°.

2. In a small bowl, combine cream cheese, 1 egg, 1 tsp. vanilla, ⅓ cup sugar, and salt. Mix until all ingredients are well combined. (If little lumps of cream cheese remain, that's OK.) Set aside.

3. In another small bowl, beat 3 eggs. Mix in ¼ cup sugar, corn syrup, and 1 tsp. vanilla. Blend well.

4. Spread cream cheese mixture over the bottom of the unbaked pie shell. Sprinkle with chopped pecans. Carefully pour the corn-syrup mixture over the pecans.

5. Bake at 375° for 35 to 45 minutes or until center is set. Refrigerate until firm.

6. Best served cold with small dollops of lightly sweetened whipped cream. Serves 8–10.

Notes: A southern belle of our acquaintance informs us that making our pecan pie with chopped pecans is tacky beyond belief. Also, we've tried fooling around with the corn-syrup mixture. A half-and-half mix of light and dark corn syrup works well. However, our attempt to make a "Connecticut Yankee" cream cheese–pecan pie with maple syrup was a dismal failure. You can gild the lily by adding 1 cup (8-oz.) semisweet chocolate chips to the corn-syrup mixture.

twenty-one. Our history books always reported his last words as "I only regret that I have but one life to lose for my country." However, the recently revealed diaries of British Captain Frederick MacKenzie, who witnessed Hale's execution, report young Nathan's final remarks as "It is the duty of every good officer to obey any orders given him by his commander-in-chief." Evidently, the spinmeisters were at work even then.

The **Nathan Hale Homestead** at 2299 South Street was once Hale's home, which is sufficient to make it some sort of landmark. Hale himself might not recognize the house in which he grew up: It was substantially

Nathan Hale Homestead

rebuilt in the then-fashionable Georgian-style the year he died. He'd probably recognize the surroundings, though. The house sits in the middle of the 1,219-acre Nathan Hale State Forest, a wooded setting not too dissimilar from the surroundings of Hale's boyhood 300-acre farm. Today the farmhouse is preserved much as it was when the Hale family lived there. On display inside the building is a collection of colonial antiques, including many of the personal possessions used by two generations of Hales. Open daily May 15 through October 15, 1:00 to 5:00 P.M. The homestead is the site of an antiques show held each July 1 and a September Nathan Hale Day celebration. Admission. Call (860) 742–6917.

By the way, while the nearby **Nathan Hale Cemetery** on Lake Street is a nice enough old graveyard, the great man isn't buried there. After they hanged him, the British dumped his remains in an unmarked grave that now lies somewhere under Sixty-sixth Street and Third Avenue in Manhattan.

Connecticut tourists almost never have the campus of the **University of Connecticut** at Storrs on their itinerary, but they should. The UConn campus is home to more than students. It also houses some attractions that leave many more heavily promoted facilities in the dust.

Almost totally ignored by travel writers, the **Connecticut State Museum of Natural History** has over two million holdings, displayed on a rotating basis. These include Indian and nature exhibits, New England's finest collection of mounted birds of prey, and the nation's largest mounted shark, a 2,779-pound 16-foot-long great white shark caught off Noank. The museum's main exhibits are spread over three buildings on the UConn campus at Storrs: the central part of the museum, housed in the Wilbur Cross Building; the gloriously scary shark exhibit in Jorgensen Auditorium; and the university's greenhouse, where more than 3,000 species of plants (including vanilla orchids, cocoa trees, and passion-fruit vines) are on display.

Housed in the former Horticultural Sales Building (a.k.a. the apple warehouse) on Hillside Boulevard are the main components of the museum's exhibits. The exhibit *One Circle Home* celebrates Connecticut's Native American heritage. This exhibit takes its name not only from the circular form of the wigwam but from the Native American belief that everything is part of the circle of life. Worked into this exhibit are an interesting series of plaques showing common English words (chipmunk, opossum, and woodchuck, among others) that have their roots in Algonquin.

The 250-bird raptor display is the finest collection of hawks and owls in New England. The birds are mounted in stunningly lifelike positions. The owls, particularly the ghostlike snowy owls, are especially fascinating to kids.

The museum is open afternoons, Thursday through Monday year-round, though hours vary depending on the day and what building you want to visit. No admission; donations gratefully accepted. Call (860) 486–4460.

One of the more interesting futuristic experiments in America shares Room 312 of the Wilbur Cross Building with the Connecticut State Museum of Natural History's main museum. There you will find something called **Video Place,** one of the first exhibits of "artifical reality" in the country.

Great Scoops on UConn

*W*ith all the attention showered on UConn's famed basketball program, it's easy to forget that UConn is also widely known for its excellent agriculture department. An offshoot of that department's activity is the UConn Dairy Bar. The Dairy Bar has been around since the 1930s, and it has been scooping up fountain treats at the current location—3636 Horsebarn Road (exit off Route 195)—since the early 1950s. Every day about twenty-five flavors of frozen treats are on the menu with old favorites such as chocolate, vanilla, strawberry, and coffee leading the pack and specialty flavors such as Jonathan Supreme (named for the school's mascot), which is peanut-butter-swirled vanilla with chocolate-covered peanuts, showing up from time to time. According to one pistachio ice-cream fanatic we know, the Dairy Bar is one of the few places in Connecticut that still churns up his favorite flavor with real pistachios, instead of green-dyed almonds. Servings are colossal. Open Monday to Friday, 10:30 A.M. to 5:00 P.M.; Saturday through Sunday, noon to 5:00 P.M. Call (860) 486–2634.

Movies under the Stars

*M*ansfield **Drive-in,** *junction of Routes 31 and 32 in Mansfield; (860) 423–4441. One of Connecticut's few remaining drive-in theaters, the Mansfield Drive-in offers good, old-fashioned double bills on its three screens. One of the best ways to enjoy the pleasures of a warm summer night. Gates open around 7:00 P.M. and first show starts at dusk. Admission.*

Pleasant Valley Drive-in, *Route 181, Barkhampstead, is one of our favorite summerime treats. It's always a beautiful drive along the river to and from the show. One screen; gates open around 6:30 P.M. and first feature starts at dusk. Admission. (860) 379–6102.*

Video Place is something like a living computer game. As you walk around or move hands, legs, arms, and feet, you can see yourself on a large TV screen interacting with an artificial world created by the computer and controlled by your activity. There's no keyboard or any of that other stuff associated with computers; just you and the picture. How you move your arms, hands, and body as you look at the screen changes the colors, views, and sounds. This experiment in "artificial reality" is ongoing, so there are new variations being added all the time.

Also on campus is the ***Ballard Institute and Museum of Puppetry*** (Willimantic Cottage, Weaver Road), a collection of more than 2, 000 puppets. Over half the puppets were created by Frank Ballard, puppetry wizard and professor emeritus of dramatic arts. Puppets and puppet lore dominate the museum's three rooms. Some of the puppets are beautiful and charming; others are dark and disturbing; all are exquisite. One fascinating fact we learned was about the origin of the marionette. Legend has it that Saint Francis of Assisi made small jointed figures to dramatize the Nativity. He called them "little Marys" or "marionettes." Open Thursday and Friday, 11:00 A.M. to 3:00 P.M.; Saturday and Sunday, noon to 5:00 P.M. Free. Call (860) 486–4605 for information about special exhibits and events.

A short distance from the busy UConn campus at Storrs, the Natchaug River rumbles through a shallow gorge and pours over a small waterfall into a clear pool at the center of a secluded, sun-dappled clearing. Winding over, under, and around the tumbled boulders on either shore are a handful of gentle walking trails. This is ***Diana's Pool,*** and it is a secret picnic ground used mainly by local fisherfolk, UConn students, and one or two enterprising travel writers.

Diana's Pool isn't easy to find, but it's worth the effort. Take Route 6 and look for signs directing you to South Chaplin or Sherman Corners. Turn right onto Diana's Pool Road. This is a dead end, but about 100 feet up the road there's an unmarked parking area on the left (look for a NO SWIMMING sign). From there walk about 100 feet down the trail; it branches a couple of times, and if you're not sure which branch to follow, walk toward the sound of the water. At the end of the trail you'll find yourself in a sylvan glade so perfect you'll expect to see dryads and fauns frolicking. If you want to picnic, you'll have to do without picnic tables, but the sun-warmed rocks above the pool are a great place to spread a blanket and watch the play of sunlight and shadow on the water. Diana's Pool is relaxing at almost any time of the year, but we like it best in the fall when cool weather kills off the mosquito population and the fall foliage is in full color. Be sure to wear boots or high-top sneakers for walking and rock climbing.

If you continue west on Route 44 from the UConn campus, you'll pass through Mansfield, home to the **Mansfield Depot** restaurant. Housed in a converted railroad station on Route 44, this place is a strange brew of surprisingly sophisticated food and student hangout atmosphere. Lunch is fairly casual, featuring salads, hearty sandwiches, burgers, homemade soups, and quiches. Things are somewhat more formal at dinner; any of the pasta or fish dishes are good bets, as well as the steaks and the veal. The wine list may surprise you, having more depth than one would expect from a small, informal place in a rural setting. The Depot is open for lunch daily except Saturday, 11:30 A.M. to 2:00 P.M. Dinner is served daily from 5:00 to 9:30 P.M. There is a Sunday brunch, 11:00 A.M. to 2:30 P.M. Call (860) 429–3663.

Continuing west along Route 44, you'll wind up in the quaint community of Ashford, home to a wonderfully thrifty, only-in-New-England version of recycling: a library in the old town dump! Even though we're From Away, we were both raised by that good old New England motto: "Use it up. Wear it Out. Make it do or do without." That's why we think this "library" at the Ashford Transfer Station is such a neat idea. It happened this way. A few years back, folks began remarking that a lot of perfectly good books were being sent to the dump, so the people down at the town's **Babcock Public Library** put their heads together to come up with a way to get some more mileage from these castoffs. What they came up with was an "annex" of the library at a central location—the, er, dump— where people could drop off or pick up used books free of charge.

So the **Ashford Transfer Station,** where everybody takes their recyclables and trash, gained a plywood shed with simple plank shelving. Now, when residents drop off their recyclables, more often than not, they stop by the "annex" to browse the shelves and pick up a couple novels. The arrangements are simple. Books are divided into broad categories such as "mysteries," "westerns," or "romance," with titles running the gamut from Stephen King and Tom Clancy to books of philosophy and children's books; drop off what you've read and take as many other books as you want. People from outside of Ashford—such as yourself—are welcome to use the library, but trash services are for Ashford residents only. The

I Scream . . .

*Y*ou didn't think they keep all those cows just for pretty did you? The Quiet Corner is home to some of the most sinful, homemade ice cream in the state. Beside UConn's Dairy Bar, here's some more super scoopers to check out.

D. Fish Family Farm, *20 Dimock Lane (off Route 85), Bolton. Here's your chance to show the kids each step in the ice cream making process, starting with petting the calves. Well, OK, that's not really an official step, but it's a nice fringe benefit. Milking occurs twice each day (5:30 to 6:00 A.M. and 4:00 to 5:00 P.M.). Bottling is more or less constant. Ice-cream making happens on Mondays. All of these activities are open for viewing. Of course, the big treat is sampling the ice cream. The dairy store is at the farm sells milk, very rich, very creamy ice cream, fresh organic produce and herbs, and locally made jams and jellies. Pony rides and other special events are offered from time to time. The dairy store is open Monday through Saturday, 8:00 A.M. to 8:00 P.M.; ice cream scooped, 11:00 A.M. to 8:00 P.M. Call (860) 646–9745 for information about tours or special events.*

Salem Valley Dairy, *200 Darling Road (near junctions of Routes 11 and 85). Rich is the word for Salem Valley Dairy's ice cream. Rich and, well, eccentric. How else would you describe an establishment that peddles outrageous flavors like ginger and espresso fudge? Actually, the menu features plenty of familiar flavors as well as an ever-changing menu of innovative items. Open from 11:00 A.M. to 11:00 P.M. daily; shorter hours in cooler months; closed January and February. Call (860) 859–2980.*

We-Lik-It, *Route 97, Pomfret. Nestled in a nineteenth-century cider mill, this ice-cream shack comes complete with farm critters and the occasional movie star. Paul Newman, whose Hole in the Wall Camp for terminally ill children is just down the road apiece, has been spotted indulging in We-Lik-It's ultra-rich frozen confections. (For those who like to star gaze, we have it on very reliable authority that when Mr. Newman is at the Hole in the Wall— usually in the summer—he often can be spotted picking up his Sunday New York Times at the Cumberland Farms in Ashford.)*

Franklin's Cursed Apples

*T*he quiet little hamlet of Franklin in the far southern reaches of the Quiet Corner has always been a farming community. One of Connecticut's most famous pieces of folklore is about dark doings and murder in this peaceful village.

In spring 1693 when Franklin's apple orchards were in blossom, an old pack peddler named Horgan spent a successful day in the village, selling his wares to the goodwives of Franklin. He asked one of the farm wives for a place to stay for the night and was directed to Micah Rood's farm. Rood often made his spare room available for travelers.

Micah Rood might have had room in his house, but throughout the village, he was known as a man with no room in his heart. He was a miserly skinflint who delighted in scaring the children who crept into his apple orchards hoping to make away with a piece of fruit. Horgan made his way to the Rood farm, where Micah agreed to put him up for the night. It's said that dinner conversation revolved around how much gold and silver the peddler had taken in that day.

The next morning, villagers were stunned to find Horgan's battered and bloody body beneath an apple tree in Rood's orchard. Micah Rood was questioned about the murder, but with little evidence, Horgan's death went

unpunished. As spring came on, the townspeople noticed the white apple blossoms on the tree beneath which Horgan had met his fate were splashed with red. Later when the fruit of the tree matured, the apples' sweet white fruit was stained with dark drops of red. The townspeople whispered the old peddler had, with his dying breath, cursed Rood and his trees. Mr. Rood never picked the fruit from that tree and later was found dead, sitting in a chair staring out at his orchard. Franklin's bloody apple tree continued to thrive and bear fruit until it was blown down in the 1938 hurricane. Today, you can still see traces of Franklin's blood-stained apples when you pick apples at some of the neighboring orchards.

Franklin, Connecticut, is located on Route 169, one of the most scenic roads in Connecticut.

Franklin's apples may be famous in folklore, but today, it's mushrooms that give Franklin its fame. Franklin Farms' mushroom caves are located at 931 Route 32 North. You can't take a tour of the mushroom caves, but you can buy fresh mushrooms at the facility. You'll find several varieties of fungus, including the familiar white mushrooms, and Portobellos, creminis, oyster mushrooms, and shiitakes.

Call (860) 642-6640 for hours and more information.

transfer station "library" (232 Upton Road; 860–429–2750) is open Wednesday, noon to 8:00 P.M.; Saturday, 8:00 A.M. to 4:00 P.M.; and Sunday, noon to 4:00 P.M.

Blue Slope Farm Inc., 144 Blue Hill Road, Franklin; (860) 642–4424.

Franklin Farms Penne with Mushroom Gorgonzola

3 cups penne pasta, uncooked

3 tablespoons olive oil

1 pound fresh white mushrooms (Franklin Farms mushrooms, naturally), cleaned and thinly sliced

1 teaspoon minced garlic

3 cups sliced zucchini or yellow squash

½ cup thinly sliced sun-dried tomatoes in oil, drained

4 ounces Gorgonzola or other blue cheese, crumbled

1 3-ounce package cream cheese, cut into several pieces, room temperature

1 teaspoon salt

½ teaspoon black pepper

Cook pasta in salted water according to package instructions. Drain and rinse under warm water. Keep warm.

In a skillet over high heat, heat oil until hot. Add mushrooms and garlic. Cook, stirring occasionally, until mushrooms are browned and most of the liquid evaporates, about 5 minutes.

Add zucchini and sun-dried tomatoes to skillet and cook, stirring occasionally, until tender, about 5 to 7 minutes.

Add reserved pasta along with blue cheese, cream cheese, and salt and pepper. Toss until cheese melts and coats pasta. Serve immediately.

Serves 6

Tiny Franklin has a surprising number of attractions. One of our favorites is this very personal collection of farm implements and tools housed in a rambling red barn. The museum offers educational programs and demonstrations relative to the importance of farming in this country. Special events in July and October. Call (860) 642–6413 or fax (860) 642–4424 for information and hours.

Tolland

As a rule, Nutmeggers understand deli about as well as New Yorkers understand chowder. Which is to say that neither understands the other very much at all. The pleasant exception is *Rein's N.Y. Style Deli-Restaurant* at 435 Hartford Turnpike (Route 30) in Vernon. This is a large, noisy place, with brisk service and small tables that would be right at home in Gotham. The only reminder that you're still in Connecticut comes from a bunch of signs making cute reference to things and places New York (with the rest rooms naturally located in Flushing). But never mind the decor. What counts is that the food is authentic deli that you wouldn't be surprised to find at Manhattan's famed Carnegie.

The half sours are crisp and briny. The firm fat chips arrive smoking hot. The turkey and pastrami are both eminently respectable. The corned beef is only a notch or two below the primo variety we used to buy at Pastrami and Things. And we like the Reubens as well as the ones we got in Manhattan at the deli from which the sandwich takes its name. Come to think of it, we also like the combo sandwiches here *better* than the ones we used to get at Reubens. If your taste doesn't run to deli meats and sandwiches, don't worry. The menu here is huge, and everything on it seems to be available all day. No matter when you stop by, you can get anything from blintzes to bagels, to lox and eggs to a full dinner to a diet plate. And all of it has that special deli touch. If you've ever wondered why New Yorkers rave about deli, here's your chance to find out without having to actually go to New York. So what more could you ask for? Open daily, 7:00 A.M. to midnight. Call (860) 875–1344.

The lights are on, but nobody's home at the **Benton Homestead** on Metcalf Road in Tolland. A ghostly figure in a military uniform seems to appear at the front door. Footsteps echo through the east wing, and then gradually trail off into silence. Occasionally the whole house shakes without making a sound.

A spokesman for the Tolland Historical Society, which acquired the Benton Homestead in the late 1960s, enigmatically notes that an old house plagued by a flying squirrel "can produce a lot of noise" but refrains from speculation on the subject of the supernatural. The society prefers to concentrate on the house's unusual architectural details, original paneling, period furnishings, and the facts that it is the ancestral home of former U.S. Senator William Benton and was used to house Hessian prisoners during the Revolution.

Area ghost watchers, on the other hand, have an abiding interest in the place and eagerly place the blame for certain strange goings-on at the homestead squarely on the shoulders of one Elisha Benton. In 1777, patriot Benton contracted smallpox while being held in a British prisoner-of-war camp. Sent home to Tolland to die, he was nursed by his seventeen-year-old sweetheart, Jemina Barrows. A little more than a month after Benton died in this house, Jemina succumbed to the same disease. Their graves lie 48 feet apart on the west lawn of the homestead.

During the years since this incident, the Benton Homestead is said to have played host to various ghostly activities. A member of the household staff claimed to have seen a weeping apparition in a white dress; a guest once reported having heard inconsolable sobbing at midnight;

a common story has a uniformed figure wandering the house with arms outstretched as if pleading.

The Benton Homestead is open daily, May through October, 1:00 to 4:00 P.M. Donation appreciated. Call (860) 872–8673.

Two other antique buildings in Tolland have a less lurid past. In colonial times the *Hicks-Stearns House* at 42 Tolland Green was first a tavern, then a private home. It was later made over in the Victorian style, a form that it retains today. The building now houses a collection of Victoriana, including some nifty faux bamboo furniture and collections of calling cards and children's toys. The house is open from mid-May through mid-October on Wednesday and Sunday from 1:00 to 4:00 P.M. or by appointment. Donation appreciated. Call (860) 875–7552.

The 1856-vintage *Old Tolland Jail Museum* on the green at the junction of Route 74 and Route 195 housed prisoners until 1968. Today the intimidating iron-and-stone structure houses the Tolland Historical Society's collection of antique manufactured goods, farm implements, furniture, and Indian artifacts. The museum is open mid-May through mid-October on Sunday from 1:00 to 4:00 P.M. Call (860) 875–7559.

Continuing north and east, you'll come to Stafford Springs. Once upon a time, the springs drew crowds to take their healthful waters. Today the remnants of life in a former Victorian spa-cum-mill-town can still be seen in many of the beautiful Queen Anne and Gothic Revival houses that crowd the town's hilly streets. Stafford Springs is also home to a raceway and a perfectly wonderful little enthusiasts' museum called *Gasoline Alley Automotive Museum* at 58 Buckley Highway (Route 190).

In the collectors' lexicon, we're not sure what comes after "car nut," but whatever the word is, Don Passardi fits it to a T. He collects everything connected with the car industry from vintage gasoline pumps and oil cans to restored autos such as a 1946 Ford Sportsman, one of only 743 manufactured. In danger of being squeezed out of his living quarters by his "collection," Don did what any sensible person in the throes of passionate collecting would do: He built a 4,800-square-foot building next to his house and christened it the Gasoline Alley Automotive Museum. Admission to the museum is by appointment only, so call (860) 684–2675.

Buell's Orchard at 108 Crystal Road in Stafford is a century-old farm stand par excellence. Starting in July with blueberries, the stand sells fresh produce throughout the growing season. August brings fresh peaches. Apples appear during the fall and can last well into the winter, depending on the size of the apple crop. The stand also sells cider, Vermont cheese, and pumpkins. The caramel apples are made with a special caramel sauce into which are dipped "good firm late apples" that Robert Buell uses especially for this purpose. We guarantee that they are among the best you've ever tasted. The season for caramel apples starts about Labor Day and ends around Halloween. On Columbus Day weekend, the Buells celebrate the harvest with an open house that includes hayrides and free cider and doughnuts. Open weekdays, 8:00 A.M. to 4:00 P.M. and Saturday, 8:00 A.M. to 3:00 P.M. Call (860) 974–1150.

North of Stafford, hard by the Massachusetts line, is Connecticut's smallest town, the diminutive settlement of Union (population 620). Most travelers pass it by, but for bibliophiles, it's a standard stop en route to Massachusetts. For here resides one of the state's unique eateries, the *Traveler Restaurant* on Route 86 (Interstate 84, exit 74). The Traveler is first and foremost a place for good, home-style cooking. Full-tilt-boogie turkey dinners and turkey pot pies at very moderate prices are the specialties here, and the Traveler reputedly serves twelve tons of the big bird a year. What we like though is one special little twist. Not only can you order a decent meal here, but customers are invited to pick out a book from the shelves lining the walls, read it while eating, and then take it home. That's right, buy a meal, get a book. Actually the folks at the Traveler are so into books, one of the servers told us: "Come in to use the rest room and we'll probably give you a book." Children are well-treated, and the supply of kid's books is great. If your one free book isn't quite enough, there's an excellent little used book shop on the lower level. There's also a cute antiques store on the property. Make sure you ask for a window table, so you can look out at the pond. Open daily from 7:00 A.M. to 8:00 P.M. The Traveler does breakfast, lunch, and dinner. Breakfast is served until 11:00 A.M., but omelettes and lighter fare are available all day. Call (860) 684–4920.

Like Union, the town of Willington, south of Stafford Springs, is one of those places most travelers pass by unknowingly. Don't you do so. For located on Route 32 (½ mile east of the junction with Route 195) in Willington is a little slice of heaven. *Willington Pizza,* with its small-town setting and decor running to carousel horses, may seem country quaint, but the pizza selection is definitely big-city sophisticated. There's a broad selection of pies and toppings, including some low-fat pies for people watching their cholesterol. But the reason most people make the pilgrimage to Willington is for the delicious Red Potato Pizza. This was the pie that gained nationwide attention on the *CBS Morning News.* Although pizza pros in New Haven would disown it, the crunchy crust, garlicky roasted potatoes, and sour cream topping make for a rich and different pie that needs to be judged (repeatedly) on its own merits. And, while we've never personally tried it this way, there are aficionados who claim that the only way to eat a Red Potato Pizza is with a side-dish of iced caviar for topping each yummy slice. Open daily from 11:00 A.M. to 11:00 P.M.; midnight on Friday and Saturday. Call (860) 429–7433.

Old Woodstock

*C*hrist Church in Pomfret is definitely not the traditional white New England church with pointed steeple. Instead, this is a stone-and-brick building with a certain Byzantine influence. The interior, decorated in what one might call "high Victorian camp," makes an ideal backdrop for six extraordinary stained-glass windows, designed by famed Arts and Crafts designer Louis Comfort Tiffany early in his career and installed in the church in 1882.

Tiffany, a native of nearby Killingly, created the windows before moving to New York City, and all but one is an original Tiffany design. It is believed that Tiffany copied the Saint George window from an original Venetian design. Interestingly, the dedications and inscriptions in all six windows are rendered in lead, not in the more common paint, and the glass used is chunkier and more faceted than later Tiffany efforts. The themes here aren't normal to Tiffany, either. Instead of the common Tiffany floral and pastoral compositions, these items feature religious subjects. Besides Saint George, there are two crosses, one with a stylized peacock, of all things. There's also a window depicting the Parable of the Wise and Foolish Virgins and one depicting the Parable of the Talents, with the inscription, "Well done my good and faithful servant." Finally, there is a rose window depicting Ezekiel and the wheel. We recommend visiting about one hour before sunset to get the full effect of sunset through the rose window. Call (860) 928–7026 for information. Ask at the church office for a tour. Make sure you take a good look at the church's interior. It's a haven of gorgeous Arts and Crafts wood carving and tile work.

Still Waters at the junction of Routes 44 and 198 in tiny Eastford is one of those shops antiques hounds, particularly lovers of vintage clothing, dream about but rarely find. Our friend Anne Goshdigian told us about this place, and we're so glad she did. The vintage clothing, especially the hats, costume jewelry, and coats, are glorious and in prime condition. And the prices aren't just right, they are a downright steal. Our friend Anne picked up a gorgeous alpaca, hand-tailored swing coat

Woodstock and Pomfret Trivia

During the mid-to-late nineteenth century, Woodstock and Pomfret were dubbed "inland Newports" due to their popularity with the rich and ostentatious, who trained up from New York or down from Boston to build lavish summer "cottages" in the Quiet Corner.

from the '50s for practically the price of a department store sweater. One of the authors of this book (*not* David) is a fan of old hats; she wears them and uses them to decorate her house, and she is in hog heaven when she visits Still Waters. The owner, a helpful and pleasant woman, promises customers "many eclectic surprises" and she's right. Visit Still Waters and be surprised. Open Thursday through Saturday, 10:00 A.M. to 5:00 P.M.; Sunday, noon to 5:00 P.M. Hours can vary in the winter, so call (860) 974– 3500 for information.

If you decide to stay in the Pomfret area, you can't do much better than **Celebrations Inn** at 330 Pomfret Street (Routes 44 and 169). Quartered in the old Pomfret Inn, this is a beautiful little B&B, with five rooms and suites, some with private baths. Lots of fireplaces and choice antiques punctuate the spacious rooms, most of which are charmingly decorated with floral patterns, giving them an airy English-garden quality. This is one of only a few accommodations in the state that welcomes not only your children, but your pets. Just let them know you're bringing a furry friend when you make your reservation. At Celebrations the breakfast included in the room rate isn't just coffee and a roll; you get the full spread, well prepared and served with much warmth and style. Call (860) 928–5492; Web site, celebrationsinn.com

Route 169 weaves south from Woodstock through Pomfret, Brooklyn, and Canterbury and has been officially dubbed one of the ten most outstanding scenic byways in the United States. We can't think of a better spot to refresh yourself on Route 169 than the **Vanilla Bean Cafe** at the corner of Routes 169, 44, and 97. After the previous edition of this book had kicked around a bit, several readers told us that they felt we had done an injustice to Pomfret's favorite hangout. So we made a trip up to Pomfret to check this cutie-pie place out again, and we have to agree that our description in previous editions did not do justice to the menu or the décor. Housed in a renovated nineteenth-century barn, this is one pretty place for lunch, dinner, or a mid-afternoon cup of cocoa. The soups here are fabulous—nothing fancy, no pear and rutabaga chowder—just beautifully prepared simple soups. We like the tomato Florentine in summer paired with a salad. In winter, go for a warmer-upper of the cheese-topped chili in either beef or vegetarian. Perhaps we don't get out much, but their sea-bass cakes were something a revelation to us, erasing memories of horrid school-cafeteria salmon cakes. The turkey sandwich tastes like the best part of

Thanksgiving dinner, the leftovers. The Vanilla Bean is family-run by the Jessuruns, and chances are, you'll run into at least one of them when you visit. We are usually too full for dessert, but the home-made ice cream really hits the spot after a chili lunch. In the evenings, you'll often find entertaining poetry readings, folk concerts, and poetry slams. (The UConn campus at Stoorss is close-by, so creative talents abound.) Open Monday and Tuesday from 7:00 A.M. to 3:00 P.M.; Wednesday through Friday from 7:00 A.M. to 8:00 P.M.; Saturday and Sunday from 8:00 A.M. to 8:00 P.M. Call (860) 928–1562 for more information.

Called by *Travel and Leisure* magazine "a Caprilands for the '90s," **Martha's Herbiary,** 589 Pomfret Street (Route 169 at the junction of Routes 44 and 97), is a sweet-smelling treasure snuggled in the carriage house and servants' quarters of an eighteenth-century house. The gift shop is packed to the rafters with potpourri, soaps, essential oils, cooking herbs, and lotions. Cooking demonstrations and classes take place in the kitchen in the back. Outside the gardens overflow with perennials, heirloom vegetables (vegetables grown from old strains of the plant, many dating back to colonial times), edible flowers, fish ponds, a sunken garden, and row upon row of herbs. Martha holds classes throughout the year on a variety of topics such as making cordials, natural cosmetics, and drying herbs. Classes are by reservation only. Call (860) 928–0009 for operating hours and class schedules.

Solair Recreation League (860) 928–9174; Woodstock. Solair is what our mothers in their most shocked voices used to call a nudist camp. It's been around since the '30s and offers 300 acres of wooded solitude. Amenities include a lake, rental cabins, pool, tennis and volleyball courts, and a social hall. Visitors are welcome provided you make reservations in advance. If you're feeling frisky, you can get a couples-only one-day trial membership for a small fee. You'll find the Solair Recreation League off English Neighborhood Road in Woodstock. Before just dropping in, call for directions, hours, more information, and reservations. Open from mid-April through late October (when it gets a bit nippy to be running around sky-clad!). Don't forget the sunscreen.

The **Brayton Grist Mill and Marcy Blacksmith Shop Museum** on Route 44, at the entrance to Pomfret's Mashamoquet Brook State Park, showcases two establishments that in 1857 made an agreement to jointly support a dam and flume on Mashamoquet Brook.

The four-story Brayton Grist Mill is a reminder of long-ago days when every town on a river or creek had a water-powered mill to shell corn and grind grain. The gristmill on Mashamoquet Brook was operated by William Brayton from 1890 until his death in 1928. The equipment on display includes the turbine, the millstone, and a corn sheller patented in 1888.

Won't Fade Away

*The **Bara-Heck Settlement** at the junction of Routes 44 and 97 in Pomfret is another of those abandoned villages that just won't go away. Founded by two Welsh families in 1780 and abandoned in 1890, stories persist that somewhere in time, the town still lives. Visitors to this abandoned spot have reported hearing the sweet silver laughter of children, cows mooing, dogs barking, mothers calling children in from play, and wagon wheels creaking along unpaved tracks. The sounds reportedly appear most prevalent near the town's old cemetery and some of the cellar holes. Some visitors have also reported seeing the ghosts of a bearded man and a small child. Take Route 97 north to the side road just north and to the left of Mashomoquet Brook, then follow the dirt road about ¼ mile to the settlement.*

The Marcy Blacksmiths also plied their trade in a shop along Mashamoquet Brook; in fact, the area became known as Marcy Hollow. In 1830, Orin Marcy of Pomfret opened the shop, which used a water-powered bellows and triphammer. The next two generations of Marcys prospered, perfecting their craft. Darius, Orin's son, won a first prize for his horseshoes at the Chicago World's Fair in 1893. There are a number of antique tools displayed at the blacksmith shop; some are farrier's tools, others are wheelwright's tools. Several tools are specially made and stamped "O. Marcy."

The museum is open weekends, May through September, 2:00 to 5:00 P.M. Admission is free.

Merchant and publisher Henry Chandler Bowen had two great obsessions: roses and the Fourth of July. He indulged both at his summer residence in the center of the town of Woodstock, in the northeastern corner of Connecticut. There, in 1846, he built himself a board-and-batten-sided, gingerbread-encrusted Gothic Revival palace. Outside he planted a rose garden, and inside he upholstered much of the furniture in pink. The house itself he painted a fashionably subdued light lavender, but it was later repainted pink with green shutters and dark green and red trim, reminiscent of the flowers that Bowen loved. He named this classic Victorian "painted lady" **Roseland Cottage,** but today most folks in Woodstock just call it "the pink house."

It was at Roseland, during the latter half of the nineteenth century, that Bowen held the most extravagant series of Fourth of July celebrations that America had ever seen. On the day before each celebration, prominent guests from all over the country would arrive by train in neighboring Putnam, whence they would be transported by carriage to Woodstock for an evening reception that featured (what else?) pink lemonade. The next day a huge American flag, with stripes a foot across, would be displayed on one side of the house. The guests would then parade down Route 169 to Roseland Park, where they would amuse the public and each other with exchanges of high-flown rhetoric until it was time to return to Roseland for further diversions of a nonalcoholic nature. (Bowen was a temperance man.) What makes all of this so remarkable is that no less than four U.S. presidents—Benjamin Harrison, Ulysses S. Grant, Rutherford B. Hayes, and William McKinley—participated in these shenanigans, two of them—Harrison and Grant—while in office, the others while they were congressmen.

Today Roseland Cottage and its grounds and outbuildings are open to the public. Everything is much as it was in the glory days. The rose garden is still there, along with an 1850s-vintage maze of boxwood hedges, and so is most of the original Gothic Revival furniture. The famous flag is displayed in its traditional location each Fourth of July. Even the bowling alley out in the barn, thought to be the oldest such facility in a private residence in America, is still as it was. One can almost imagine Ulysses Grant—who seems to have coped well at Roseland despite the fact that he was most definitely not a temperance man—bowling his famous strike there during his July 4 visit.

Roseland Cottage is open Wednesday through Sunday, 11:00 A.M. to 5:00 P.M., June 1 though October 15. Admission. Call (860) 928–4074.

The Christmas Barn on Route 169 in Woodstock is more than just a red barn full of Christmas paraphernalia. The year-round display of Christmas decorations upstairs is balanced by displays of country furniture, crafts, lace curtains, curios, collectibles, quilts, craft supplies, and Victoriana suitable for all seasons. Besides, owners Joe and Kris Reynolds are that rare breed of people who seem able to keep the Christmas spirit alive all year. Open (until 7:00 P.M. Thursday). These hours change seasonally. Call (860) 928–7652.

Roseland Cottage

Glorious Fall Drive

In the Quiet Corner, there's no prettier fall drive than Route 169 north. Start at the intersection of Rocky Holly Road in Lisbon and head off to Woodstock and points north.

Not long after you cross the township line into Woodstock driving north on Route 198, you'll see on your left, right next to the side of the road, a rambling wooden structure built into a looming wooded hillside. The sign says **Stoggy Hollow General Store,** but it's not really a general store in the old-fashioned sense. These days, it's more of a restaurant, deli, and local hangout. It's also where folks in the know stop to pick up picnics on their way to the shaded glens of **Bigelow Hollow State Park,** about 5 miles north on Bigelow Hollow Road (Route 171).

Stoggy Hollow specializes in great overstuffed sandwiches. The best of which is the Stoggy Special, a stack of roast beef, turkey, and ham with your choice of cheese, lettuce, tomato, and Russian dressing. We think Stoggy Hollow makes some of the best crab cakes we've ever wrapped a tooth around—grilled, not fried, and served with a toothsome tomato-garlic mayonnaise. The cakes, pies, and cookies are all homemade and include the kind of simple-yet-exotic varieties (like caramel–apple pie) that tend to arise out of successful home experiments.

You can eat inside in a dining room across the hall from the deli area or, if the weather's nice, take your meal out on the porch and visit with some of the animals who live at the store. We really like the exceptionally cheeky rooster, a revelation to kids who've never seen a chicken except as a McNugget. Open daily from 7:00 A.M. to 8:00 P.M. (9:00 P.M. on Friday). Call (860) 974–3814.

Originally constructed in 1814, as a stagecoach tavern, **White Horse Tavern** on Route 193 in Thompson was used throughout the nineteenth century for various purposes. One of its last incarnations was as a tavern owned by Captain Vernon Stiles, a distinguished, if slippery, local politician.

Located near the Rhode Island and Massachusetts borders, Captain Stiles's establishment seems to have been a hole-in-the-wall for fugitives fleeing neighboring states and runaway lovers, who used Captain Stiles's good offices to join in the bonds of holy matrimony. Newlyweds became such a common presence that the tavern's kitchen routinely baked a wedding cake every Sunday.

Like so many older New England establishments, the White Horse Tavern doesn't claim that Washington slept or dined there. Using reverse snobbery, the inn claims that Washington selected a rival inn in 1775 and pronounced the accommodations "not good." The Marquis de Lafayette did, however, dine and sleep here in 1824. Call (860) 923–9571 for current hours. Last we checked, the tavern was open to the public only for Sunday brunch, 11:00 A.M. to 2:00 P.M.

You know you've found *Zip's Diner* when you see the neon sign that towers over the building advertising with commendable brevity: EAT. Located at the junction of Routes 101 and 12 (exit 93 off Interstate 395) in Dayville, Zip's is an original O'Mahoney diner, built in 1954. That makes it something of a holdover from another era.

The diner is actually a New England invention. Its progenitor, the lunch wagon, was invented by Walter Scott in 1872 in Providence, Rhode Island. More improvements followed and, in 1906, the Worcester Lunch Car Company was born. It soon was the primary popularizer of the art deco, neon-crowned, nickel alloy (later stainless steel) structure that we now associate with the American diner.

Zip's is one of the last of the original stainless steel diners still in operation and is especially notable for its pristine condition. The quilted and beveled stainless steel and the blue-accented chrome just gleam. This isn't some embalmed cultural icon, though. It's an honest-to-goodness working diner owned by local boy Thomas Jodoin, whose father managed the forerunner of the current Zip's in Danielson back in the 1940s. Thomas's brother Robert is the head chef; his son, Michael, also works in the kitchen. Brother James is the general manager. It's that kind of place. Truckers really do eat here. So do the locals, who call the place "Town Hall North."

Zip's menu is diner classic, featuring freshly prepared food, most of it made from scratch. The roast turkey with all the trimmings and the Yankee pot roast are both big dinner favorites. For lunch, we recommend the Zip burger (an especially good cheeseburger on a bulky roll) and the turkey club (made with freshly roasted turkey); these examples of the sandwich-making art are as well executed as you will find anywhere. But what Zip's is really famous for are its desserts, especially its homemade puddings and custards and the strawberry shortcake made with a flaky biscuit—all topped with real whipped cream, beaten with a wire whisk. It takes something special to stand out in this crowd, but the one dish that manages to do so is the Grape-Nuts Pudding, a house specialty.

Open daily 6:00 A.M. to 9:00 P.M. No credit cards. Call (860) 774–6335.

Head south from Zip's on Route 12 and you'll hit *Logee's Greenhouse* at 141 North Street. With the revival of all things Victorian, violets have

Zip's Own Grape-Nuts Pudding

¼ cup Grape-Nuts cereal
2 cups milk and 1 cup light cream (or
   3 cups milk)
½ cup sugar
4 eggs, at room temperature, beaten
dash salt
good splash of vanilla (about 1½ to
   2 teaspoons)
cinnamon and freshly grated nutmeg
   mixed together for topping (about
   ½ teaspoon cinnamon and
   ¼ teaspoon nutmeg)
Soft butter or non-stick cooking spray
   for greasing the baking dish

Preheat oven to 325 degrees.

Generously butter a 1½- or 2-quart
baking dish. (Or spray with non-stick
cooking spray.)

Line the baking dish with the Grape-Nuts. Just dump them in and shake the dish around until the bottom and sides are coated with a thin layer of the cereal.

Mix the eggs, sugar, salt, and vanilla together.

Pour the egg-sugar-milk mixture over the Grape-Nuts in the baking dish and then sprinkle with cinnamon-nutmeg mixture.

Bake at 325 degrees for about one hour or until a knife inserted in the center comes out clean. (Ovens vary; start checking at 45 minutes.)

Serve slightly warm with freshly whipped cream.

never been more popular, and the best place to see and buy violets is Logee's. The business has been a family operation since 1893, so when it comes to plants they speak gospel truth. The eight greenhouses have the feel of Victorian conservatories with their displays of orchids, jasmine, ferns, and a dazzling variety of begonias. Logee's publishes a mail-order catalog that's available at a small charge. Logee's is open year-round; Monday through Saturday, 9:00 A.M. to 4:00 P.M.; Sunday, 10:00 A.M. to 4:00 P.M. Call (860) 774–8083 for information.

Windham

Mention the **Golden Lamb Buttery** in a roomful of Connecticut foodies, and chances are that the initial reverent silence will shortly be followed by exclamations of "Isn't it just the best!" While we're extremely partial to Farmington's Apricots, Brooklyn's Golden Lamb Buttery at Hillandale Farm, 499 Wolf Den Road (off Route 169), just may be the most romantic restaurant in the state.

Owners Jimmie and Bob Booth (cook and host respectively) do know how to set a scene. During the warmer months, cocktails are served on a tractor-drawn hay wagon that carries you to the restaurant through

Danielson Trivia

In 1855, R. R. Jones of Danielson became the country's first woman dentist.

the opalescent summer twilight. During northeastern Connecticut's chilly winters, dinner is served by a roaring fireplace. The pieces of eclectica scattered about the vintage Jaguar, the telephone box, the country-costumed waitresses, tell you that you're in for a memorable dinner from the time you enter the barn.

Dinner starts with soup, always seasoned with fresh herbs from the garden and always a knockout. There's usually a choice of several entrees. Duck is a perennial, but lamb and beef are common, and there's almost always some kind of fish or seafood. Veggies, lots of them, are served family-style with the meal; marinated mushrooms always seem to be on the menu, and other vegetables ebb and flow with the output from the farm's garden. Everything is fresh, and it's all cooked without salt or preservatives. The desserts here are endearingly homey, especially the cakes.

Dinner is prix fixe and is served Friday and Saturday at 7:00 P.M.; there's one seating only, and you *must* have a reservation. Tuesday through Saturday the restaurant also serves lunch from noon to 2:00 P.M. (without the stage dressing, but still quite wonderful). Dinner seatings are booked months in advance; lunch is easier to get into. The restaurant is closed from January through May. No credit cards. Call (860) 774–4423.

Creamery Brook Road in bucolic Brooklyn is bordered by the usual Quiet Corner collection of quaint stone walls and verdant pastures. That's as expected. What's completely unexpected is the herd of shaggy bison. After all, Connecticut isn't exactly known as the home where the buffalo roam. Except that they do now. Austin and Deborah Tanner started out buying one bison for their dairy farm and ended up with a small, shaggy herd of American bison on their ***Creamery Brook Bison Farm,*** at 619 Purvis Road (Interstate 395, exit 91).

The Tanners offer a forty-minute tour of their farm, including a visit and petting session with Thunderbolt, their enormous, but gentle, show bison. Farm tours also include watching cows being milked and trying your hand at churning butter or ice cream. The Tanners and their employees will happily teach you about the healthful qualities of lean, red bison meat, and you can purchase various cuts of bison meat and souvenirs at the farm store. The Tanners suggest bison burgers are a good way to start. Tours are held July through September on Saturdays and Sundays at 1:30 P.M. Admission. Call (860) 779–0837 for tour information or store hours.

Antiquing in the Northeast

*W*oodbury may boast Connecticut's "antique alley," but in **Putnam** you've got a whole town full of antiques shops. OK, some carry merchandise that's somewhere just above "tag sale stuff" on the antiques food chain, but most are chockablock with high-quality, well-maintained furnishings, collectibles, and jewelry.

When its main industries quite literally went south, the town of Putnam and its citizens could have held a pity party and thrown in the towel. Instead they revitalized the town into one of the hottest antiques shopping districts in the state. Today, more than 450 dealers make Putnam their home, with most scattered throughout the Main Street area in a former factory, a renovated courthouse, and an old department store.

The anchor attraction in Putnam is the **Antiques Marketplace** at 109 Main Street, a 22,000-square-foot, renovated Victorian department store that houses about 300 dealers. For us, the best reason to visit the Antiques Marketplace is the Mission Oak Shop on the second floor. We love browsing among the authentic Gustav Stickley furniture, the reproduction Van Erp lamps, and the Arts and Crafts–style pottery from Woodstock, New York. The Antiques Marketplace isn't just for big stuff, though, there's lots of good collectible jewelry, china, and glassware, as well as vintage Christmas ornaments. Check the handwritten tags carefully, though. On one buying trip, one of us obligingly paid $55.00 for a charming, blown-glass fish Christmas ornament that had

been firmly placed in the Ritchie shopping basket by our more near-sighted half under the mistaken impression that it cost $5.00! The entire antiques district is open from 10:00 A.M. to 5:00 P.M. daily. Call (860) 928–0442.

Other stores we like to browse include:

Arts and Framing, 88 Main Street; (860) 963–0105. Lots of antique mirrors and frames, restoration, custom hand gilding, some antique furniture, and accessories.

Brighton Antiques, 91 Main Street; (860) 928–1419. Mostly imported eighteenth-, nineteenth-, and twentieth-century furniture and accessories.

Jeremiah's, 26 Front Street; (860) 963–9485. Large, multidealer shop, with an ever-changing display of estate jewelry, china, and glass. Victorian and primitive furniture.

If all that walking about has left you a tad peckish, Putnam center offers a modest selection of handy eateries offering everything from a sophisticated lunch to a light nosh. For lunch, we like the **Vine Bistro** at 85 Main Street. The dining is informal, but the contemporary menu is more sophisticated than it looks at first glance and includes some interesting pastas and a selection of artful sandwiches. There are also daily specials, which on our last visit included a very nice cold apricot soup and a grilled Portobello mushroom sandwich. Open Tuesday through Sunday. Call (860) 928–1660.

*If you're more in mind of a snack, try **Mrs. Bridges Pantry,** 136 Main Street, which features food, teas, and gifts from the British Isles. You'll find lots of neat stuff, such as tea cosies, lemon curd, and imported cards. One of the owners is a cat-fancier, so cute kitties abound. You can order a light tea of scones and a cuppa or a complete tea with sandwiches and desserts. We found their low-fat ginger scones and ginger peach iced tea just the pick-me-up we needed after a long afternoon of antiquing. The tearoom is open Wednesday through Monday from 11:00 A.M. to 5:00 P.M. call (860) 963–7040 for information.*

We don't fish, but if you do you'll probably want to put Plainfield on your itinerary. The modern **Quinebaug Valley Trout Hatchery** on Hatchery Road in the township's Central Village is one of the largest hatcheries in the East, producing 280,000 pounds of trout annually. The operation is open to the public year-round, and visitors can view the hatchery through a big glass wall. The state allows restricted fishing in the nearby waters. Open daily, 10:00 A.M. to 4:00 P.M. Call (860) 564–7542.

Keep driving west from the Plainfield area on Route 14A until you're almost in Rhode Island. There, in the hamlet of Oneco (where Route 14A is known as Pond Road), you'll find something called **River Bend Mining Attraction and Gem Stone Panning** (41 Pond Road). We're not sure what to call this place. Maybe a "Dude Mine?" In any event, while you won't exactly find the treasure of the Sierra Madres here, prospective prospectors—including small ones—can don miner's hats and delve underground in search of gemstones, fossils, or shells, or try their luck panning the sluice. Open Tuesday through Thursday, 10:00 A.M. to 5:00 P.M.; Friday, 10:00 A.M. to 8:00 P.M.; Saturday, 10:00 A.M. to 7:00 P.M.; Sunday, 9:00 A.M. to 5:00 P.M. Open early April through mid-October. Admission. Call (860) 564–3440 for information.

Prudence Crandall opened New England's first academy to admit black females on April 1, 1833. Within a month, the Connecticut General Assembly passed the "Black Law," making it illegal to establish any institution for the purpose of instructing "colored persons who are not inhabitants of this state." Miss Crandall was convicted of breaking the new law, but her conviction was overturned on a technicality, and the school remained open. After a mob attacked the school in September of 1834, however, Prudence Crandall reluctantly closed the institution and left the state. Half a century later Canterbury (and, within a few months, Connecticut) initiated an annuity on Crandall's behalf.

The 1805-vintage building in Canterbury where Miss Crandall's academy was housed is preserved as the **Prudence Crandall House Museum,**

Prudence Crandall House Museum

a site for both permanent and changing exhibits on the history of black Americans in pre–Civil War Connecticut. There are also exhibits dealing with the life of Prudence Crandall and the development of Canterbury. The museum has a gift shop and a research library. You'll find the facility at the junctions of Routes 14 and 169. Open January 15 through December 15, Wednesday through Sunday, 10:00 A.M. to 4:30 P.M. Call (860) 546–9916.

Cackleberry Farm Antiques at 16 Lisbon Road in Canterbury is a piece of inspired goofiness located just off Route 14. For the uninitiated, "cackleberries" are eggs. You'll wonder which came first, the chicken or the egg cup, when you visit this homey antiques store. Run by Robert Forest and his wife, Barbara, with crafts supplied by their daughter Jackie, Cackleberry Farm is fantasy land for collectors of country crafts and a mecca for fanciers of *Gallus gallus* (chickens to you and me).

Barbara Forest has a private collection of more than 2,000 egg cups, and you'll discover egg cups galore at Cackleberry Farms. But you'll rarely see the egg cups displayed there for the use that God intended them. Instead, Barbara and Robert show off their treasures in unexpected and unique ways. The Forests also have other chicken-related collectibles in their store. If chickens aren't your thing, there are also lots of country craft items (soft sculpture dolls, placemats, and the like) for sale. Open by chance or by appointment; Barbara says they're around most of the time, but call ahead (860–546–6335).

When we think of collections, what usually comes to mind are coins, stamps, dolls, antiques, and such small easily displayed items. The

Yaworski family has bigger ideas. Their **Haul of Fame** is a collection of antique trucks!

Inside a 21,000-square-foot warehouse on Route 14A in Canterbury, T. A. Cox, the curator, keeps fifty-seven antique vehicles and a collection of antique toys and models of heavy equipment (made by prison inmates) in tip-top shape. One of the jewels of the collection is a 1917 Mack truck. Probably the most famous item is a 1939 FK Model Mack truck, which, during World War II, hauled 70-foot 16-inch-bore cannons for coastal defense emplacements from Maine to Virginia. If your tastes run to flash, take a gander at the 1953 LTL Model Mack truck with buttery soft leather upholstery and exquisite hand-painted decals, which Cox modestly calls the most "dressed-out truck in the collection." So how does a museum like this get started? Yankee thrift, of course. The Yaworski family simply wanted to see the old trucks cared for and appreciated, not cast aside like junk. They plan on adding more space to the warehouse and upping the number of trucks in the collection to an even hundred.

The museum keeps a pretty low profile. A lot of Canterbury residents don't even know it exists. So if you have problems finding it, go to the post office for directions. (By the way, this getting-directions technique works just about everywhere in New England.) Open weekdays from 11:00 A.M. to 4:00 P.M. and Saturday from 8:00 A.M. to noon.

Scotland is one of those "blink and you're past it" places just west of Canterbury on Route 14, but for as long as we can remember, tea drinkers have been wending their genteel way there. That's because Scotland is home to Pearl Dexter's **Olde English Tea Room,** 3 Devotion Road at the junction of Routes 14 and 97. Pearl devotes several downstairs rooms of her house to the art of tea. One room holds her extensive collection of teapots, another tea trinkets, and in a third, the tearoom where you sit at lace-bedizened tables to partake of tea. The menu includes light lunch items and different types of teas. We suggest you go for the full-tilt tea, featuring tea sandwiches, scones, shortbread, sweet breads, dessert, and, of course, a pot of tea. You'll discover lots of interesting teas to taste and try and you can buy tea goodies such as the shortbread and teas to take home. Open Wednesday through Saturday, 11:30 A.M. to 5:00 P.M. by reservation only.

Willimantic (Willi to locals) is home to the largest thread mill in America and is sometimes called the "thread city." So where else would you locate a museum dedicated to the history of the textile industry? The **Windham Textile and History Museum** at 157 Union-Main Street.

Quiet Corner Trivia

The tiny settlement of Sterling near Canterbury in the Quiet Corner is named for a doctor who reneged on his promise to build the village a library if they named the town after him. Guess it was too much trouble to change the town's name yet again to Piker.

The museum occupies two 1877-vintage buildings inside the mill complex of the old Willimantic Linen Company. Dugan Mill is a two-story brick building housing a factory setting re-creating conditions of a century ago. There's a fully equipped shop floor with a spinning frame, carding machine, loom, and 1880s cast iron proof printer. Overlooking the shop is an 1890-vintage overseer's office.

The museum's three-story main building houses a re-creation of the company store that once occupied the site; it's now set up as a gift shop. The museum also offers re-creations of a nineteenth-century mill owner's mansion and a mill worker's home. The Dunham Hall Library, on the third floor, contains a one-of-a-kind collection of books, photographs, and manuscripts, including a collection of old textile industry pattern books. Open Wednesday through Sunday, 1:00 to 4:00 P.M. Admission. Call (860) 456–2178.

Is **Moosup** (pronounced Moose-up) Connecticut's most patriotic town? Come visit them on the Sunday closest to August 14 (V-J Day, the day Japan surrendered) and find out. One of our fathers fought in the Pacific theater in World War II, so it always warms our hearts to see those brave veterans honored. The whole town turns out for its "Victory

Independence Day, Willi-Style

*O*n July 4, Willimantic, like most towns in New England, celebrates Independence Day with a patriotic parade. Nothing very off-the-beaten path about that, except Willimantic's parade is a Boombox Parade. That's right, thousands of marchers all bopping along, boomboxes held high, all tuned into the town's radio station, WILI–AM. The radio station obliges by playing stirring patriotic marches and music. Anyone can join in as long you obey a few simple rules: wear red, white, and blue; tune your box to WILI; and be prepared to have a heck of a good time and not take anything too seriously. Aside from those few simple rules, your costume is limited only by your imagination (and good taste). Marchers costumed as George and Martha Washington, rocket ships, snowmen, and frogs (Windham is nearby) are regular participants. No preregistration is necessary. Participants usually assemble in downtown Willimantic and the area is well marked with signs. The Willimantic Recreation Department can usually answer questions about this year's parade. Call (860) 465–3046.

over Japan" parade—sadly, the last of its kind in the country. You'll see flags, brightly costumed marching bands, and baton twirlers, but the day really is for the vets. You'll probably have to brush away a tear or two as you watch these brave men, some wearing chests full of medal, walking in the parade or lining the sidewalks. The marchers parade from North Main Street to Prospect Street. The parade starts at 1:01 P.M. (the time Japan surrendered) and lasts until around 3:30 P.M. The parade is free; come early and bring your own lawn chairs. Call (860) 564–8005.

If you head west on Route 6 out of Willie, you come across the **Hurst Farm** at 746 East Street in Andover. If your kids have never seen livestock up close and personal, then we suggest a visit. You'll find lots of standard farm critters such as cows, goats, and lambs, as well as some of those exotic chickens with the punk-rocker hairdos. Big people will probably find more than enough to interest them at the food shop with James Hurst's own salsas, jams, and dried herb blends, and lots of "only in Connecticut" food products. In the fall there are hayrides, and pick-your-own pumpkin and dig-your-own chrysanthemums patches. Call ahead (860) 646–6536 for hours and information about special events such as the hayrides.

The sleepy village of Windham isn't well known these days. Two centuries back, however, the **Windham Frog Pond** was famous throughout England and her colonies. During the long hot summer of 1754, war and drought endangered Windham. As that summer drew to a close, ponds and streams across Connecticut were almost dry; a catastrophe for an agricultural community. That year, though, Windhamites had other worries. With the French and Indian War in full swing, they could expect especially ferocious Indian raids at the end of summer. One hot night, worried residents heard an uproar coming from a marshy pond outside the village. It sounded, they thought, like the chanting of hundreds of Indians working themselves up to an attack. Some even thought they heard someone utter the words "Colonel Dyer and Elderkin, too." Dyer and Elderkin were the community's leaders.

All night long the sound continued as the town marshaled its defenses. In the last hour before dawn, the noise rose to a crescendo before dying out at first light. Their nerves drawn taught as bowstrings, the desperate colonists prepared to fend off the expected attack. But it never came. After a while, a scouting party crept through a swamp to the pond from whence the startling noises had come. There, they found not the expected French and Indians, but the corpses of thousands of dead bull frogs choking in the shallow waters of the pond. No one could explain what had happened, but it was a wonder and no mistake. Some speculated that the night-long noises were the sounds of the frogs fighting for territory in the restricted waters, but it was only speculation.

The Frog War story eventually became well known in Europe, so much so that it was made into a popular operetta that brought notoriety, if not fame, to the small town of Windham. As recently as thirty years ago, school children in Ohio still performed the operetta. In honor of the frogs, the town renamed the site Frog Pond. Windham Frog Pond can be seen today about a mile east of Windham Center on the Scotland Road (Route 14); the pond is on your left as you cross Indian Hollow Brook.

A few years ago, Windham announced that it was adopting a new town seal. The winning entry featured—you guessed it—a frog.

Don't Miss

Here's a brief look at other cool stuff in the Quiet Corner.

Attractions

Marlborough eagle, Route 66 between Route 2 (Marlborough) and Route 85 (Hebron). A stunning piece of road art, a beautiful depiction of an eagle spanning the rocky sides of a hill. Not far from the Marlborough Country Barn and Sadler's Ordinary.

Pauchaug Forest, Route 49, Sterling (Voluntown); (860) 376–4075. A rare rhododendron sanctuary of 23,115 acres.

Special Joys Antique Doll and Toy Museum, 41 North River Road, Coventry; (860) 742–6359. Open April through October, Wednesday through Sunday, 11:00 A.M. to 5:00 P.M.; November through March, 11:00 A.M. to 4:30 P.M.

Diamond A Ranch, 975 Hartford Turnpike, Dayville; (860) 779–3000. Trail rides, Wild West cookouts, riding lessons, camp outs. Open year-round, weather permitting. By reservation only.

Shopping

Eastern Connecticut Flea Market, Mansfield Drive-in, 228 Stafford Road, (junction of Routes 31 and 32), Mansfield; (860) 456–2578. Eastern Connecticut's largest weekly outdoor flea market. Antiques and old and new crafts, household goods, and so on. Open Sundays, April through November, 9:00 A.M. to 3:00 P.M.

Stone of Scone Antiques, Books & Firearms, 19 Water Street (off Route 14 west), Canterbury; (860) 546–9917. Out-of-print books, black-powder rifles, antique jewelry, and maps.

Open Saturday, 11:00 A.M. to 5:00 P.M.; Sunday, noon to 5:00 P.M. Call about weekday hours.

Freudenwald Antiques,
26 Route 87 (one mile from Route 6), Columbia; (860) 228-1245. Americana, folk art, and pottery. Open Saturday and Sunday, 10:00 A.M. to 5:00 P.M.

LODGING

Bird-in-Hand B&B,
2011 Main Street, Coventry; (860) 742-0032. A 1731 colonial filled with antiques and six fireplaces. Very private and romantic. Hearth cooking demonstrations available. Three bedrooms, private baths, full breakfast. Children over twelve welcome. Moderate.

French Renaissance House B&B,
550 Norwich Road (Route 12), Plainfield; (860) 564-3277. Large rooms and a very friendly host. Four bedrooms, some with private baths, full breakfast. Children welcome. Moderate.

Chickadee Cottage B&B,
375 Wrights Crossing, Pomfret; (860) 963-0587. Very private (ten acres) renovated cape. Lots of antiques and beautiful gardens. Two bedrooms, one private bath, continental breakfast. Children welcome. Moderate.

Captain Parker's Inn at Quinebaug B&B,
32 Walker Road, Thompson (Quinebaug); (800) 707-7303. Gourmet Polish cooking in a beautiful home. Very relaxed and romantic. Six bedrooms, private baths, full breakfast. Children over thirteen welcome. Moderate.

General Attractions Index

A

Abbey of Regina Laudis, 92
Abbott's Lobster in the Rough, 185
Action Wildlife Foundation, 77
Al Forno, 191
Albany Turnpike, 63–75
Aldrich Museum of
    Contemporary Art, 125
Allegra Farm, 169
Allen, Ethan, 95
Allis-Bushnell House & Museum, 152
American Clock & Watch Museum, 27
American Legion State Forest, 69
American Radio Relay League, 25
Amistad Revolt, 40
Amy's Udder Joy Exotic
    Animal Farm Park, 19
Ancient Burying Ground, 4
Ancient Muster, 159
Antiq's, 59
"Antique Avenue" (Woodbury), 88
Antiques and Accommodations, 182
Antiques and Herbs, 68
Antiques at Canton Village, 52
Antiques Marketplace, 218
Antiques on the Farmington, 46
Apricots, 44
Arts and Framing, 218
Ashford, 202
Ashford Transfer Station Library, 202
Avery's Beverages, 25
Avon, 43
Avon Cider Mill, 46
Avon Congregational Church, 47
Avon Old Farms School, 43

B

Babcock Public Library, 202
Bacco's, 140

Balcony Antiques, 52
Ballard Institute and Museum
    of Puppetry, 201
Bamboo Grill, The, 52
Bantam, 85
Bantam Baking Company, 85
Bantam Cinema, 85
Bara-Heck Settlement, 212
Barbara Farnsworth, Bookseller, 101
Barker Character, Comic, and
    Cartoon Museum, 137
Barnum Museum, 116
Bart's Drive-In, 36
Battle of Ridgefield, 124
beaches,
    Calf Pasture Park, 113
    Hammonasset Beach State Park, 154
    Meigs Point Nature Center, 154
    Rocky Neck State Park, 186
Beardsley Zoological Gardens, 118
Bear Mountain, 73
Beaumont home, 174
Bee and Thistle Inn, 171
beer and brewery tours,
    Hammer and Nail Brewers, 131
Belgique Choclatier and Podisserie, 96
Belltown Hill Orchards, 22
Benedict Arnold's birthplace, 174
Benton Homestead, 206
Bethany, 133
Bethel Cinema, 126
Bethlehem, 92
Bethlehem Christmas Town
    Festival, 92
Bible Rock, 160
Bigelow Hollow State Park, 214
Birches Inn, The, 105
Birdcraft Museum and
    Sanctuary, 142
Bird House Antiques, 59

Bird-in-Hand B&B, 225
Bishop Farm and Winery, 142
Bishop's Orchards Farm
    Market, 152
Bittersweet Herb Farm, 148
Blackrock Castle, 143
Black Swan Antiques, 94
Blessing of the Fleet, 179
Bloodroot, 118
Bloomfield, 37
Bloomfield Seafood, 38
Blue Sky Foods, 65
Blue Slope Farm, Inc., 204
boat trips,
    Clarke's Outdoors, 99, 100
    Mountain Workshop, Inc., 100
    North American Whitewater
        Expeditions, 100
    Small Boat Shop, 100
    Sunbeam Express, 190
Bolton Notch Park, 193
Born in America Pizza, 149
Boulders Inn, 93
Bovano Enamelware, 142
Branford, 150
Branford Craft Gallery at Bittersweet
    Herb Farm, 148
Brayton Grist Mill and Marcy
    Blacksmith Shop Museum, 211
Bridgeport, 116
Brighton Antiques, 218
Bristol, 26
Brix Restaurant, 137
Brookfield, 123
Brookfield Craft Center, 123
Brooklyn, 218
Brookside Bagels, 60
Bruce Museum, 109
Buckingham Galleries, 67
Buell's Orchard, 207
Bull's Bridge, 98
Burr Pond State Park, 75

Bushnell Carousel, 5
Bushnell Park, 5
Butler-McCook Homestead, 7
Butternut Farm, 62
Buttolph-Williams House, 17

C

Cackleberry Farm Antiques, 220
Cafe Routier, 191
Calf Pasture Park, 113
Campbell Falls, 71, 97
Canaan, 105
candy,
    Chocolate Lace, 153
    Dryden & Palmer Rock
        Candy, 153
Canfield Corner Pharmacy, 89
Cannery, The, 105
Cannon Square, 179
Canterbury, 221
Canton, 52
Canton Barn Auction Gallery, 52
Canton Historical Museum, 55
Caprilands, 195
Captain James Francis House, 17
Captain Parker's Inn at Quinebaug
    B&B, 225
Captain's Walk, 187
Carole Peck's Good News Cafe, 89
carousels,
    Bushnell Carousel, 5
    Five-Mile Point Light, 131
    Lake Compounce Amusement
        Park, 26
Carville's Ranch House, 61
Catnip Mouse Tea Room, 68
Cedar Hill Cemetery, 6, 28
Celebrations Inn, 210
Chaiwalla, 73
Chamard Vineyards, 155
Charles R. Hart House, 61
Cheney Homestead, 20

Cheshire, 137
Chester, 163
Chester-Hadlyme Ferry, 169
Chez Lenard, 114
Chickadee Cottage B&B, 225
Chief Waramaug, 90
Children's Museum of Southeastern
    Connecticut, 176
Chocolate Lace, 153
Christ Church, 209
Christ Church Cathedral, 4
Christmas Barn, 213
Christmas Shop in Bethlehem, 92
Christopher Leffingwell House, 174
cider, 46
Claire's Cornucopia, 143
Clarke's Outdoors, 99, 100
Clinton, 154
Clinton Crossing Premium Outlet
    Mall, 154
Coast and Country, 145–92
Cochegan Rock, 176
Coffee An', 115
Colchester, 175
Collinsville, 54
Collinsville Antiques Co., 55
Colonel Amos Palmer House, 179
Compensating Reservoir, 66
Comstock Bridge, 173
Comstock, Ferre & Company, 17
Connecticut Department of
    Environmental Protection Marine
    Headquarters, 172
Connecticut Fire Museum, 34
Connecticut Notable Tours Project, 58
Connecticut River Museum, 156
Connecticut Sports Museum and
    Hall of Fame, 4
Connecticut State Museum of
    Natural History, 199
Connecticut Trolley Museum, 34
Copernican Space Science Center, 24

Copper Beech Inn, 159
Cornwall Bridge Pottery Store, 100
Cottage Restaurant, 60
Coventry, 195
covered bridges,
    Bull's Bridge, 98
    Comstock Bridge, 173
    Cornwall Bridge, 100
Cow's Outside, 121
Cracovia, 23
craftpersons and craft galleries,
    Branford Craft Gallery at
      Bittersweet Herb Farm, 148
    Brookfield Craft Center, 123
    Cornwall Bridge Pottery Store, 100
    Fair Haven Woodworks, 132
    Farmington Valley Arts
      Center, 49
    Guilford Handicrafts Center, 150
    Kent Carved Signs, 96
    Lorenz Studios, 85
    Merry-Go-Round of Fine Crafts, 89
    United Crafts, 142
Creamery Brook Bison Farm, 217
Cricket Hill Gardens, 104
Cromwell, 69
Curtis House, 105

D

D. Fish Family Farm, 203
Danbury, 120
Danbury Railway Museum, 120
day trips,
    Antiquing in Putnam, 218–19
    Connecticut River Valley
      day trip, 160–61
    fall foliage day trip, 46
    leaf-peeping day trip, 66
    Litchfield County day trip, 80
    Plantsville antiquing, 30–31
Dayle's Antiques, 30
Dayville, 215

Deacon John Graves House at Tunxis Farm, 153
Deep River,
Demonstration Forest Trail, 41
Des Jardins Oriental Rugs, 88
Desserts by David Glass, 10
Devil's Den Preserve, 111
Devil's Hopyard, 167
Diamond A Ranch, 224
Diana's Pool, 201
Dick's Antiques, 27
DiGrazia Vineyards & Winery, 123
diners,
    Norm's Diner, 185
    O'Rourke's Diner, 164
    Philips Diner, 89
    Quaker Diner, 14
    Sheik Diner, The, 105
    Skee's Diner, 76
    Winsted Diner, 70
    Zip's Diner, 215
Dinosaur State Park, 18
dinosaurs,
    Dinosaur State Park, 18
    Yale Peabody Museum of Natural History, 129
Discovery Museum, 117
Dr. Mike's, 127
drive-ins
    Mansfield Drive-in, 201
    Pleasant Valley Drive-in, 201
Dryden & Palmer Rock Candy, 153

E

1840 Stone House, 159
eagle watching, 83
East Granby, 32
East Haddam, 165
East Hartford, 19
East Lyme, 172
Eastern Accents, 54
Eastern Connecticut Flea Market, 224

Egg & I Farm, The, 104
Eiko Japonalia, 13
Elbow Room, The, 12
Elephant's Trunk Flea Market, 105
Eli Whitney Museum, 132
Elizabeth Park Rose Gardens, 10
Elms Restaurant & Tavern, 126
Epicure Market, 41
Essex, 156
Essex Saybrook Antiques Village, 191

F

Fabiola's Bistro, 47
Faces, 141
Fair Haven Woodworks, 132
fall foliage, 46
Farm Implement Museum, 37
Farmington, 39
Farmington Antiques Weekend, 44–45
Farmington Polo Grounds, 44–45
Farmington Valley Arts Center, 49
farms and dairy stores,
    Buell's Orchard, 207
    Creamery Brook Bison Farm, 217
    D. Fish Family Farm, 203
    Egg & I Farm, 104
    Fisher Old Farms, 43
    Miller Foods, 49
    Pickin' Patch, 48
    Rose's Berry Farm, 59
    Town Farm Dairy, 59
    Tulmeadow Dairy Farm, Inc., 59
Feast of Saint Anthony, 122
Feast of Saint John, 122
Fire Museum, The, 19
First & Last Tavern, 61
Fisher Old Farms, 43
Fishing Derby, 69
Five-Mile Point Light, 131
Flanders Fish Market & Restaurant, 172
Florence Griswold Museum, 170

Fort Griswold Battlefield
    State Park, 183
Fort Shantok State Park, 176
Franklin, 204
Freja Park, 193
French Renaissance B&B, 225
Freudenwald Antiques, 225
Front Parlour at The British
    Shoppe, 154

G

Gail's Station House, 125
Garden of Light, 60
gardens and flower farms,
    Cricket Hill Gardens, 104
    Elizabeth Park Rose Gardens, 10
    Glebe House, 91
    Hillside Gardens, 104
    Logee's Greenhouse, 215
    Morosani Farms, 84
    Sunflower Farms, 134
    White Flower Farm, 82
Gasoline Alley Automotive
    Museum, 207
ghosts,
    Bara-Heck Settlement, 212
    Benton Homestead, 206
    Huguenot House, 18
    Simsbury's Charthouse
        Restaurant, 55
    White Lady, 135
Ghost Train, 158
Gillette Castle, 168
Giovanni's Bakery and Pastry Shop, 24
Glastonbury, 21
Glebe House, 91
Golden Lamb Buttery, 216
Goodspeed Opera House, 166
Goshen, 76
Goulash Place, 121
Governor's Horse Guards, 49, 122
Granby, 33

Granby Oak, 33
Great American Trading Company
    Factory Outlet Store, The, 161
Greenwood Gates, 72
Griswold Inn, 157
Groton, 183
Guida's Drive-in, 165
Guilford, 150
Guilford Handicrafts Center, 150
Gunn Memorial Library and
    Museum, 94

H

Haddam, 171
Haight Vineyard & Winery, 82
Hallmark Ice Cream, 191
Hamden, 134
Hammer and Nail Brewers, 131
Hammonasset Beach State Park, 154
Harney & Sons Tea, 74
Harry's Pizza, 16
Hartford, 1
Hartford Exhibit, The, 1
Hartford Police Museum, 4
Hat City, 120
Haul of Fame, 221
Haunted Graveyard, 28
Haystack Mountain State Park, 71
Hebron, 43
Henry B. duPont Planetarium, 117
herb farms,
    Bittersweet Herb Farm, 148
    Caprilands, 195
    Martha's Herbiary, 211
    Sundial Herb Garden, 163
Heublein Tower, 58
Hibachi, 54
Hicks-Stearns House, 207
Higganum, 165
Higgies, 160
Highland Festival, 79
Hillside Gardens, 104

Hillside Historic District, 139
Hill-Stead Museum, 38
Hilltop Haven, 101
Historical Museum of Medicine
    and Dentistry, 9
Historic Ship *Nautilus* and
    Submarine Force Museum, 183
Hitchcock Chair Factory Store, 67
Hitchcock Furniture Factory, 67
Holy Land (miniature), 140
Homestead Inn, The, 143
Hopkins Inn, 93
Hopkins Vineyard, 93
Horse and Carriage Livery Service, 71
hot dogs,
    Carville's Ranch House, 61
    Chez Lenard, 115
    Guida's Drive-in, 165
    Higgies, 160
    Rawley's Drive-in, 115
    Saint's, 31
    Super Duper Weenie, 115
Hotchkiss-Fyler House, 75
Housatonic Railroad Company, 103
House of 1833 B&B, 192
House on the Hill B&B, 143
Howland-Hughes Department
    Store, 141
Huguenot House, 18
Hurlbut-Dunham House, 17
Hurst Farm, 223
Hyland House, 150

I

ice cream,
    D. Fish Family Farm, 203
    Dr. Mike's, 127
    Hallmark Ice Cream, 191
    Hurst Farm, 223
    Mystic Drawbridge Ice Cream
        Shoppe, 178

Salem Valley Dairy, 203
Shady Glen, 21
Sweet Claude's, 139
UConn Dairy Barn, 202
We-Lik-It, 203
Wentworth's, 133
Images, 142
Indian Leap, 175
Institute for American Indian
    Studies, 94
Institute of Living, 7
Irish Country Furniture, 161
Isaac Stevens House, 17
Islander, 147
It's Only Natural, 191
Iwo Jima Survivors' Monument, 26

J

J. Seitz & Co, 94
James Pharmacy, 162
Jeremiah's, 218
Johnny Ad's, 162
Jonathan Trumbull House, 174
Jonathan Trumbull, Jr., House, 174
Jones Family Farm, 136
Joseph Carpenter House, 175
Joseph Stewart's Hartford Museum, 3
Joseph Webb House, 17
Joshua Hempsted House, 187
Judie's European Baked Goods, 148
Jumping Frog, The, 11

K

Kasulaitis Farm and Sugarhouse, 66
Keeler Tavern Museum, 124
Kent, 96
Kent Carved Signs, 96
Kent Falls State Park, 96
Kerosene Lamp Museum, 70
King House Museum, 34
Kitchen Little, 178

L

Lake Compounce Amusement Park, 26
Lake Waramaug, 92
Lakeside, 85
LaMothe's Sugar House, 46
Last Post, The, 102
leaf-peeping day trip, 66
Lebanon, 176
Ledyard Power-Up—Power-Down
    Sawmill, 186
Lenny and Joe's Fish Tale
    Restaurant, 156
Lenny's Indian Head Inn, 147
Leo's, 142
Lieutenant Walter Fyler House, 37
lighthouses,
    Five-Mile Point Light, 131
    Ledge Lighthouse, 190
    Old Lighthouse Museum, 179
    Sheffield Island Lighthouse, 113
Lighthouse Inn, 190
Lime Rock Park, 101
Litchfield, 77
Litchfield Green, 77
Litchfield Historical Society
    Museum, 79
Lock 12 Historical Park, 137
Lock Museum of America, 86
Logee's Greenhouse, 215
Long Ridge Tavern, 143
Lorenz Studios, 85
Louis' Lunch, 130
Lourdes in Litchfield Shrine, 82
Lucius Pond Ordway Devil's
    Den Preserve, 111
Luddy/Taylor Connecticut Valley
    Tobacco Museum, 59
Luke's Donut Shop, 48
Lutz Children's Museum, 22
Lyman Allyn Art Museum, 189
Lyman Orchards, 28

M

Madison Beach Hotel, 192
Madison Trust Antiques, 190
Maggie Dailey's Fine Celtic Wares, 53
Manchester, 19
Manor House, 105
Mansfield Depot, 202
Mansfield Drive-In, 201
maple syrup, 43
Maria's Italian Restaurant, 53
Marcus Dairy Bar, 122
Maritime Center of Norwalk, 112
Marjolaine, 143
Mark Twain House, 10
Marlborough, 198
Marlborough Country Barn, 196
Marlborough eagle, 224
Martha's Herbiary, 211
Mashantucket Pequot Museum &
    Research Center, 180
Massacoe Indians, 55
Massacoe Plantation, 55
Massacoh Plantation, 56
Mattatuck Museum, 140
Matthews 1812 House, 103
Mayflower Inn, 105
Mazes,
    Jones Family Farm, 136
    Steck's Nursery, 136
    Valley Farm, 136
Mazotta's Restaurant & Bakery, 165
McConney's Farm, 134
Me & McGee Restaurant, 163
Meeker's Hardware, 142
Meetinghouse, 17
Meigs Point Nature Center, 154
Memory Lane Countryside Antique
    Center, 196
Merchant House, 166
Merry-Go-Round of Fine Crafts, 89
Merrywood, 58

Michaele's Coffee and Tea, 12
Mid-Connecticut Resources Recovery
    Authority, 8
Middlesex Fruitery, 165
Middletown, 166
Middlesex County Historical Society, 28
Milford, 111
Military Historians Headquarters &
    Museum, 155
Military Museum of Southern
    New England, 119
Mill House Antiques, 88
Miller Foods, 49
Milton Barn, 81
miniature golf,
    Hidden Valley, 42
    Riverfront Miniature Golf and
        Ice Cream, 42
    Safari Golf, 42
Mohawk Mountain State Park, 102
Mohegan Congregational
    Church, 176
Monroe, 137
Monte Cristo Cottage, 188
Montville, 178
Moodus Noises, 170
Moosup V-J Day Parade, 222
Morosani Farms, 84
Morris, 104
Morris Historical Society Museum, 104
Mother Earth Gallery &
    Mining Company, 123
Mountain Workshop, Inc., 100
Mount Frissel, 72
Mount Riga, 72
movie theaters,
    Bantam Cinema, 85
    Bethel Cinema, 126
Mozzicato De Pasquale's Bakery
    & Pastry Shop, 8
Mrs. Bridges Pantry, 219
Mrs. White's Tea Room, 87

Murder Mystery Train, 158
Museum of American
    Political Life, 13
Museum of Fife & Drum, 158
Music Mountain Chamber
    Music Festival, 103
Mystic, 177
Mystic Drawbridge Ice Cream
    Shoppe, 178
Mystic Hilton, 177
Mystic Pizza, 178
Mystic Seaport, 177

N

Nathan Hale Cemetery, 199
Nathan Hale Homestead, 198
Nathan Hale Schoolhouse, 166
National Audubon Society's
    Northeast Center, 98
Natural Resource Center, 7
Nature Center for Environmental
    Activities, 116
New Britain, 23
New Britain Industrial Museum, 24
New Britain Museum of
    American Art, 24
New England Air Museum, 33
New England Carousel Museum, 29
New England Jukebox and
    Amusement Company, 20
New Hartford, 67
New Haven, 128
Newington, 25
New London, 187
New London County Courthouse, 187
New London Maritime Society, U.S.
    Customs House, & Museum of
    American Maritime History, 187
New Milford, 104
New Preston, 94
Newtown, 124
Niantic, 198

Noah Webster Museum, 14
Noank, 187
Nodine's Smokehouse, 76
Norfolk, 73
Norfolk Chamber Music Festival, 71
Norm's Diner, 185
  Texas Beef Stew (recipe), 184
North American Canoe Tours, Inc., 65
North American Whitewater
    Expeditions, 100
North Stonington, 184
Northfield, 84
Norwalk, 112
Norwalk's City Hall, 112
Norwich, 177
Nothing's New, 30
Nut Museum, 171
Nutmeg Vineyard, 196

O

Old Academy Museum, 17
Old Avon Village, 47
Old Bank Antiques, 190
Old Customs House, 179
Old East Street Burying Grounds, 26
Old Lighthouse Museum, 179
Old Lyme, 173
Old Lyme Inn, 192
Old New-Gate Prison and
    Copper Mine, 31
Old Norwichtown Burial
    Ground, 28
Old Riverton Inn, 69
Old Saybrook, 162
Old State House, 3
Old Tolland Jail Museum, 207
Olde English Tea Room, 221
Olde Weathersfield, 17
O'Neill, Eugene, 190
One-Way Fare, 56
Orange, 126
O'Rourke's Diner, 164

outlets,
    Clinton Crossing Premium
      Outlet Mall, 154
    Cow's Outside, 121
    Hitchcock Chair Factory Store, 67
    Woodbury Pewter Outlet, 90

P

Paris–New York–Kent Gallery, 95
Pasta Nostra, 112
Pat's Kountry Kitchen &
      Pat's Kountry Kollectibles, 191
Pauchaug Forest, 224
Paul's Pasta Shop, 191
peach orchards,
    Belltown Orchards, 22
    Starberry Farm, 22
Peoples State Forest, 67
Pepe's Pizzeria Napoletana, 130
Peter B.'s Espresso, 12
Pfau's Hardware, 13
Philips Diner, 89
Pho Tuong Lai, 15
Pickin' Patch, 48
Pilot House, 161
Place, The, 152
Plantsville, 30–31
Plantsville Station Antique Shops, 30
Plainville, 61
Pleasant Valley, 201
Pleasant Valley Drive-In, 201
Podlasie, 23
Polish National Home, 9
Pomfret, 210
Portland, 163
Portuguese Day, 122
Project Oceanology, 184
Prudence Crandall House
      Museum, 219
Pub, The, 72
Putnam, 126
Putnam Memorial State Park, 124

INDEXES

Q

Quaker Diner, 14
Quaker Diner Meat Loaf (recipe), 14
Quinebaug Valley Trout Hatchery, 219

R

R.W. Commerford & Sons
    Circus Animals, 76
racing,
    Lime Rock Park, 101
Railroad Museum of New England, 142
Randall's Ordinary, 181
Rawley's Drive-in, 114
recipes,
    Almost-Sadler's Ordinary
        Pecan–Cream Cheese Pie, 198
    Chili-Dog Sauce, 115
    Norm's Texas Beef Stew, 184
    Penne with Mushrooms
        Gorgonzola, 205
    Quaker Diner Meat Loaf, 14
    Zip's Diner Grape-Nuts Pudding, 216
Red Brook Inn, 177
Rein's N.Y. Style Deli-Restaurant, 205
Restaurant du Village, 163
Revolutionary War Office, 174
Rich Farm Ice Cream Shop, 134
Richard D. Scofield Historic
    Lighting, 191
Ridgefield, 126
River Bend Mining Attraction and
    Gem Stone Panning, 219
Riverdale Farms Shopping, 50
Riverfront Miniature Golf and
    Ice Cream, 42
Riverton, 68
Riverton General Store, 68
road food,
    Brookside Bagels, 60
    Chez Lenard, 114
    Coffee An', 115
    Guida's Drive-In, 165
    Louis' Lunch, 130
    Marcus Dairy Bar, 122
    Pilot House, 161
    Saint's, 31
    Sea Swirl, 178
    Super Duper Weenie, 114
Roaring Brook Falls, 137
Rock Candy , 153
Rocky Hill, 17
Rocky Hill–Glastonbury Ferry, 22
Rocky Neck State Park, 186
Rose's Berry Farm, 59
Rose & Thistle, The, 106
Roseland Cottage, 212
Roseledge Farm B&B, 192
Route 10, 26
Royal Indian Burial Ground, 175

S

1768 Holley-Williams House, 74
Sadler's Ordinary, 197
Safari Golf, 42
Saint's, 31
Salem Valley Dairy, 203
Salisbury, 75
Salmon Brook Shops, 33
Samuel Huntington House, 175
Sands World Wide Games
    Factory Outlet, 173
Sankow's Beaver Brook Farm, 170
Sarah Whitman Hooker House, 13
Satan's Kingdom, 65
Schaghicoke Indian Reservation, 98
Science Center of Connecticut, 16
Scotland, 79
Scott-Fanton Museum, 119
Scottish Festival, 79
Sea Mist II, 147
Sea Swirl, 178
Second Company of the Governor's
    Horse Guards, 122
Shad Derby Festival, 36

Shady Glen, 21
Sharon, 98
Sheffield Island Lighthouse, 113
Sheik Diner, The, 105
Shelton, 136
Shenipisit Trail, 193
Shore Line Trolley Museum, 131
Silas Deane House, 17
Silo, The, 104
Silvermine Tavern, 113
Simsbury, 53, 54
Simsbury 1820 House, 56
Simsbury's Charthouse Restaurant, 55
Skee's Diner, 76
Slater Memorial Museum, 175
Sleeping Giant State Park, 132
Sloane-Stanley Museum, 98
Small Boat Shop, 100
Solair Recreation League, 211
SoNo, 114
Southbury, 107
Southford Falls, 97
Southington, 31
Special Joys Antique Doll &
    Toy Museum, 224
Spiritus Wines, 12
Stafford, 209
Stafford Springs, 209
Stamford, 111
Stamford Cone, 109
Stamford Museum and Nature
    Center, 110
St. Andrew's Society, 79
Stanley-Whitman House, 39
Starberry Farm, 22
Starbucks, 12
State Capitol Building, 5
Steamboat Dock, 157
Steck's Nursery, 136
Sterling, 224
Still Waters, 209
St. James Church, 142

Stoggy Hollow General Store, 214
Stone House, 151
Stonehenge, 126
Stone of Scone Antiques, 224
Stonington, 177
Stony Creek, 148
Stony Creek Market, The, 148
Storrs, 201
St. Peter Church, 142
Stratford, 110
St. Stephen's Church, 166
Submarine Library Museum, 164
Sunbeam Express, 190
Sundial Herb Garden, 163
Sunflower Farms, 134
Super Duper Weenie, 114
Sweet Claude's, 138
Sycamore, 127

T

Talcott Mountain, 57
Talcott Mountain State Park, 57
Tantaquidgeon Indian Museum, 176
Tapping Reeve House &
    Law School, 81
Tarrywile Mansion and Park, 142
teas and tearooms,
    Catnip Mouse Tea Room, 68
    Chaiwalla, 73
    Front Parlour at The British
        Shoppe, 154
    Harney & Sons Tea, 74
    Mrs. Bridges Pantry, 219
    Mrs. White's Tea Room, 87
    Olde English Tea Room, 221
Ted's Restaurant, 136
Thames River, 148
Thankful Arnold House, 190
Thimble Islands, 147
Thomas Griswold House, 150
Thomaston, 67
Thomaston Clock Company, 68

Thompson, 228
Three Dog Bakery, 12
Tidewater Inn, 192
Timbertown Swing Set Company, 111
Timexpo Museum, 139
Timothy's, 6
Tir'na nO'g Farm B&B, 106
Tolland, 208
Topsmead, 84
Torrington, 78
Town Farm Dairy, 59
Trading Post, The, 54
Trash Museum, 8
Travelers Insurance Companies, The, 3
Traveler Restaurant, 208
Trinity College Chapel, 6
Trumball Family Store, 174
Tulmeadow Dairy Farm, Inc., 59
Tunxis Plantation Golf Course, 42
Twain, Mark, 10

U

UConn Dairy Barn, 202
Uncle Willie's, 141
Under Mountain Inn, 72
Union Cemetery, 135
Union Station, 103
Unionville Museum, 45
United Crafts, 142
United House Wrecking Company, 110
University of Connecticut, 199
U.S. Coast Guard Academy, 186
USS *Nautilus* Memorial, 183

V

Valley Falls Park, 193
Valley Farm, 136
Valley Railroad Company, 157
Vanilla Bean Cafe, 210
Victoria Rose, 30
Video Place, 200
Village Barn and Gallery, 94

Village Sweet Shop, 68
Vine Bistro, 218
vineyards and wine tastings,
    Bishop Farm and Winery, 142
    Chamard Vineyards, 155
    DiGrazia Vineyards & Winery, 123
    Haight Vineyard & Winery, 82
    Hopkins Vineyard, 93
    Nutmeg Vineyard, 196
    Spiritus Wines, 12
Vintage Radio & Communications
    Museum, 59
Vintage Shop, 60
Volsunga IV, 149

W

Wadsworth Atheneum, 3
Wadsworth Stable, 174
walking and hiking hints, 35
War & Pieces, 13
Warren Occult Museum, 135
Washington, 96
Waterbury, 139
waterfalls,
    Campbell Falls, 71, 97
    Kent Falls, 97
    Roaring Brook Falls, 137
    Southford Falls, 97
Watershed Balloons, 87
Webb-Deane-Stevens Museum, 17
Weir Farm, 122
We-Lik-It, 203
Wentworth's, 133
West Avon Congregational Church, 48
West Cornwall, 102
West Hartford, 12
West Street Grill, 78
Westbrook, 156
Westport, 114
Wethersfield, 16
Wethersfield Historical Society, 28
Whale Oil Row, 187

whale-watching cruises, 190
Whistle Stop Muffin Co., 143
White Flower Farm, 82
White Horse Tavern, 214
White Lady, 135
White Memorial Foundation and
    Conservation Center, 81
Whitfield House Museum, 150
Whitfield Jewelry, 150
Whitlock Farm Booksellers, 133
Whitney Museum of American Art
    at Champion, 109
Willimantic, 221
Willington Pizza, 208
Wilson Museum, 37
Windham, 223
Windham Frog Pond, 223
Windham Textile and History
    Museum, 221
Windsor, 33
Windsor Locks, 33
Winsted, 72
Winsted Diner, 70
Wisdom House Retreat Center, 83
Witch's Dungeon, 31
Wonder Workshops, 117

Wood's Pit BBQ & Mexican Cafe, 86
Woodbury, 88
Woodbury Guild, The, 88
Woodbury Pewter Outlet, 90
Woodstock, 210

X

XYZ Bank Robber, 159

Y

Yale Center for British Art, 128
Yale Peabody Museum of Natural
    History, 129
Yale Summer School of Music, 71
Yale University, 128
Yale University Art Gallery, 129
Ye Ancient Burial Ground, 187
Ye Olde Tavern Mill, 187
Yellow Victorian, 68
Your Just Desserts, 15

Z

Zip's Diner, 215
Zip's Diner Grape-Nuts Pudding
    (recipe), 216

Kid Stuff Index

Action Wildlife Foundation, 77
Allegra Farm, 169
Amy's Udder Joy Exotic Animal
    Farm Park, 19
Avon Cider Mill, 46
Ballard Institute and Museum of
    Puppetry, 201
Barker Character, Comic, and
    Cartoon Museum, 137
Barnum Museum, 116
Beardsley Zoological Gardens, 118
Bushnell Carousel, 5
Bushnell Park, 5

Calf Pasture Park, 113
Children's Museum of Southeastern
    Connecticut, 176
Connecticut Department of
    Environmental Protection Marine
    Headquarters, 172
Copernican Space Science Center, 24
Creamery Brook Bison Farm, 217
D. Fish Family Farm, 203
Danbury Railway Museum, 120
Dinosaur State Park, 18
Discovery Museum, 117
Egg & I Farm, 104

Five-Mile Point Light, 131
Governor's Horse Guards, 49, 122
Henry B. duPont Planetarium, 117
Institute for American Indian
    Studies, 94
Kasulaitis Farm and Sugarhouse, 66
Lake Compounce Amusement Park, 26
LaMothe's Sugar House, 46
Last Post, The, 102
Lutz Children's Museum, 22
Maritime Center of Norwalk, 112
Mashantucket Pequot Museum &
    Research Center, 180
Mazes,
    Jones Family Farm, 136
    Steck's Nursery, 136
Meigs Point Nature Center, 154
Mid-Connecticut Resources Recovery
    Authority, 8
Mother Earth Gallery & Mining
    Company, 123
Mystic Seaport, 177
National Audubon Society's
    Northeast Center, 98
New England Air Museum, 33
New England Carousel Museum, 29
Old New-Gate Prison and Copper
    Mine, 31

Pat's Kountry Kitchen & Pat's
    Kountry Kollectibles, 191
Project Oceanology, 184
Railroad Museum of New England, 142
Sankow's Beaver Brook Farm, 170
Science Center of Connecticut, 16
Second Company of the Governor's
    Horse Guards, 122
Special Joys Antique Doll & Toy
    Museum, 224
Stamford Museum and Nature
    Center, 110
Sweet Claude's, 138
Thimble Islands, 147
Timbertown Swing Set
    Company, 111
Town Farm Dairy, 59
Trash Museum (Mid-Connecticut
    Resources Recovery Authority), 8
Tulmeadow Dairy Farm, Inc., 59
Valley Railroad Company, 157
Video Place, 200
War & Pieces, 13
Windham Frog Pond, 223
Yale Peabody Museum of
    Natural History, 129

Only in Connecticut Index

Amistad Revolt, 40
Ashford Transfer Station Library, 202
Bara-Heck Settlement, 212
Benton Homestead, 206
Gasoline Alley Automotive
    Museum, 207
Haul of Fame, 221
Iwo Jima Survivors'
    Monument, 26
Joseph Stewart's Hartford Museum, 3
Kerosene Lamp Museum, 70

Last Post, The, 102
Lock Museum of America, 86
Luddy/Taylor Connecticut Valley
    Tobacco Museum, 59
Marlborough eagle, 224
Nut Museum, 171
Thimble Islands, 147
United House Wrecking Company, 110
U.S. Coast Guard Academy, 186
Windham Frog Pond, 223

A Taste of Connecticut Index

Abbott's Lobster in the Rough, 185

Blue Sky Foods, 65

Carole Peck's Good News Cafe, 89

Flanders Fish Market &
    Restaurant, 172

Johnny Ad's, 162

Lenny and Joe's Fish Tale
    Restaurant, 156

Louis' Lunch, 130

Me & McGee Restaurant, 163

Nodine's Smokehouse, 76

O'Rourke's Diner, 164

Pepe's Pizzeria Napoletana, 130

Randall's Ordinary, 181

Rich Farm Ice Cream Shop, 134

Sadler's Ordinary, 197

Sea Swirl, 178

Shady Glen, 21

Stony Creek Market, The, 148

Sycamore, 127

Ted's Restaurant, 136

Traveler Restaurant, 208

About the Authors

Transplanted Midwesterners turned born-again Yankees, David and Deborah Ritchie live in Avon, Connecticut, with their three feline companions, Gremlin, Magpie, and Vlad.

Both the Ritchies have worked as editors, staff writers, and game designers. Today, they are freelance writers who specialize in business and technical writing. Most of their work involves helping clients such as Morgan Stanley Dean Witter, J. P. Morgan Chase and Co., Bayer Pharmaceutical, Pratt & Whitney, British Airways, DuPont Pharmaceuticals, and United Technologies Corporation to develop online documentation systems, Web sites, and intranets. In their spare time, the Ritchies frequently contribute travel, food, and lifestyle articles to several regional and national magazines.

They love hearing from readers and welcome your comments and travel tips. You can write them in care of Globe Pequot or e-mail them at CTOBP@aol.com.